STUDENT AFFAIRS ASSESSMENT

STUDENT AFFAIRS ASSESSMENT

Theory to Practice

Gavin W. Henning and Darby Roberts

Foreword by Marilee J. Bresciani Ludvik

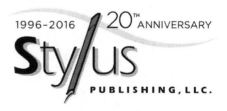

1996-2016 20TH ANNIVERSARY

Stylus
PUBLISHING, LLC.

STERLING, VIRGINIA

Published by Stylus Publishing, LLC.
22883 Quicksilver Drive
Sterling, Virginia 20166-2102

Library of Congress Cataloging-in-Publication Data
Names: Henning, Gavin, author. | Roberts, Darby M., author.
Title: Student affairs assessment : theory to practice /
Gavin Henning and Darby Roberts ; foreword by
Marilee Bresciani Ludvik.
Description: Sterling, Virginia : Stylus Publishing, 2016. |
Includes bibliographical references and index.
Identifiers: LCCN 2015036524|
  ISBN 9781620363355 (cloth : alk. paper) |
  ISBN 9781620363362 (pbk. : alk. paper) |
  ISBN 9781620363379 (library networkable e-edition) |
  ISBN 9781620363386 (consumer e-edition)
Subjects: LCSH: Student affairs services--United States--Evaluation. |
Student affairs services--United States--Administration |
Student affairs administrators--United States.
Classification: LCC LB2342.92 .H46 2016 | DDC 371.4--dc23
LC record available at http://lccn.loc.gov/2015036524

13-digit ISBN: 978-1-62036-335-5 (cloth)
13-digit ISBN: 978-1-62036-336-2 (paperback)
13-digit ISBN: 978-1-62036-337-9 (library networkable e-edition)
13-digit ISBN: 978-1-62036-338-6 (consumer e-edition)

Printed in the United States of America

All first editions printed on acid-free paper
that meets the American National Standards Institute
Z39-48 Standard.

Bulk Purchases

Quantity discounts are available for use in workshops and for
staff development.
Call 1-800-232-0223

First Edition, 2016

10 9 8 7 6 5 4

CONTENTS

FOREWORD

Gavin W. Henning and Darby Roberts set out to write one book that would be useful for student affairs preparation programs and student affairs professionals to reference as they begin their inquiry journey. Gavin and Darby have accomplished their goal. This book is filled with references to several approaches for inquiring into whether student affairs professionals are accomplishing the work they intend to do at the level of quality they desire. In addition, Gavin and Darby share their wealth of wisdom from years of experience in the field. This book will be very useful to many professionals as they look inside it for answers and reference it in a way that raises additional questions for their developing inquiry practices.

As I considered the privilege of writing the foreword to this book, I wondered how I could contribute to their already thoughtful compilation of work. Gavin and Darby introduce student affairs practitioners to several facets of inquiry, including addressing ethics and politics, and do so in a way that will empower practitioners to seek additional resources as their inquiry skills grow. So, what could I genuinely contribute to this conversation? As I mulled this question over and over, I chose to step back and invite you, the reader, into an inquiring mind-set.

How do you know what you know? How do you know the "best" way to solve a problem, answer a research question, or evaluate the effectiveness of the program? How you have come to respond to ways of knowing and inquiring is likely steeped in your personal and academic history. As such, we tend to celebrate our ways of knowing and doing. There is nothing wrong with that; I am happy to celebrate your ways of knowing and doing with you.

Consider now, for just this moment, that the greatest disservice we can do to our profession is actually thinking we "know." What do I mean by that? Allow me to illustrate with a personal story.

I have always been driven by my curiosity. I just wanted to "know" stuff. I like solving problems, finding answers to questions, and sharing the methodology I am learning with others as we join together to seek answers, solve problems, improve student success, and help make the world a better place to live. Along this inquiry journey, I made many disastrous choices—so many of which I have lost count (thankfully). The cool part of these disasters is that, while painful, I learned as much from *not knowing* as I have from *knowing.* As such, I am holding many more questions today than I am holding anything that resembles an answer.

I still really like to know stuff; yet, I am arriving into this space where I am fascinated with what I don't know. And I am discovering that there is a lot of amazing learning and development in the don't-know space; there is a lot of possibility of seeing something different when I come from a place of inquiry—a place of "I don't know."

To connect this personal story to its relevance with student success, we must ask ourselves the following: How do we arrive at a place of knowing how to intentionally foster student success, while making the experience affordable and accessible, as well as sustainable and healthy for all? That line of inquiry is our journey. There is a lot we *know* about how to do that and there is a lot more that we *don't know.* For example, when I get to work with neuroscientists and psychologists and we explore unpacking how to intentionally foster specific malleable characteristics of student success—such as mind-set (which at the time of writing this foreword is considered to be the number one predictor of student success)—we recognize that there is *a lot we don't know* and there is some stuff we do know.

As I consider what we do know, I wonder how higher education faculty, student affairs professionals, administrative staff, and students can collaborate to become aware of how each person's mind-set toward the other is influencing success. Can we do this in an affordable, sustainable way that heightens access, expedites time-to-degree as well as degree completion, and increases employability without harming each person's well-being? *I don't know.* And I am motivated to stay in inquiry, to play with possibilities and do so within a historically grounded inquiry framework. But I am also interested in trying out emerging methods and epistemologies of inquiry to discover what has not yet been discovered. How fun is that?

This book presents a framework for looking into what we intentionally design every day, and how it is either contributing to student success or detracting from it. It is a great book to ground yourself in historically accepted methodology and ways of seeking answers, solving problems, and discovering what works well. I am grateful to Gavin and Darby for integrating their expertise and making this available for me to learn from as well as others.

And while you are learning from this book, my invitation to you is to remember this quote attributed to Albert Einstein: "We can't solve problems by using the same kind of thinking we used when we created them." As such, continue to inquire, and avoid resting in the space of feeling you know the answer or even know the best ways to inquire into the problem. Continue to stay in inquiry, and challenge others to do the same. Try out new forms of inquiry, and be careful to not violate human subjects or ethical principles but simply to explore in childlike wonder.

And if you are concerned that coming from a place of not knowing may cause you to appear as if you are unprofessional or incompetent, I offer this reflection: When Jeff Lichtman from Harvard University, one of the world's leading neuroscientist researchers, was asked how much we know about how the brain functions—the very mechanism we tend to attribute to learning and development—he responded with something like this: "If the journey to discover the brain's secrets is a journey from earth to the moon and back, we have traveled about three miles."

So, how can one book be your one-stop shop—a place to go where you find all the answers? Well, it can't—no book can—*but* it can be your one-start shop—a place to go where you find answers and questions and references that lead you on in your never ending inquiry journey. So, as you read, consider this thoughtfully compiled book your one-start shop and discover how you can stay in inquiry about how to improve student success, whatever that may mean to you.

Enjoy the journey!

Marilee J. Bresciani Ludvik, PhD
Professor, ARPE, San Diego State University

ACKNOWLEDGMENTS

A book of this kind includes the efforts of more than just the authors. First is a publisher who shares a vision for its need not only from a market standpoint but also, and more importantly, from an educational standpoint. We thank John von Knorring and Stylus Publishing for creating the space for this type of resource for the field.

A book like this also includes a host of individuals who are willing to give their time, talents, and energy to support the work. Many friends and colleagues provided thoughtful feedback, making the content of this book stronger and more valuable. We wish to thank Rob Aaron, Stefanie Baker, Brian Bourke, Stephen Britt, Dan Bureau, Brandon Carlson, Kathy Collins, Amber Garrison Duncan, Becki Elkins, Ted Elling, Sonia Deluca Fernandez, Joseph Granado, Waylon Hastings, Justin Keen, Dena Kniess, Rachel Mansolillo, Andy Mauk, Daniel Newhart, Lindsay Peck, Steve Schuh, David Sweeney, Kevin Valliere, Sherry Woosley, and Kim Yousey-Elsener. We would also like to thank the numerous graduate students whom we have taught and learned from over the years.

We would also like to thank the members of Student Affairs Assessment Leaders who provided feedback and suggestions on the content of the book when we were developing the concept. It is truly motivating to see so many professionals committed to improving student affairs and the lives of college students.

Finally, our thanks go out to Marilee J. Bresciani Ludvik, who selflessly has offered her knowledge and support over many years and provided the thoughtful foreword that frames this book. We would not be the assessment educators and professionals we are today without her.

PREFACE

S tudent affairs assessment is a rapidly growing field. In today's complex and sometimes turbulent higher education context, student affairs professionals need to be fluent in the language and skills of their field in an environment that expects demonstration of effectiveness, value, student learning, and contributions to the academic mission of institutions. Staff should consider themselves educators and, as such, understand their responsibility to continually determine how well they are delivering programs, services, and activities that enhance students' experiences in their college careers. While relatively few staff work in student affairs assessment as a primary functional area, all student affairs staff have a stake in the process and thus must be competent in this work.

The idea for this book came out of discussions with colleagues about the need for a textbook specifically focused on student affairs assessment to be used in student affairs and higher education master's programs. There was not one text that covered important assessment topics within the student affairs context, specifically theory to practice. While there are several excellent books that address higher education assessment, they mostly focus on curricular assessment and accreditation. The few student affairs assessment books seemed outdated, as the field has quickly changed.

Professional associations also saw a need to address expectations of administrators working in student affairs. ACPA—College Student Educators International published the *Assessment Skills and Knowledge (ASK) Standards* (2006) to clarify what all student affairs professionals should know and be able to do regardless of functional area. In 2010, ACPA partnered with NASPA–Student Affairs Administrators in Higher Education to produce professional competencies: They determined that the area of assessment, evaluation, and research (AER) was important enough to have its own category. The competencies describe skills and abilities at the beginner, intermediate, and advanced levels to guide staff in their professional development. Rubrics were created for each competency area and similar outcomes were grouped in categories called *dimensions* (Yousey-Elsener & Elkins, 2012). The competencies were updated, revised, and published in the fall of 2015. Similar to the original framework of the competencies, the 2015 version has three levels. However, the first level is described as "foundational" rather than basic. The competencies at this level

TABLE P.1

Comparison of ACPA/NASPA Assessment, Evaluation, and Research Competency Dimensions and Book Chapters

Chapter	*Competency Dimension(s)*
1. Assessment in Student Affairs	Define terms and concepts, value
2. Epistemology	Define terms and concepts
3. The Assessment Process	Define purpose
4. Planning and Designing Individual Assessment Projects	Design
5. Types of Assessment	Design
6. Outcomes	Define purpose
7. Quantitative Design	Design, analysis, interpreting results
8. Survey Design	Data collection
9. Statistical Overview for Assessment	Analysis, interpreting results
10. Qualitative Design	Design, analysis, interpreting results
11. Interviews and Focus Groups	Data collection
12. Additional Assessment Methods	Data collection
13. Sharing Assessment Results	Reporting
14. Using Assessment Results	Use of results
15. Ethics	Ethics
16. Politics	Politics
17. A Culture of Assessment	Creating systems
18. Technology	Data collection, analysis
19. The Future	No corresponding dimension

are those that every student affairs professional should possess regardless of functional area. At the time of this printing, the rubrics for the 2010 competencies were not updated to reflect the revisions in the 2015 edition. However, upon review, the dimensions identified for the 2010 edition of the AER competency also apply to the 2015 version. This comprehensive book addresses the foundational level of the AER competency area. Table P.1 demonstrates the alignment between the AER rubric dimensions and the book chapters.

Audience

There are several key audiences for this text. Graduate students in student affairs or higher education programs will gain an understanding of key assessment concepts before they enter the profession, being prepared to perform assessment on the first day they begin a job. Because more preparation programs include a required or elective course in assessment, younger professionals are developing skills that their more seasoned counterparts may not have been exposed to years ago.

Another audience is those new to student affairs, who may not have graduated from a traditional preparation program or who have come into the profession from a different field altogether. They need foundational knowledge about the context of student affairs assessment and how it might differ from other professions.

More seasoned professionals may also find the book a good resource, either for themselves or as a professional development opportunity for staff. It can bring administrators up to date regarding current discussions and methods as well as provide clarity and demystify key concepts in assessment that may have seemed complicated in the past. For divisions, departments, or units getting started with assessment, the discussion questions at the ends of the chapters can engage staff in the process of developing an effective assessment culture.

Organization of the Book

This book is arranged in an order that sets the stage for assessment. It then moves into specific methods, current issues, and the future. Chapter 1 provides a history and context of how student affairs assessment developed into a vibrant field. Chapter 2 reviews the epistemological perspectives that guide methodological choices. Chapter 3 builds upon that foundation to then describe the big picture when developing an assessment program. Because assessment requires understanding the philosophical foundations, Chapter 4 describes the assessment cycle in more detail as individual projects are implemented. Chapter 5 highlights common types of assessment used in student affairs. Because student affairs and higher education are focused on program and student learning outcomes more than they were in the past, Chapter 6 delves into the importance of developing quality outcomes to guide assessment.

To provide knowledge about specific methods, Chapters 7 and 8 address quantitative design and survey methods that are common in student affairs. Building on that information, Chapter 9 reviews common statistical methods useful to student affairs staff. Chapters 10 and 11 delve into qualitative design and methods, addressing data-collection methods of focus groups and interviews and the analysis options. Chapter 12 focuses on additional methods that are appropriate in a variety of student affairs contexts.

The next two chapters describe how to put assessment into action. Chapter 13 addresses the topic of sharing assessment results to enable student affairs professionals to tell their story and communicate with a variety of stakeholders. Chapter 14 closes the assessment loop, providing guidance about using assessment results for improvement.

Chapter 15 explains key areas of ethical beliefs and behaviors regarding assessment and evaluation. In Chapter 16, the political environment is illuminated because professionals need to understand the reality of their contexts. In addition, Chapter 17 focuses on building a culture of assessment in student affairs. These chapters address the human side of assessment.

The book ends with how student affairs assessment has changed based on technological advances Chapter 18 and where the profession is headed in the future (Chapter 19).

This book was developed to provide foundational knowledge and skills to perform student affairs assessment. It can be used as a text for courses to be read from beginning to end, a resource for professional development activities with a focus on certain chapters, or simply a tool to be pulled off the shelf and consulted as needed.

I

ASSESSMENT IN STUDENT AFFAIRS

Setting the Stage

Assessment in student affairs has evolved into a vibrant field of study and practice. This unique environment provides opportunities and challenges for assessing programs, services, experiences, student development, and learning. Until recently very few publications have comprehensively addressed the distinctive topics that new professionals, assessment coordinators, midmanagers, and senior student affairs officers (SSAOs) address in their day-to-day work of planning and communication with stakeholders.

Before focusing on the current and future state of assessment, it is important to know about the roots of assessment in higher education and student affairs. Although the field is dynamic, there remain foundational publications that continue to influence the environment and provide guidance about the commitment to quality and student learning and development.

History

Although more attention has been paid to student affairs assessment in the past decade, the topic has been addressed since the development of the student affairs profession. In 1937, the American Council on Education published *The Student Personnel Point of View (SPPV)*. That document proposed providing functions and services for the whole student in conjunction with the educational and business areas of the institution. In addition to providing admissions, orientation, career services, mental and physical health services, housing, food services, and more, the *SPPV* recommended evaluating extracurricular activities, social life and interests, and religious life and interests. The final entry in the list of services suggested "carrying on studies designed

1

to evaluate and improve these functions and services" (American Council on Education, 1937, p. 4). In addition, the authors of the 1937 *SPPV* proposed a research agenda in four areas: student out-of-class life, faculty-student out-of-class relationships, financial aid to students, and a follow-up study of college students. In terms of the out-of-class experiences, they wrote:

> College students spend the majority of their time outside the classrooms and laboratories. We have, however, no significant data as to the activities in which they engage. In order to understand the educational importance of their activities we propose that on a score of campuses throughout the country data be collected. Incidentally, this research would be relatively inexpensive since on every campus individuals may be found to do the work without compensation. (p. 13)

After World War II, the American Council on Education revisited its philosophical stance as it saw changes in the United States and higher education. Building upon the 1937 document, it published a revised edition of *The Student Personnel Point of View* (American Council on Education, 1949), expanding the elements of the student personnel program to provide for the development of the individual as a member of society. Once again, assessment was a key component of the student affairs functions. The council encouraged "a continuing program of evaluation of student personnel services and of the educational program to ensure the achievement by students of the objectives for which this program is designed" (American Council on Education, 1949, p. 29). Moreover, it requested that every staff member devote significant time to planning and evaluation to improve services and develop students. The 1949 *SPPV* outlined the following criteria for evaluating programs: (a) student satisfaction and dissatisfaction with services should be assessed, either formally or informally; (b) faculty should be asked about their satisfaction and dissatisfaction with the student personnel program; (c) student use of services should be recorded; (d) staff development and training needs to be continually improved and recognized; and (e) the relationship between student personnel staff and faculty and other staff needs to be evaluated for quality and cooperative efforts. These criteria are still relevant in the twenty-first century.

In the middle of the twentieth century, the concept of student development theory gained acceptance out of human development theory as social scientists began to research how students changed and grew throughout their college careers. Researchers focused on the transition from adolescence through adulthood, how people affect and are affected by their environment, and how students view their world. Based on that research, the role of student affairs professionals shifted and the expectation to measure student development grew (Evans, Forney, & Guido-DiBrito, 1998). Assessment methods, both qualitative and quantitative, emerged as a way to capture growth and learning over time.

In 1979, the Council for the Advancement of Standards in Higher Education (CAS) (2012d) created a coalition of functional area student affairs and higher education associations to promote professional standards and assessment to improve the programs and services across the institution. With focus on quality, CAS established a set of guidelines for a variety of functional areas and continues to adapt, hone, and create more standards and expectations as the nature of higher education and student affairs changes. The standards can be used for program review and self-study, as well as external review. In 2006, CAS created specific standards for assessment services, giving recognition to the importance of the growing field. The assessment services standard follows the format of the other functional areas but also provides specific verbiage about collaborating with institutional research; assessing needs, learning, and effectiveness; consulting literature; acknowledging limitations; and connecting to strategic initiatives.

The American Association for Higher Education (Astin et al., 1992) published *Nine Principles of Good Practice for Assessing Student Learning*, which provided criteria to incorporate assessment into higher education, particularly student learning. Although the document does not specifically address the cocurricular area, the statements are broad enough to include student affairs practice. These statements are as follows:

1. The assessment of student learning begins with educational values.
2. Assessment is most effective when it reflects an understanding of learning as multidimensional, integrated, and revealed in performance over time.
3. Assessment works best when the programs it seeks to improve have clear, explicitly stated purposes.
4. Assessment requires attention to outcomes but also and equally to the experiences that lead to those outcomes.
5. Assessment works best when it is ongoing, not episodic.
6. Assessment fosters wider improvement when representatives from across the educational community are involved.
7. Assessment makes a difference when it begins with issues of use and illuminates questions that people really care about.
8. Assessment is most likely to lead to improvement when it is part of a larger set of conditions that promote change.
9. Through assessment, educators meet responsibilities to students and to the public.

These nine criteria emphasize the importance of the need for assessment to be thoughtfully incorporated into the student experience, coordinated across the campus, and forward thinking. In higher education and student affairs in the late twentieth century, there was a clear shift from satisfaction and informal assessment to student learning and formal assessment. For example, whereas departments of residence life have been (and still should be) concerned with student satisfaction, there is more of an emphasis on what students are gaining through their on-campus experiences, such as living-learning communities. Administrators may want to know if living on campus has a positive impact on grades, first- to second-year retention, and the ability to work in diverse groups. Assessment in those areas has become more sophisticated and focused.

In more recent years, ACPA, recognizing the changing higher education environment, published *The Student Learning Imperative* (1994) to move the student affairs profession forward with an intentional focus on student learning, not simply student services. Once again, assessment was a key issue. Specifically, one of the characteristics of a learning-oriented student affairs division was defined as follows: "Student affairs policies and programs are based on promising practices for the research of student learning and institution-specific assessment data" (p. 4). Student affairs professionals were expected to not only be experts on students and how they spent their time but also integrate and synthesize information from faculty and others and then to disseminate that information to stakeholders. In order to contribute to the body of knowledge about student learning and development, student affairs staff must collect and report information about their contribution to the institution's mission. This includes assessing policies, practices, programs, and services. One of the challenges is that in academic affairs the reporting may focus on curricular assessment and student grades, whereas student affairs assessment is less structured. In order to demonstrate their contribution, staff must be versed in assessment and student learning, and graduate programs should prepare new professionals in the area.

In 2004, NASPA and ACPA published *Learning Reconsidered: A Campuswide Focus on the Student Experience* (Keeling, 2004), recognizing that learning is a complex endeavor in which student affairs plays an important role in the integrated process. Learning is "a comprehensive, holistic, transformative activity that integrates academic learning and student development, processes that have often been considered separate, and even independent of each other" (p. 4). Further, student affairs staff provide an additional benefit because of their role in working with students who are applying what they are learning in the classroom as well as developing life skills. Staff are able to engage students in application, integration, and reflection in out-of-class experiences.

At the institutional level, student affairs should collaborate with academic affairs and others to assess and document learning experiences and

Learning Evidence ✓

expected graduate outcomes. At the same time, Keeling (2004) recognized that satisfaction assessment plays a role and that multiple methods should be used to develop a clear understanding of students' experiences. In sum, "all institutions should establish routine ways to hear students' voices, consult with them, explore their opinions, and document the nature and quality of their experience as learners" (Keeling, 2004, p. 28).

The Current Higher Education Context

Higher education has become increasingly complex in a political environment. "Assessment in public higher education is no longer simply an 'add-on' or something that is peripheral to the institution's overall education program. It is at the center stage of colleges and universities" (Sandeen & Barr, 2006, p. 136). In student affairs, the expectation is to assess and address issues such as sexual assault, alcohol and drug abuse, mental health, and the climate for diversity, in addition to focusing on efficiency, effectiveness, and cocurricular learning. Student affairs needs to be included in the institutional strategic plan and assessment, even when it is not directly connected to the larger picture. These political, environmental, and ethical issues lead to a focus on accountability.

Wehlburg (2008) has suggested that higher education has been more concerned with accountability than quality improvement:

> Data have been collected (and filed, piled, and stored) for the benefit of others. But it seems clear that higher education has not done a very good job of using assessment data to improve student learning or the quality of the undergraduate experience. (p. 2)

There is a tension between data collection for external stakeholders (accountability) and internal audiences (improvement). Although both are essential, how people actually spend their time and resources will be guided by campus leaders. Showing others what is happening at the institution may take precedence over focusing on improving the teaching, learning, and engagement.

The federal government has been increasingly concerned with education—more specifically higher education as a preparation for career success. "As a result of President Obama's goal to increase the number of college graduates by 60% by 2020, colleges and career readiness have become focal points for K–12 reform" (Finley, 2012, p. 28). There are concerns with the cost of education, time to complete a degree, student debt, and employment rates. Smith and Sponsler (2014) have recognized the importance of communication with employers in this area:

The process surrounding creation of Gainful Employment regulations provides a reminder to college administrators to engage employers in discussions about higher education. It would be wise to confirm with employers that academic preparation, cocurricular programming, and support services are well aligned with the needed skills and competencies, and that sufficient job openings exist (or are projected to exist) before institutions offer and administer new career-oriented programs. (p. 30)

Career services, academic advising, financial aid, and other support areas need to be proactive in their efforts to serve students. Assessment of these areas, which may or may not belong in a division of student affairs, can provide more information about career preparation and success.

Higher education has been under more scrutiny in recent years, with statements from the president of the United States to accreditation agencies to individual institutions. President Obama (White House, n.d.) saw the importance of higher education as an economic issue, recognizing the fact that the United States has fallen behind in degree attainment. He has also challenged Americans to enroll in college or other forms of postsecondary education for at least a year. At the same time he understands that everyone has a responsibility to keep cost down, that community colleges occupy an important place in the education market, and that there needs to be more transparency and accountability to the American public.

Stakeholders are questioning the value of a college degree, the cost, and preparation for the world of work. State legislators debate funding models and reporting requirements. Employers are expressing some discontent with the preparation of recent graduates. Graduates should not only be proficient in their content field but also able to work with people who are different from themselves, communicate effectively to a variety of audiences, and make decisions considering the consequences (Hart Research Associates, 2015). Institutions are grappling with issues of retention, persistence, time to graduation, containing costs, and improving the student and faculty experience. As Keeling, Wall, Underhile, and Dungy (2008) have stated, "Assessment in higher education primarily responds to two forces: external demands for accountability and internal commitment to improvement" (p. 1). The need for assessment, in many forms, is increasing.

Regional accrediting agencies have the task of deciding whether institutions meet quality standards. For example, the Southern Association of Colleges and Schools Commission on Colleges (2012) determines whether institutional missions are appropriate, institutions have the resources and activities to meet that mission, and the institutional objectives are appropriate and measured (p. 1). When institutions do not meet these standards during a regular review or when specific information surfaces, the association can put the institution on notice that its accreditation is in danger.

Traditional four-year universities are not the only institutions that feel the pressure for assessment. Bresciani Ludvik, Kline, and Moore Gardner (2014) have recognized the unique position of community colleges in assessment and student success:

> Postsecondary institutions are currently facing common challenges, including greater numbers of students; shrinking capital and human resources; and diminishing public confidence. These challenges have resulted in higher demands for accountability by stakeholders across the board. Community and two-year colleges face the additional challenge of serving the needs of a variety of programs including traditional academic, vocational, and continuing education programs, and more remedial course offerings. (p. 25)

Although challenges may be common across colleges and universities, each institution has its own nuances in terms of purpose, goals, values, type of students, and resources that impact its assessment priorities, methods, and processes.

Bresciani, Zelna, and Anderson (2004) have explained that institutions now are "expected to provide evidence to their internal and external constituencies that the quality of education and the student experience is commensurate with rising costs, with their statements of excellence, and with their desire to retain the competitive edge" (p. 1). Staff must assess more than satisfaction and needs to show the cocurricular contribution to an institution's mission and values. This can be a challenging but beneficial paradigm shift for student affairs professionals who work in an unstructured learning environment with students who are still developing. Now, student affairs assessment must become more focused and meaningful while providing opportunity for collaboration with faculty and institutional research offices. Rather than happening haphazardly, assessment should be incorporated into the strategic and operations planning processes. This integration allows for a consistent timeline of program delivery, data collection, reflection, sharing, and use of results.

Kimbrough (2011), a college president who moved up through student affairs, has stated that the current environment demands that institution presidents need to be "more engaged in campus assessment and must be familiar with national studies that may provide information that affects that particular campus. Student affairs professionals have access to a tremendous amount of data" (p. 187). As more college presidents see the need for data, they will be expecting an SSAO to provide information about major current student issues (e.g., alcohol use and abuse, sexual assault, preparation to enter the work world, contribution to timely graduation) in a way that a president can easily digest and share. More than ever, college leaders are being asked by various stakeholders—such as state legislators, parents, and the media—to provide answers to challenging questions regarding the student experience. "The concept of accountability has grown more complex with changes in society, broader access to higher education, rising public expectations, and the emergence of competition, positioning, and marketing among postsecondary institutions" (Keeling et al., 2008, p. 1). Institution leaders are much more in tune with expectation of accountability than they had been in previous years. The authors also emphasized the importance of assessment for improvement in student success. Leadership should not only be concerned with the external accountability pressure, but also continue to examine internal processes and programs that support student success, business practices, and student learning for the greater good.

The Current Student Affairs Context

Student affairs, as a subset of the higher education environment, impacts and is impacted by what happens at the institutional level. Because SSAOs provide information to the institution, they should be actively seeking information from a variety of campus resources. Carreon (2011) has provided advice to SSAOs regarding assessment, indicating that they should continually assess college data to understand the institutional demographics and functions, ensure that each functional area is aligned with larger institutional priorities and student needs, and understand how the institutional community perceives the division and departments. In addition, student affairs leaders need to understand how various subpopulations experience the campus through the departments that serve students (Schuh & Gansemer-Topf, 2010). SSAOs set the overall assessment tone and expectations of the division that can be delegated through each department.

An SSAO is concerned with cost effectiveness and operational efficiency while also promoting the "institution's purpose through clear and strategic messaging to constituents. At the same time, SSAOs must help students prepare for employment and learn to present their achievements in ways that highlight their potential for success in the work world" (Pate, 2014, p. 36). The complexity of the position continues to grow, placing more emphasis on the focused evaluation of programs, services, and processes in a division of student affairs and departments in the division. SSAOs rely on staff to provide accurate assessment results so they can tell a story to a variety of audiences and make informed decisions.

Although SSAOs know that assessment is important, they may also be cautious about how assessment is used. "There are obvious risks for student affairs leaders in assessment, as results from various studies may reveal some embarrassing weaknesses and shortcomings in various programs" (Sandeen & Barr, 2006, p. 144). Leadership is held accountable and may face repercussions for poor results, even if those results are beyond their control. On the other hand, "assessment may be the best way to ensure a strong educational and ethical commitment to quality services and programs in student affairs" (Sandeen & Barr, 2006, p. 144). By being transparent with assessment and implementing needed changes, a division can be proactive in addressing student needs and supporting the institution mission. By building a culture of evidence with leadership support, staff will be more likely to naturally include assessment in the planning and execution of programs and services.

Related to the collaboration between employers and institutions, the Association of American Colleges and Universities (AAC&U) sponsored a survey of employers about their identified essential learning outcomes (Finley, 2012). Employers were asked on what areas they wanted colleges to place more emphasis. The following examples include those outcomes that could and should be addressed by student affairs professionals (with the percentage of employers in agreement in parentheses): written and oral communication (89%); critical thinking and analytic reasoning (81%); applied knowledge in real-world settings (79%); complex problem solving (75%); ethical decision making (75%); intercultural competence (teamwork skills in diverse groups) (71%); intercultural knowledge of global issues (67%); and civic knowledge, participation, and engagement (52%) (Finley, 2012, p. 3). Employers may not care in what context students learn those skills, but student affairs staff should incorporate those skills in their student engagement and development opportunities and then assess students to determine their level of accomplishment and ability to articulate and demonstrate these skills. By the nature of student organization involvement, many students practice communication skills, make difficult decisions, work with others who are different from themselves, and practice applying what they learn in a variety of settings.

Similarly, the Education Advisory Board (2011) collected information from 80 institutions specifically about cocurricular outcomes. The top outcomes identified included community involvement (99%), values and ethics (91%), diversity (91%), self-esteem (86%), critical thinking (85%), teamwork (84%), and communication (82%). Most if not all student affairs staff would agree that the cocurricular experiences provided to students address those issues. The challenge is to assess how these experiences enhance those outcomes.

evidence for a co-curricular model

In 2014, AAC&U again sponsored a survey with 400 employers and 613 college students (Hart Research Associates, 2015). Similar to previous findings, employers were looking for broad learning and skill development across majors that can be used in real-world settings. They value applied learning and project-based experiences such as internships and capstone projects. Unfortunately, employers do not have much confidence in students' ability: "Just 14% of employers think that most of today's college students are prepared with the skills and knowledge needed to complete a significant applied learning project before graduation" (p. 6). In this study, students also valued those applied experiences, although they were more likely than employers to think that their institution prepared them well for entry-level positions. Student affairs staff need to specifically articulate the learning outcomes related to cocurricular experiences (employment, student leadership, service-learning, etc.), engage students in active learning and reflection strategies, and teach students how to articulate their learning and ability to translate those skills and competencies to the world of work. Students may be having amazing learning experiences, but if they are unable to describe and transfer knowledge, employers will continue to see much room for improvement. One of Finley's (2012) conclusions is still relevant today:

> The mandate of the twenty-first century isn't to conduct assessment; it is to be able to *articulate* how well students are learning on campuses and to demonstrate the collective worth of higher education. Doing this will take more than assessment. It will also take an understanding of the outcomes we seek, as well as an understanding of the practices needed to achieve them and the tools with which to capture them. (p. 28)

Recently, institutions and accrediting agencies have placed more emphasis on how and to what extent student affairs contributes to student learning and the academic mission. Inherently, student affairs professionals know that learning takes place in cocurricular experiences. Student leaders learn valuable lessons about teamwork, communication, and project management, for example, in the course of such experience. Many student employees have opportunities to develop critical thinking skills, ethics, and working in a diverse environment. Advisors and supervisors observe students performing these skills and have reflective conversations. They also provide students with important feedback to improve performance and integrate learning in other areas. One of the challenges, though, is that student affairs does not give grades as validation of learning. Typically, students do not receive standardized credentials of their learning in a coordinated way. However, as technology improves and emphasis on holistic learning increases, there could be institutional records that document learning and competence. Accrediting agencies, such as the Southern Association of Colleges and Schools Commission on Colleges (2012), have stated that institutions need to have a campuswide quality enhancement plan to address student learning while also identifying outcomes, assessing those outcomes, and providing evidence that assessment has been used for improvement. Student affairs is included in the process.

In terms of financial resources, higher education is a complex environment with many moving parts and stakeholder opinions. Many public institutions have been struggling with decreasing state appropriations (Blumenstyk, 2015) and need to increase tuition and fees. Private institutions rely on student enrollment to cover their expenses. Community colleges face their own complexities of funding and student enrollment. Institutions may also be seeking grant funding, donor endowments, and other streams of revenue to support their efforts. On the campus level, this means difficult decisions are made to determine where those scarce resources are to be allocated. For student affairs, there is pressure to indicate the efficient use of current resources and to document the need for additional funds to enhance the institution's priorities.

Student Affairs' Responsibility

In the mid-1980s, assessment in higher education really gained traction. Sandeen and Barr (2006) concluded that student affairs had already been using studies about student characteristics, learning, diversity, needs, and satisfaction. Since then, student affairs assessment has become more focused to answer more complex questions, especially as student demographics and needs continually change. Higher education assessment professionals also recognized that student affairs has played a key role in student success and assessment. To emphasize that point, Wehlburg (2008) stated:

> Many cocurricular activities are crucial to the student development process and should be assessed. In addition, many elements within institutional mission statements focus on areas of leadership, citizenship, and global diversity issues. These types of broad goals are often not part of a student's academic major but are intentionally developed within residence life and student affairs areas. (p. 79)

As the student affairs profession has moved from a student services perspective to a student development perspective and now a student learning perspective, student affairs staff are beginning to see themselves as educators. "By focusing on learning outcomes, Student Affairs leaders are making a change that requires a significant mind shift as practitioners move

↳ FOCUS ON LEARNING OUTCOMES

from viewing themselves as program facilitators to thinking of themselves as educators" (Education Advisory Board, 2011, p. 54), and that change can be challenging. Many practitioners enter student affairs to have direct contact with students, plan programs and activities that support student development, and encourage students to develop a balanced life. Few, if any, practitioners enter the profession specifically to collect, analyze, and share data. If student affairs professionals were forced to assess, their focus has generally been on tracking attendance and satisfaction, which are much easier to assess than something as complex as learning (Education Advisory Board, 2011).

As the student affairs profession changes, so do the expectations placed on an individual staff member. "One of the primary implications of understanding oneself professionally as an educator is the obligation to assess the learning that happens in one's programs and services" (Keeling et al., 2008, p. 8). Being an educator implies the responsibility to have a prepared curriculum, deliver learning, and assess for learning. No longer can student affairs staff create and implement programs on a whim—there should be some evidence of need, which might be based on current research, and a plan to assess to determine student learning and program success. As Schuh and Gansemer-Topf (2010) recommended, staff "need to have the empirical evidence to be confident that these programs, activities, and experiences actually do contribute to student learning. This is the point in student affairs practice where assessment is vital" (p. 12). If there is not assessment, people external to student affairs will continue to question the value of student affairs. To demonstrate effectiveness, staff need to be proficient in not only student learning assessment but also the entire assessment process. In a broader sense, student affairs staff may need competence in pedagogic and instructional design concepts to further increase the quality of educational programs.

Banta and Palomba (2015) identified several reasons that student affairs need to be engaged in the assessment process: demonstrating their worth, measuring their success against their goals and objectives, helping students connect in-class and out-of-class experiences, assessing skills and competencies identified by the institution, and meeting standards and expectations for accountability. Because of the educational backgrounds of many student affairs professionals, they may be better prepared to focus on assessing students' out-of-class learning experiences than some faculty and others who are new to assessment (Banta & Palomba, 2015). Student affairs preparation programs typically have topics such as student development theory, counseling, advising, diversity, assessment, and law as part of the curriculum that gives professionals a broad-based knowledge of students' experiences.

Student affairs professional associations have published standards to provide guidance in the area of assessment knowing the importance of the topic in higher education today. ACPA's (2006) *ASK Standards* describe 13 focus areas for assessment skills and knowledge: assessment design, articulating learning and development outcomes, selection of data collection and management methods, assessment instruments, surveys used for assessment purposes, interviews and focus groups used for assessment purposes, analysis, benchmarking, program review and evaluation, assessment ethics, effective reporting and use of results, politics of assessment, and assessment education. This document provides specific outcomes for each area in which all student affairs professionals should develop competence regardless of their functional area. The standards provide a framework for professional development as staff identify areas that need improvement.

ACPA and NASPA (2010) joined together to publish a description of 10 areas in which student affairs professionals should be proficient regardless of functional area. The competencies are described in three levels of proficiency: beginner, intermediate, and advanced. Those competencies were updated, revised, and published in the fall of 2015. The assessment, evaluation, and research (AER) competency area includes using qualitative and quantitative methods, critiquing assessment, managing processes, and shaping the political environment. Similar to the *ASK Standards*, the *Professional Competency Areas for Student Affairs Practitioners* provides a framework for growth by describing what each level of competence entails. Both associations provide professional development in the areas through conferences, institutes, webinars, and publications. The competencies were being reviewed and updated in 2015.

Some institutions have created specialist positions in student affairs to address assessment coordination. Although it may be no one's job, a portion of one person's job, or the main responsibilities for one person, few institutions have more than one professional working solely on student affairs assessment. Kuk (2012) made a case that student affairs organizations need to create some specialist roles/cross-organizational positions to meet increasing demands while under resource constraints. Bresciani (2012) emphasized that student affairs professionals need to improve their ability to use outcomes-based assessment to evaluate our programs; to connect results and resources needed for improvement to research or lack thereof in our profession and to various stakeholders; and to explain how what student affairs does aligns with student learning, current higher education research, and stakeholder values. In the future, Bresciani (2012) has suggested that staff become more collaborative, be able to communicate clearly with the public, allocate time for reflection, and use technology effectively as assessment becomes incorporated into the day-to-day student affairs environment. All staff, regardless of the percentage of job description devoted to assessment, should be developing their assessment skills to evaluate programs, services, and student learning. Student affairs as a profession needs to be more proactive in conducting assessment, sharing results, and demonstrating how assessment is used for improvement.

The Council for the Advancement of Standards in Higher Education (2012a), also known as CAS, developed evaluation criteria for 44 functional areas. One of the 12 general standards included in each functional area centers on assessment and evaluation. Each functional area is expected to have an assessment plan, provide resources to implement assessment, use a variety of methods, and use and share assessment results for improvement. These widely accepted standards provide structure for units to review their performance and make plans for improvement. The standards are reviewed on a regular basis. For those institutions with an assessment office, CAS developed standards for assessment services. Because most institutions do not have multiple staff solely working in student affairs assessment, the standards can provide guidance for their current efforts and indicate a need for more resources, including staff.

Challenges of Student Affairs Assessment

As student affairs assessment becomes pervasive, there are still challenges. In the past, assessment was not a priority for leaders or staff. Although it is identified as a priority now, there is still disagreement about what should be assessed and who does the assessment. In addition, student affairs used to rely on scholars outside of student affairs practice for assessment and research (Sandeen & Barr, 2006). Unfortunately, student affairs professionals are not always rewarded for or encouraged to participate in assessment activities even when the division mission supports the institution. Banta and Palomba (2015) have suggested that "the reward of collaboration with professionals outside the division is perhaps more elusive than it should be" (p. 213). In order for student affairs and higher education assessment to truly take hold, institutions have to commit to developing processes, policies, and cultures that encourage collaboration and coordination.

For some divisions, having a professional staff member reporting to the SSAO level provides a broader and coordinated effort. That person might be tasked with assessment, strategic planning, and possibly budgeting or even professional development. Having someone who can see the entire landscape allows for better implementation and success:

> An alternative benefit or reward from engaging in assessment is to have assessment results valued in broader processes, and this does not happen in many student affairs divisions. The function of assessment is often com-

bined with those of program review and planning, greatly increasing the likelihood that assessment results will be used. (Banta & Palomba, 2015, p. 213)

Although devoting one or more staff members to assessment efforts is a significant investment in resources, it can also provide a great benefit for direction, coordination, and staff buy-in. If there is not a dedicated staff person, resources could be provided to develop competence among multiple staff members.

As the assessment effort evolves in student affairs, skill development and resources are even more important, especially with the lack of full-time student affairs assessment professionals. In 1999, about 40 institutions had a full-time student affairs assessment person (Malaney, 1999) Current estimates indicate about 130 institutions have a director or dedicated assessment person, about 140 people with at least 75% of their job description, and 192 staff with at least 50% of time spent on student affairs assessment (T. W. Elling, personal communication, June 30, 2015). Some universities have multiple full-time staff, others have one person, still others have assessment as only a portion on one person's job, and yet others do not have a formal designation for assessment staff. Still others rely on their institutional research office to provide support and assistance. Devoting human and financial resources to the student affairs assessment effort can be challenging in the current economic environment when there are many priorities to be addressed.

Sandeen and Barr (2006) have identified several shortcomings related to student affairs assessment: staff acting alone (e.g., being too close to the program and not relating assessment to academic outcomes), being isolated from campus institutional assessment efforts, focusing on narrow issues and personal agendas, staying in their comfort zone, lack of coordination in assessment (e.g., oversurveying students), a disconnect from core undergraduate academic programs, and a lack of support from SSAOs. It is easy for staff members to be comfortable doing what they have always done, not assessing in a meaningful or challenging way, and working within a very narrow perspective. Staff need to proactively collaborate with academic affairs and the institution as a whole in learning and assessment efforts to best serve the students. This could include developing institutional learning goals and an institutional assessment plan.

Meeting the Challenges

Taking a holistic view of student development and student learning is an important part of understanding areas such as retention trends and graduation rates. More than likely, these topics are not the concern of an individual academic program or department, but student affairs addresses those areas well. "Student affairs areas often have several ongoing benchmarks focusing on alcohol awareness, student safe sexual practices, and diversity. These areas for assessment are useful for the institution as a whole, and these data can inform teaching and classroom practices" (Wehlburg, 2008, p. 83). One of the major challenges on many campuses, though, is finding a way for student affairs and academic affairs to partner in student learning and success. Both areas have their own theories, priorities, and reporting structures that may interfere with the ability to collect and use data about students.

Sandeen and Barr (2006) offered several suggestions to address the challenges: Strong leadership by SSAOs is the most important change that could improve student affairs' role in assessment. Those directly engaged in student affairs assessment activities should broaden the focus of their interests by working cooperatively with faculty on the core academic programs on their campuses. SSAOs frequently report directly to the president, and this may enable them to have access to institutional resources and to influence major policies and programs. Leaders in the student affairs assessment movement should urge collaboration between student affairs professional associations and generalist higher education associations.

Because most institutions do not have one or more full-time staff devoted to student affairs assessment at the division level, there are ways to maximize human and other resources. SSAOs may hire someone to report specifically to them while working on broader assessment topics. Some departments have created positions that have assessment as one component or as the main responsibility. That person may also work on larger divisional assessment processes and practices as needed. Another model is to hire a part-time person (graduate student or staff) when a full-time position is not provided for in the budget. This could include someone who works in the institutional research office but supports student affairs work. Alternatively, the division could create a committee to move assessment initiatives forward. These committees could be composed of volunteers interested in the topic, or the membership could include a representative from each department. There is no one perfect model, but the implementation of a sound model can lead to additional future resources as assessment is embedded in processes.

Assessment in higher education has become such a highly visible and volatile issue that it cannot be ignored by student affairs professionals, even when they find it confusing or frustrating or when priorities are driven by external bodies that are not as committed as they are to diverse and substantive approaches to student learning. The excellent assessment initiatives now being conducted by student affairs professionals are commendable, are contributing to the improvement of programs and services on many campuses, and should be continued and enhanced (Sandeen & Barr, 2006, pp. 148–153). Student affairs staff can continue to improve by having divisional assessment committees, serving on campus committees, providing professional development, and sharing credible assessment information with interested stakeholders (Banta & Palomba, 2015).

Wehlburg (2008) also offered some advice about assessing student learning at the institution. She has suggested an initial discussion about the need for collaboration, then determining educational goals and creating outcomes across the institution. In creating these, representatives from across campus should be included in a small, manageable committee. They can all share ideas for how student affairs can partner with faculty in the student learning and assessment process. By coming together, all faculty and staff can be more efficient and effective in providing and assessing student learning. For example, residence life departments can closely partner with faculty in living-learning communities, student activities departments can work with faculty in leadership studies, and the multicultural affairs office can coordinate with the study abroad office. Student affairs staff and faculty can collaborate to provide students internships, service-learning experiences, and other activities that enhance deeper learning. The possibilities are endless.

Kuh, Gonyea, and Rodriguez (2002) offered several other strategies that could move student development assessment forward to address policies and practices. Like other authors, they have suggested that influential stakeholders be included in assessment processes and policies. In addition, they proposed that staff use a variety of assessment methods, collect enough data to be disaggregated at the unit level and with underrepresented students, and use national research programs and other organizations to provide information and leadership. As with all assessment, there should be a connection with the process, results, and changes in policies. Kuh et al. (2002) suggested that scholarly and systematic approaches work best when there is a culture of assessment as well as clear student development goals.

Student affairs assessment is dynamic, maturing, and complex. A practitioner has a responsibility to his or her unit, department, division, institution, and profession to ask hard questions about student learning, program effectiveness, and contribution to higher education. New professionals and those new to assessment can begin now to frame their work in student affairs with an evaluation state of mind. All staff should be recognized for their contribution to assessment, although they should not be penalized for negative results (Banta & Palomba, 2015).

Conclusion

Assessment in student affairs has a long history and continues to be shaped by the current complexities of higher education. As the subsequent chapters describe student affairs assessment in more detail, staff should continue to reflect on the development of the field, the current context, and the future of student affairs and higher education. Student affairs assessment is not only a field but also a process. "Assessment is a means, not an end" (Keeling et al., 2008, p. 5). As the field grows and develops, student affairs professionals need to continue to grow and develop in their knowledge and application.

Key Points

- Student affairs assessment occurs in a dynamic environment.
- Professionals need to follow higher education current events and campus issues, as these shape assessment priorities, decision making, and resource allocation.
- Assessment will continue to be an important area of professional development.

Discussion Questions and Activities

- How is the current higher education climate affecting your campus?
- What are the assessment priorities at your institution?
- How is student affairs assessment implemented on your campus?
- Describe your role in assessment activities in your department or division.
- In which areas do you need to develop in terms of knowledge, skills, and abilities?

EPISTEMOLOGY

↱ how do we know what we know

*E*pistemology is one of those big words that some people may find puzzling. Gall, Gall, and Borg (2007) defined this term as "a branch of philosophy that studies the nature of knowledge and the process by which knowledge is acquired and validated" (p. 15). In other words, epistemology is concerned with how people come to know something and how knowledge is confirmed. For example, how do kids understand that a pot on a heated stove is hot? They could listen to authorities who tell them so. They could also touch the pot and burn their fingers. Although this term is often specifically used in research to discuss how research (or the process of acquiring knowledge) should be constructed, it is also a helpful concept to consider in assessment, as assessment is also the acquisition of knowledge. However, the goal of assessment is to document student learning or program performance, not necessarily the generation and dissemination of generalizable knowledge. In assessment, knowledge, derived in some way, is used to make decisions about the effectiveness of programs and services or what students learn. In considering how knowledge is acquired it is necessary to examine "ways of knowing." In other words, how do college student educators acquire knowledge to make decisions on the effectiveness of programs and services?

Ways of Knowing

Before we discuss how to perform assessment, it is important to consider how knowledge is gathered—or "ways of knowing"—and decisions are made. It is critical to understand this because some ways of knowing are more valid than others. For example, by touching a pot on a heated stove, a child learns directly that the pot is hot. However, if the child learns this indirectly, as from her mother's warning, she is receiving this knowledge and not constructing it herself. Fraenkel, Wallen, and Hyun (2014) described and defined five ways of knowing: *sensory experience, agreement with others, expert opinion, logic, scientific method, and logic models.*

Sensory Experience

One of the most basic ways in which data are gathered is through the senses: sight, hearing, touch, taste, or smell. People learn about their surroundings through personal data-collection tools. However, senses may be inaccurate. People may sense that it is warm or cold outside, but most can't gauge the exact temperature, humidity, or atmospheric pressure. Senses may be not only unspecific but also inaccurate. Someone may smell smoke and assume it is coming from a neighbor's fireplace when in fact it's a brush fire. Senses are also incomplete. There is the story of five blind men who were asked to touch different parts of an elephant. Each creates an image of the object he is touching based on his senses. The ear is a fan, the tail a snake, the legs tree trunks, and the body a wall. But since each does not have all the possible data, each fails to imagine that he is touching an elephant. Whereas sensory experience provides immediate information, this is only one way of knowing, and a way of knowing that may share only part of the whole picture.

Agreement With Others

People often use others to challenge or confirm what they know. This may be because they lack the experience that another person has, they perceive another person as being an expert on a topic, or they do not feel confident in their own knowledge. Consider the blind men with the elephant. Although each had an image in his head based on his sensory experience, none compared his experience with that of the others. If each described to the others what he was touching—a tail, a foot, an ear, a trunk, or a toenail—they might as a group realize that they were likely touching the same object, given their proximity to one another, even though they were sensing different parts of the same whole. However, others can be wrong. Whereas the five men might agree that they were touching different parts of the same object, they still might not conclude that they were touching an elephant. They still might not have enough information to draw the correct conclusion.

Expert Opinion

Another way of knowing is talking with experts. Perhaps the five blind men would decide to call on expert opinion to synthesize their information. They know that the object is large. If they suspected that the object was an animal, they could consult a veterinarian specializing in large animals. After hearing the descriptions of what each one found, the expert might be able to identify the examined object. But experts can be wrong, or the wrong experts might be consulted. Having touched the long, tubular trunk, the men might believe that it was some sort of hose and contact a gardener or firefighter. Neither of these experts would be able to help the men identify the object they were touching.

Logic

Another way of knowing is logic, or the use of reason. This process would require additional information. Besides touch, the men might use smell and describe the odors they were able to detect. They might also listen to the sounds the object made. They might also be more detailed in their description, also noticing texture, hardness, and other qualities. Then, integrating all of this information, the men might begin to deduce the nature of the object. However, there are challenges to this process as well. Multiple pieces of information may yield a number of logical results. Consider the childhood riddle "What's black and white and red all over?" The answers could include a newspaper (read, not red), a sunburned penguin, a zebra with a bloody nose, or a skunk in a red evening dress. Although most of these answers are unrealistic, the riddle does illustrate that there may be multiple results for a set of parameters.

Scientific Method

Another way of knowing involves the scientific method. According to Fraenkel et al. (2014), the scientific method requires the testing of an idea in the public arena (p. 5). The general idea is to test guesses about a problem or issue under controlled conditions. These tests do not constitute the scientific method unless the procedures and results are shared in the public arena so others may replicate the test. The steps are as follows:

1. Identification of the problem to be solved or questions to be answered
2. Identification of the data that would be needed to answer the question
3. Collection of the data needed (which could be data that already exist or new data yet to be gathered)
4. Analysis of the data
5. Interpretation of the data
6. Sharing of the procedures and results

Given the steps in the scientific method and the precise expectations of how each step should be implemented, the understanding resulting from this way of knowing is often more trusted than that derived from other ways of knowing. A key characteristic of the scientific method is the collection and analysis of data in such a way that alternative explanations are identified.

Thus, the goal is to find disconfirming evidence. If the goal of an assessment is to demonstrate the effectiveness of a program rather than to show that the program was effective, the assessor will be trying to find evidence that it was *not* effective. If this type of evidence cannot be found, then the assessor can confidently assert that the program was effective.

Consider once again the blind men and the elephant. To determine what they were touching, they would then need to know what data they needed to collect—perhaps samples of what they were touching, other sensory experience, or even the opinions of others. The men would then develop a process for analyzing and interpreting the data and thus coming to a conclusion. Finally, they would share their procedures and results with the public. This may sound very similar to the logic example, and it is. The scientific method is a logical process; the difference is that here it is a systematic process with rigorous steps. A similar methodical approach is used in assessment.

Logic Models

A way of knowing used in assessment is the logic model. Wyatt Knowlton and Phillips (2013) defined the *logic model* as a visual method of presenting an idea that offers an understanding of relationships among the elements needed to operate a program or change effort (p. 4). As depicted in Figure 2.1, the assessment cycle is a logic model.

One goal of using a logic model is to determine causation. Like hypotheses, logic models are tested in evaluative settings to determine if the causation or relationships depicted in the model are true. In addition to being a way of knowing, logic models are also used for planning and implementation. A theory-of-change model is a representation of how one believes change will occur, whereas a program logic model details resources, planned activities, and their outputs and the outcomes that result (Wyatt Knowlton & Phillips, 2013, p. 5). Much assessment uses this way of knowing.

Paradigms of Inquiry

Whereas ways of knowing provide a basic understanding regarding how people gain knowledge, there are paradigms of inquiry that lay out specific details regarding how knowledge is acquired, constructed, and verified. Schwandt (1997) defined a *paradigm* as a "worldview or general perspective" (p. 109). In other words, a paradigm is the set of rules and assumptions that guide an understanding of how knowledge is constructed and verified. There are many paradigms of inquiry; positivism and interpretivism are the two major examples, each with its own set of rules.

Figure 2.1 Assessment as logic model.

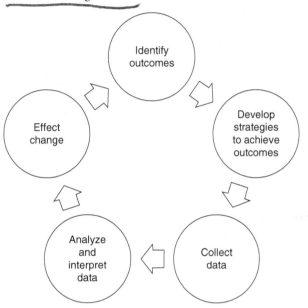

Positivism

Positivism is the doctrine that "physical and social reality is independent of those who observe it and that observations of this reality, if unbiased, constitute scientific knowledge" (Gall et al., 2007, p. 16). In other words, only verifiable claims based on experience could be considered knowledge (Patton, 2015). For positivists, there is an objective reality that can be understood through observed experience. In this perspective, there is one Truth (with a capital *T*), and knowledge is "objective, measurable, and generalizable" (Egbert & Sandeen, 2014, p. 33). The use of logic through the scientific method is the primary "way of knowing" or acquiring and validating knowledge in this paradigm. In positivism, hypotheses are developed to be tested by instruments that have been created with the goal of showing that there is not interaction between the subject and the researcher. By keeping this distance the researcher attempts to ensure objectivity.

Postpositivism

Critics have identified issues regarding the ability to be truly objective in social science research, saying that this is impossible. Researchers are inherently biased, even in attempting to control for bias. In addition, social science research is also value-laden, and the values cannot be separated from the research itself. Because of the weaknesses seen in the positivist paradigm, postpositivism has emerged. In this view, objectivity is useful but not necessarily attainable, particularly in the natural settings where much educational research takes place (Egbert & Sandeen, 2014, p. 33). The same issues involving objectivity with social science research are applicable to student affairs assessment. The individuals doing the assessment are biased because it is impossible to fully set aside all assumptions about an assessment project. In addition, the work is value-laden as importance is placed on different aspects of the college experience. For example, the in-class experience is often valued more highly than the out-of-classroom experience—although that value may be misplaced.

Interpretivism

Unlike positivism, which has a foundational belief that reality is objective and observable, the basic assumption of interpretivism is that "reality is multi-layered and complex and a single event can have multiple interpretations" (Egbert & Sandeen, 2014, p. 32). It posits that "reality is socially constructed by the individuals who participate in it" (Gall et al., 2007, p. 21). Knowledge is acquired by individuals based on their experience in the world and how they interpret that experience. As a result, reality comprises multiple subjective truths (small t) rather than just one objective Truth (capital T).

Rather than trying to observe the objective reality in positivism, the purpose in the interpretivism paradigm is to understand the realities of individuals close to the phenomenon under study. Interpretivism is an inductive paradigm centered on theory generation by observing the human contact with a phenomenon to identify patterns that may suggest a theory. The researcher is the research instrument and subjectivism, meaning the ongoing interaction between the researcher and the data, is valued knowledge and is socially constructed and not objective, static, or immutable.

Constructivism

Some scholars consider constructivism a subcategory of interpretivism (Egbert & Sandeen, 2014), although Holstein and Gubrium (2011) have suggested that it should not be associated with other modes of qualitative inquiry. Constructivism seeks to understand social action through interpretation (Jones, Torres, & Arminio, 2006) and transactional knowledge acquisition. Tenets in this paradigm center on the importance of social interactions and the interpretation of reality by the individual. Multiple realities are constructed by different groups, and these constructions and their implications affect individuals and their interactions with others (Patton, 2015). Knowledge is "subjective, contextualized, and personally experienced rather than acquired from the outside" (Egbert & Sandeen, p. 33), and "everyday realities are actively constructed in and through forms of social action" (Holstein & Gubrium, p. 341). In addition, language and prior knowledge affect individual realities. Constructivism seeks to understand phenomena through the interpretation and meaning constructed by the individual.

Critical Theory

Critical theory is a research paradigm that seeks to understand the interrelationships between power and reality. This way of thinking recognizes power and oppression in society and seeks to address that oppression throughout the research process. A basic assumption is that reality is moderated by historically and socially created power relations (Merriam & Tisdell, 2015). Critical theorists posit that social, political, and historical forces influence individuals and their experiences and that people must be understood in relation to these forces to truly clarify how they construct meaning from their experiences. Research based on critical theory does not necessarily focus on power and oppression as the subject of research, but it can. However, the research process must include strategies for examining the interaction of individuals and their sociopolitical context. Kincheloe, McLaren, and Steinberg (2011, p. 164) have identified the following assumptions of critical theory:

- All thought is fundamentally mediated by power relations that are socially and historically constructed.
- Facts can never be isolated from the domain of values or removed from some form of ideological inscription.
- The relationship between concept and object and between signifier and signified is never stable or fixed and is often mediated by social relations of capitalist production and consumption.
- Language is central to the formation of subjectivity (conscious and unconscious awareness).
- Certain groups in any society and particular societies are privileged over others and, although the reasons for this privileging may vary widely, the oppression that characterizes contemporary societies is more forcefully reproduced when subordinates accept their social status as natural, necessary, and inevitable.
- Oppression has many faces, and focusing on only one at the expense of others (e.g., class oppression versus race oppression) often elides the interconnections among them.
- Mainstream research practices often contribute to the reproduction of systems of class, race, and gender oppression.

Implications of Paradigms for Methodologies and Methods

Each paradigm affects the way the assessor will approach an assessment project. Someone coming from a positivistic perspective will likely try to uncover the static, knowable "facts" regarding the effectiveness of a program, whereas an assessor coming to the same project from an interpretivist perspective would be interested in understanding the participants' experience in the program and how they made sense of it. Because there are distinct sets of procedures and assumptions for each paradigm, each gives rise to one of two groups of methodologies: quantitative and qualitative. Each methodology dictates specific methods. Whereas methodology and method are often used interchangeably, they are different concepts. Egbert and Sandeen (2014) have defined *methodology* "as a reasonable plan for gathering and analyzing information that corresponds to a line of research inquiry" (p. 75). *Methods* are defined as "specific procedures that accomplish the task of gathering and analyzing data in a research study" (p. 75). A research design is predicated on a methodology, and once a design is determined, methods can be identified. Schwandt (1997) has described methodology as the "theory of how inquiry should proceed" (p. 93), whereas method is the "procedure, tool, or technique used to generate data, analyze data or both" (p. 91).

Quantitative methodologies include survey, correlation, causal-comparative, experimental, quasi-experimental, or existing data analyses. Data-collection methods include surveys/questionnaires, self-report measures, and tests; experiments and analytic methods include a variety of statistical tests such as frequencies, cross-tabulations, *t*-tests, and analyses of variance. Biography, phenomenology, ethnography, case study, and grounded theory are qualitative methodologies. The data-collection methods for these methodologies include interviews, focus groups, and document/text review. Analytic methods include content analysis, thematic analysis, open coding, and axial coding.

A paradigm, or the way in which someone approaches inquiry, has an impact on data assumptions about knowledge, as described previously, as well as on data collection and analyses. Table 2.1 demonstrates some of the differences between positivism and constructivism.

Another implication for paradigms in assessment is the use of mixed methods, meaning both quantitative and qualitative methods in the same assessment project. For example, a survey may be followed up with interviews to provide breadth to the survey data. Although qualitative and quantitative methods complement each other, their methodologies may be in conflict. However, the paradigm may be pragmatism (Gall et al., 2007,

TABLE 2.1
Comparing Positivism With Constructivism

Positivism	*Constructivism*
Reality is objective and observable	Reality is subjective and constructed
Data are static	Data are evolving
Attempts to control bias and errors	Bias is addressed openly and is part of the construction and interpretation of data
Researcher is disconnected from the data	Researcher is connected to the data
Data are often numbers	Data are often words, stories, pictures, and images
Quantitative methodologies are used	Qualitative methodologies are used
Data-collection methods include surveys, tests, and quasi-experiments	Data-collection methods include interviews, focus groups, and narratives
Analytical methods include frequencies, cross-tabs, *t*-tests, analysis of variance	Analytical methods include content analysis, thematic analysis, open coding, and axial coding

p. 32) or simply a rationale (efficiency of breadth and depth) for perform-ing it (Creswell & Plano Clark, 2010, p. 3). Creswell and Plano Clark have provided a definition of *mixed methods* that identifies key components:

- Collects and analyzes persuasively and rigorously both qualitative and quantitative data (based on research questions)
- Mixes (or integrates or links) the two forms of data concurrently by combining them (or merging them) sequentially by having one build on the other or embedding one within the other
- Gives priority to one or to both forms of data (in terms of what the research emphasizes)
- Uses these procedures in a single study or in multiple phases of a program of study
- Frames these procedures within philosophical worldviews and theoretical lenses
- Combines the procedures into specific research designs that direct the plan for conducting the study (p. 5)

Though challenging to combine well, mixed-methods assessment can be extremely fruitful in providing a fuller picture of a phenomenon.

Standards for Rigor

Rigor is the quality of the methodology and methods used to acquire knowledge. There are accepted ways of implementing research methods for qualitative and quantitative methods. Standards exist related to how the data are verified, which helps to ensure that rigorous methods have been employed. In quantitative methodology, reliability and validity are standards of rigor, whereas trustworthiness is the standard used in qualitative work.

Reliability

In quantitative methodology, *reliability* refers to the consistency of data. This includes consistency of scores on a test from one administration to another (test-retest reliability) or from one set of items for another (parallel forms reliability). Reliability also includes consistency of raters of a phenomenon, also called interrater reliability. If data are not consistent, there was an error in observing a phenomenon.

In assessment, *reliability* has a similar meaning. It refers to consistency and objectivity (Goff et al., n.d.). In assessment, the assessor wants to be sure that two students who learn similar skills perform similarly on an assessment. The challenge comes when embedded, authentic assessments are used. These types of assessments are situational and context-specific, which may increase the variability between assessments (Goff et al., n.d.). One way of addressing this, suggested by Goff et al. (n.d.), is to focus on trustworthiness and credibility of the information from the assessment. These are concepts of rigor used in qualitative settings and discussed later in this chapter. Another solution is the use of multiple methods to assess the same outcome. This approach, called *triangulation*, helps to increase the credibility of judgments when results of multiple data sources converge (Goff et al., n.d.).

Validity

Validity is a more complex concept to explain. Fraenkel et al. (2014) have defined *validity* as "the appropriateness, correctness, meaningfulness, and usefulness of specific inferences researchers make based on the data they collect" (p. 149). It is important to note that validity is related to the inferences made about the data rather than the data themselves. There are three main types of validity: instrument validity, internal validity, and external validity.

Instrument validity centers specifically on the data-collection instrument. This type of validity can be described by asking, "Does the instrument measure what it purports to measure?" To validate such an instrument, researchers may then collect additional data. These additional data may fall into three categories (Fraenkel et al. 2014): content-related evidence of validity, criterion-related evidence of validity, and construct-related evidence of validity. Assessors want to determine that the content they collected regarding the phenomenon at issue was appropriate and comprehensive. For example, if staff wanted to create a survey to assess orientation, they would analyze the instrument to make sure that it contained items related to all elements of orientation. Researchers may also gather data to determine the relationship of their instrument as compared with another instrument, thus ensuring that they are both measuring the same criteria. If assessors had created a tool to predict retention of students from the first year to the second year of college, they would want to correlate the scores on their tool with the actual retention rates of the students taking the instrument. Finally, researchers may want to validate the constructs in the data-collection tool. Many institutions use the National Survey of Student Engagement (NSSE) because research has suggested that engagement is highly associated with student success. Test developers performed analyses to determine that the NSSE actually measured engagement and not something else.

Internal validity, or "the extent to which extraneous variables have been controlled by the researcher" (Gall et al., 2007, p. 383) is another type of validity. In the positivist paradigm, the researcher must be able to observe the phenomenon objectively. Thus, other variables should not cloud or interfere with that objective observation. If other variables do "moderate" the variables under study, the inferences made from the observations will be flawed. Here is an example: A career development advisor may offer a program on effective communication, as this is a skill that college students should develop and is often an institutional learning goal for colleges and universities. After the program, the hall director may use empty outlines, a classroom assessment technique that is often used to assess learning, to determine if the students learned what was intended. The hall director may infer that the participants learned a great deal based on their completed empty outlines. The hall director may then assume that the learning acquired was a result of the program, but there may be other reasons why students were able to successfully complete the program assessment. One of those reasons could be that students already had this knowledge of effective communication. They could have acquired it through past experience or learned it in high school or other college courses. It is important to consider the moderating variables before making inferences from assessment data. There are a number of issues that can affect the internal validity. They are not covered in this text because more comprehensive discussions are included in texts on research design.

Although internal validity is associated with the impact of variables extraneous to the study, external validity relates to the applicability of findings from a study to individuals or settings beyond those that were studied (Gall et al., 2007, p. 388). External validity, often called *generalizability*, can vary across settings. An assessment can be applicable across departments in a division, but it may not be applicable to a similar department at a different institution. Connected to external validity is ecological validity, where the focus is not necessarily setting but specific conditions (Gall et al., p. 390).

An example of external validity may be useful. The benefit of professional conferences is the opportunity to hear what is working well at other institutions. A student affairs educator may have the opportunity to learn about the assessment of a leadership program at a small private liberal arts college. Every college culture is unique. What one may find in assessing a leadership program at a small private liberal arts college may not be the same when assessing the same program at a large state research university. Whereas the implementation of the program may be transferable to other schools, the findings themselves may not be. It is important to keep this in mind in looking at the impact of programs across settings.

In assessment, *trustworthiness* is defined similarly: Does the assessment assess what it is supposed to assess? (Goff et al., n.d.). To be valid, assessment strategies should reflect not only the learning that should take place but also the level of that learning and the context in which it takes place (Goff et al., n.d.). In addition to learning within a specific domain, such as critical thinking, there are also levels of learning that range from basic to complex. Learning taxonomies such as Bloom's revised cognitive taxonomy (Anderson et al., 2000) outline frameworks for such leveling. Chapter 6, on outcomes, discusses leveling in more detail.

Trustworthiness

In qualitative research, the positivist concept of validity is often replaced with trustworthiness (Lincoln, Lynham, & Guba, 2011, p. 100). Trustworthiness describes the quality or characteristics of the research that make the findings believable to the audience. In a classic text, Lincoln and Guba (1985) have defined *trustworthiness* as the ability of an "inquirer to persuade his or her audience (including self) that the findings of the inquiry are worth paying attention to, worth taking account of" (p. 290). Kincheloe and McLaren (1994, pp. 151–152) have identified the following criteria used to evaluate the trustworthiness of findings, the first criterion being credibility of how the phenomenon is portrayed. In other words, do the findings match reality? (Merriam & Tisdell, 2015). According to Lincoln and Guba (1985), there are two components to credibility. First is implementing the research in a way that is seen as credible. In other words, observers believe that the research is rigorous. The second component of credibility involves being approved by those who shared the information in the first place (p. 296). The second criterion used to evaluate trustworthiness of findings is the similarity or transferability between the context of the findings and the context to which it is being applied. The second criterion used to determine of trustworthiness is dependability. This concept is the extent to which the research methods decisions are made consistently and appropriately throughout the course of a study (Elkins, 2009, p. 9). The third criterion of trustworthiness is confirmability, which is the extent to which results make sense and can be confirmed by others (Elkins, 2009). Whereas quantitative studies use reliability and validity to ensure rigor, qualititative studies use trustworthiness to ensure rigor.

Implications for Assessment

As noted earlier, assessment is not research, although applied research methods are used. Assessment does not attempt to develop or confirm theory but seeks to demonstrate the impact of programs and services. As Upcraft and Schuh (2002) point out, there are a number of issues that affect assessment but not research. These include resource limitations, time limitations, design limitations, political contexts, and organizational contexts (pp. 18–19). When faculty perform research to confirm a hypothesis or build a theory, they often have years to collect and analyze the data and then publish the findings. College student educators do not have years to determine if a program or service is effective because resource allocation decisions need to be made. They may also simply lack sufficient resources to prolong an assessment project. In addition, assessment occurs within a political context (as described in Chapter 16), which also affects how the assessment is carried out.

Approaching Assessment Projects

Although the discussion thus far has related to research methods, the epistemology background is informative for assessment projects as well. It is useful to consider how the person performing the assessment sees the world, because that will influence the data collection and analysis used. If one sees the world as relatively static and believes that behavior can be observable, a positivist approach may likely be used, which would dictate the use of quantitative data collection and analysis. However, if the person doing the assessment sees knowledge and experience as being constructed by individuals, an interpretivist approach may be used, resulting in qualitative data collection and analysis.

Unfortunately, assessment is not as simple as this. The person engaged in assessment does not operate in a vacuum, and many others have a stake in the assessment, each with his or her own paradigm for understanding the world. Given the political nature of assessment, as discussed in Chapter 16, it is critical that assessors be attuned to the paradigms of stakeholders, including those of divisional and institutional leaders. Assessment is ultimately about change and making improvements. Therefore, if leaders who are often the ones with the ability and resources to make change have an epistemological approach differing from that of the assessor, change will be more difficult. This is one reason why mixed methods are often a useful approach to assessment projects as they address both epistemological positions.

Data Collection

As discussed earlier, one's epistemological approach to research, or in this case assessment, influences the data-collection methods used. If one approaches assessment from a positivist perspective assuming that there is just one Truth, then surveys and tests may be the dominant form of data collection. Unfortunately, these data-collection methods are often the default methods, not because the assessment is aligned with the positivist epistemology but because they seem to be the easiest and quickest methods to use. However, many quantitative methods are actually more complex than they appear. There is both a science and an art to survey and test development. Given the predominance of surveys and the proliferation of easy-to-use online survey tools, these methods have resulted in survey fatigue and poor data on college campuses. Students are inundated with surveys from college officials, other students, the stores at which they shop, and social media. Students have become numb to surveys; as a result, participation rates for assessment-based surveys on campus have dropped. This popular data-collection method has lost its value. However, tests and surveys that are administered at the "point of service" do result in higher participation rates because students are more compelled to respond. Point-of-service surveys are brief surveys administered during or directly after a person has used a service.

People subscribing to an interpretivist epistemology are more inclined to use qualitative assessment methods, including interviews, focus groups, and reflection papers. Participants are able to construct their own understanding of an experience through these methods rather than being forced to choose from a small number of responses to a very narrow question. Although these methods do allow for more authentic responses from students, they take longer to collect as well as to analyze the resulting data. As Harper and Kuh (2007) note, "Qualitative inquiry requires more expertise than simply drafting some questions, starting the audio recorder, and reading prompts from an interview protocol" (p. 11). The need for time for collection and analysis is off-putting to many of those who perform assessments because they usually want to get a quick answer to their assessment question. But it is critical to recognize the interaction effect between researcher and participant, which could lead to changes in the questions, sample, and process in the middle of the assessment. Although this adds more time to the process, these adaptations improve the quality of the assessment.

There are also assessment methods called classroom assessment techniques (CATs), which do not necessarily fit neatly into data-collection methods rooted in research methodology. Angelo and Cross developed CATs after extensive research regarding effective methods of assessing learning in college classrooms. Their book, *Classroom Assessment Techniques* (Angelo & Cross, 1993), includes 50 assessment techniques, many of which can be used in student affairs assessment. Most of these methods would be considered qualitative, as they seek to have students describe what they have learned from an activity or experience. As such, the assumption is that they are constructing their own knowledge. However, there are some more positivist or quantitive methods that include the categorizing grid, defining features matrix, and empty outlines. See Chapter 12 for several examples that could apply in student affairs settings.

As with research, the assessment question should influence the data-collection method used. Thus, it is critical to be clear what will be assessed. The type of question often provides a clue regarding the epistemological approach needed. Questions regarding "what" (e.g., "What was learned or what impact did this program have?") are often but not always quantitative in nature, especially if the assessor has a list of the items to be learned or the effect that should occur. However, "what" questions can also be qualitative if the assessor wants the student to construct his or her own understanding of his or her experience. This construction can then be compared with intended outcomes of the program or service. Questions such as "how" or "why" (e.g., "How did they learn x?" or "Why did this program not have the intended impact?") are often qualitative and require data-collection methods that are exploratory and narrative in some form. Although it is not critical to perform a philosophical analysis regarding the appropriate epistemological approach to an assessment project, it is essential to clearly define the assessment question itself, as it will dictate the methods needed to answer it. However, it is important to note that an epistemological approach can affect data collection and analysis.

Ensuring Rigor in Assessment Projects

Whereas there are different concepts of rigor, depending on the epistemological approach to a topic, the assessor, as in data collection, does not have to engage in in-depth mental olympics to determine which approach to rigor is needed. The basic question to be answered regardless of approach is: "How does one know that the results of an assessment are accurate and how important is it that they be accurate?" Researchers would deconstruct this question into reliability, validity, or trustworthiness (and its components). But for someone performing assessment, the focus is on the most basic question of accuracy and thus on determining how to ensure accuracy. A key concept to consider here is triangulation. Schwandt (1997) defined *triangulation* as a means of verifying the integrity of inferences made. Janesick (1998) outlined four approaches to triangulation in qualitative research:

1. Data triangulation: the use of a variety of data sources in a study
2. Investigator triangulation: the use of several different researchers or evaluators
3. Theory triangulation: the use of multiple perspectives to interpret a single set of data
4. Methodological triangulation: the use of multiple methods to study a single problem (pp. 214–215)

Although these four types of triangulation refer to qualitative research, they are transferable to all types of assessment. This provides stronger evidence for conclusions drawn from interpreting the results.

To draw from the quantitative tradition, it is also important to consider the generalizability of assessment findings. The goal is to ensure that the experiences of a sample are comparable to those of the larger group from which the sample was drawn. For example, if 300 students living in the residence halls were surveyed and asked about their on-campus experience, it would be important to policy and practice to know to what extent the responses from the sample were similar to those of the students who were not sampled. This topic is covered in more detail in Chapter 9.

The use of multiple methods may be one of the most popular and easiest ways to triangulate assessment data. Suskie (2014) has suggested the use of multiple methods because any one method is imperfect and imprecise and in this way you can be more confident in your findings (pp. 38–39). It is important to note the difference between multiple methods and mixed methods. *Multiple methods* simply means the use of more than one method to collect data, whereas *mixed methods*, as discussed earlier, means using both qualitative and quantitative methods. Though seemingly similar, both approaches have distinct purposes. Maki (2010) has reiterated the importance of using multiple methods in assessment, specifically in the course of assessing learning. She outlines the following benefits of using multiple methods:

- Reduces straitjacket interpretations of student achievement based on the limitations inherent in one method
- Provides students with opportunities to demonstrate learning that they may not have been able to demonstrate within the context of another method
- Contributes to comprehensive interpretations of student achievement at both institution and program levels
- Values the dimensionality of learning
- Values the diverse ways in which humans learn and represent their learning (p. 157)

An example may be useful to demonstrate what ensuring rigor looks like in an assessment project. Residence halls provide a fertile opportunity for student growth. If a director of residence life at a college wanted to assess what first-year students learned from their experience of living in the residence halls, she could employ a variety of ways to ensure rigor. If she wanted to use data triangulation, she could look at different data sets that had already been collected from the first-year students, which might include results from institutional surveys, grades, placement tests, program attendance, and so on. The director could also use investigator triangulation by gathering data regarding what students learned from the students themselves, resident assistants who lived on the floors, and hall directors who lived in the buildings. Each of these groups would have a different perspective, but the data collected from each group should reinforce and confirm the data from other groups. Theoretical triangulation could be applied using multiple theories, such as Chickering and Reisser's Theory of Identity Development (1993) and Perry's Schema of Epistemological Growth (1968), to understand reflection papers written by the students describing what they learned from living in the residence halls. Finally, the mixed-methods approach to triangulation would be used if survey data were analyzed alongside focus group data in the hope that the results from those two data-collection methods would converge on similar outcomes from the experience of living in the residence halls.

Conclusion

In approaching assessment projects in student affairs, it is helpful to understand the epistemological approaches to research. The philosophy regarding how knowledge is constructed helps us to understand how to approach assessment and also informs us on how to collect and analyze data. However, it is important to remember that assessment is not research, and while there are specific concepts related to rigor in research, the key concern regarding assessment results is the accuracy of the results and interpretations made from them. Triangulation is a concept that can help to ensure this accuracy, and there are multiple ways to triangulate assessment data. One does not have to be an expert in research to engage in assessment. To ensure a high-quality assessment, it is important to understand the differences and similarities between research and assessment as well as how research methodology and methods inform assessment.

Key Points

- There are multiple ways of gaining knowledge, called *ways of knowing*.
- A paradigm of inquiry is a set of beliefs regarding how knowledge is acquired, constructed, and verified.
- *Methodology* is a theory of how inquiry should be done, whereas *method* is a procedure to collect and/or analyze data.
- There are standards of rigor for evidence, which vary slightly by methodological paradigm.

Discussion Questions and Activities

- In your own words, how would you explain the concept of epistemology?
- Why is epistemology important to student affairs assessment?
- How would you paraphrase each paradigm of inquiry?
- Which paradigm of inquiry most aligns with your view of the world? How might this paradigm impact how you implement assessment?
- What are the similarities and differences between the tenets of positivism and interpretivism?
- What are some strategies for ensuring rigor in quantitative assessment? In qualitative assessment?

3

THE ASSESSMENT PROCESS

The Big Picture

A s Banta, Jones, and Black (2009) have noted, "Student affairs professionals have long recognized the need to move from counting the number of students who attend an event to collecting meaningful information about how effectively the goals of the event or program are being met" (p. 199). In order to be meaningful, student affairs units need to have a systematic and ongoing plan to collect information from their audiences at the right time.

Unfortunately, even if assessment is done, it is sometimes done in a haphazard and disjointed way. You may have heard (or voiced!) the following lament: "They did an assessment, but the results just sat on the shelf." Or "They never bothered to close the loop by using the results and then assessing the changes to see if they made a difference." Suskie (2009) aptly said, "Assessment reports that end up briefly perused and then filed without any resulting action are, to be blunt, a waste of time" (p. 297). To prevent that from happening, student affairs staff need to plan for an overall assessment implementation strategy and priorities that are manageable and consistent. Such planning includes determining unit needs, defining language, engaging stakeholders, adopting a cycle, and setting expectations.

Banta et al. (2009) have suggested engaging stakeholders in assessment planning from the very beginning: "Faculty members, academic administrators, and student affairs professionals must play principal roles in setting the course for assessment, but students can contribute ideas and so can trustees, employers, and other community representatives" (p. 3). They also suggest connecting assessment to the goals and processes that the institution has deemed important and developing a written plan/template that both staff and faculty can use to document progress. Assessment should be built into a unit's strategic plan and new programs but also scheduled in a manageable way to collect a variety of information using different methods over a set period of time (Banta et al., 2009). In order for assessment to be the most successful, there should be a coordinated plan. One important note related to student affairs assessment is this: "Unlike research, assessment does not need to *prove* that a certain learning experience alone produced a certain learning outcome—only that students who completed that learning activity had, at the end of it, the desired competency" (Keeling, Wall, Underhile, & Dungy, 2008, p. 34). We know that students learn from a variety of experiences, and many institutions define what they want their students to obtain by the time they graduate in terms of goals, outcomes, or domains. In terms of quality improvement, student affairs staff are concerned with the effectiveness of a given program at a given time, rather than making broad generalizations about the test of a theory (which is more of a description of research).

Common Language

One of the most important foundational steps is to determine a common language. Usually this takes place at the institutional level, but divisions or departments may do that as well. For the purposes of this book, we will use the following definitions:

> *Assessment:* Collecting, analyzing, interpreting, and disseminating data applied for accountability and program and learning improvement
>
> *Evaluation:* Using data to make judgments regarding programs or services
>
> *Research:* Collecting data for the purpose of testing a theory to produce generalizable knowledge
>
> *Strategic plan:* A long-term plan that designates what a unit will accomplish
>
> *Vision:* An inspirational statement regarding the ideal success of an organization
>
> *Mission:* The purpose of an organization
>
> *Values:* Foundational beliefs that guide an organization
>
> *Goals:* The end results of an activity, a program, or a service written in broad terms
>
> *Learning outcomes:* What students know or are able to do at the end of an experience
>
> *Program outcomes:* What the program is expected to provide
>
> *Objectives:* Specific accomplishments attained to meet a goal—also called operational outcomes or administrative outcomes
>
> *Assessment methods:* The measures used to collect data to determine whether a program has met its goals and outcomes and/or a student has learned
>
> *Action plans:* Documents to improve programs and services that units create after collecting and interpreting data

The time it takes to agree on definitions will vary by institution, but it is a worthwhile investment. Some definitions may be imposed by external accreditation agencies, but even those may vary by regional accrediting agency as well as by academic and functional area accrediting agencies. Because student affairs language differs from academic affairs language, this step is extremely important in getting everyone in the organization on the same page. An Internet search for assessment glossaries and common terms is a useful way to get started. Staff new to a campus should proactively learn the language as soon as possible.

Rationale and Expectations

Once language has been established, the next step is to set the foundation of why assessment is taking place and the expectations for performance. As mentioned, there are multiple reasons to engage in assessment; two that are frequently cited are accountability and program improvement. Different areas within the institution may prioritize them differently. For example, the provost may be particularly concerned with accreditation requirements, rankings, and documentation, while the senior student affairs officers (SSAO) may place more emphasis on program evaluation to be able to tell the story of the division to others. Units may focus on the learning that takes place during a particular program. As a part of that foundational discussion, other areas should be addressed, such as acknowledging the political environment, building a support network, identifying resources, and documenting current assessment practices and results (Bresciani, Zelna, & Anderson, 2004). In setting this stage, it is helpful to set up regular meetings with specific staff to review progress and continue collaborative efforts.

Because of the expectations at the institutional level, SSAOs (and therefore their reporting staff) are typically taking a more active role in assessment plans than they did in the past. They may be facing more scrutiny about the effectiveness and efficiency of their programs and services. Assessment planning should be incorporated into the budget and strategic planning processes. SSAOs may be looking for synergies across programs or offices that will improve efficiency and effectiveness, or they may be looking at the division structural changes. They may be requesting information from their staff about program accomplishments and contributions to institutional priorities such as academic success, retention, and graduation. The president of the institution may ask the SSAO to report on specific metrics each year including budget requests and expenditures. For example, the president is concerned with the overall budget of a division of student affairs but may also want to know how efficient and effective the division is in terms of promoting student persistence through programs and services. The SSAO also wants to know that the departments are being good stewards of funds, and he or she wants to know that the units are contributing to the division goals. Let's say that one of the goals addresses diversity and inclusion; the SSAO wants to know what programs and initiatives the departments are working on and how effective they have been (e.g., Have reports of bias incidents decreased? Have residence hall students reported increased feelings of inclusion on the biannual campus climate survey?). Individual departments may offer specific diversity programs and workshops, while SSAOs assess the learning outcomes with each activity.

Resources

Creating a new assessment program requires investments of resources at the university, division, and department levels. Keeling et al. (2008) have described three dimensions of planning for assessment costs: "(1) determining and gathering appropriate human resources, (2) planning appropriate time frames for activities, and (3) developing authentic and reasonable budgets" (p. 79). Staffing considerations include who is going to be coordinating any divisional and departmental efforts and providing appropriate training and support. Several factors determine time commitment for assessment: professional development, planning, development of assessment tools, implementation, analysis, reporting, and action planning and program improvement. Inevitably, assessment initially takes more time than expected, especially if it is a new endeavor. Factors determining cost include types of assessment, existing organizational capacity, level of existing internal professional expertise, and technical demands (hardware and software). The most expensive budget elements include technological systems and support, staffing, and professional development for all staff expected to implement assessment. Other costs need to be considered in the entire budgeting process. These costs include data-gathering expenses (e.g., incentives for participants or travel to a data-collection site), data entry or analysis costs, and reporting expenses.

Timeline

As part of the assessment planning process, a timeline should be established. For example, accreditation reviews may occur every 10 years (typically with a 5-year smaller review), although data should be collected all the time. The institutional effectiveness office may have a documentation process to collect assessment data in a consistent manner across the campus that examines institutional learning outcomes and/or the general education requirements. The division of student affairs may have an annual reporting process to share assessment results in support of the division's strategic plan. A department may expect that an assessment report be prepared following a particular program or service delivery. Those reporting requirements can also look different and may be more or less structured.

Assessment Cycle

As the assessment cycle develops, Bresciani et al. (2004) have identified several questions that should be answered throughout the process:

- What are we trying to do and why?
- What is my program supposed to accomplish?
- How well are we doing it?
- How do we know?
- How do we use the information to improve or celebrate successes?
- Do the improvements we make work? (p. 9)

Understanding and following a systemic and continuous process helps student affairs professionals make the most of assessment. Bresciani et al. (2004, p. 10) have proposed a cycle of assessing student learning, which also applies to other assessment types. At the center of assessment lie the mission, goals, and outcomes. Those serve as a foundation for the program and the assessment process. As staff determine the delivery strategies, they also determine the assessment methods. Once the assessment has been implemented and data have been collected, the analysis and interpretation phases move the staff member toward the decisions that need to be made. Those improvements could be about particular policies and practices, but they could also be about the program changes or fiscal priorities.

The Bresciani cycle, shown in Figure 3.1, provides a road map for student affairs professionals to take, rather than wandering aimlessly and forgetting important landmarks. It is also important to understand the context in which you are operating. Politics, power, budget, literature, and campus culture all influence the decisions and actions at every step along the way.

Student affairs professionals have an obligation to read and reflect on current literature about their functional area or program. Recent published research results as well as current events inform campus and unit practice. The diversity of students coming to campus influences how staff

Figure 3.1 The Bresciani cycle.

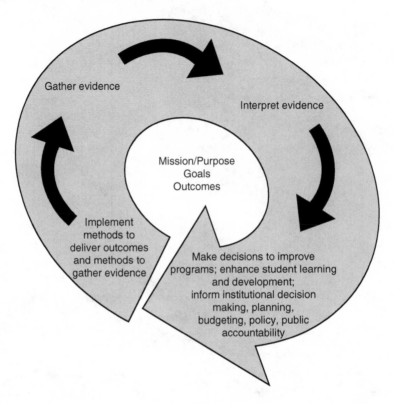

Gather evidence

Interpret evidence

Mission/Purpose
Goals
Outcomes

Implement
methods to
deliver outcomes
and methods to
gather evidence

Make decisions to improve
programs; enhance student learning
and development;
inform institutional decision
making, planning,
budgeting, policy, public
accountability

implement programs and services. Programs that worked two decades ago may not be appropriate today. In addition, how students receive and interpret information has changed (think about marketing efforts prior to the Internet and social media), and their needs have changed. Has the institution's new student orientation stayed the same, although the student population is older and includes more adult students and veterans? Are the counseling center's staff seeing more serious mental health issues than they did five years ago? Are students of color feeling isolated and excluded? Are sexual assault survivors comfortable reporting such incidents to campus officials and confident that they will receive needed services? How has the cost of education affected students' behavior in terms of employment and involvement? How are international students experiencing their stay on campus?

Keeling et al. (2008) have proposed a practical stage model for assessment planning with four stages and 10 steps (pp. 69–71):

Stage 1: During this stage, a foundation is established that anchors and provides ballast to future assessment activities.

Step 1: Determine who within the institution, division, or department will take leadership of assessment activities; clearly communicate the dimensions of that person's leadership role and expectations. This role is often defined as an *assessment champion.*

Step 2: Consider the talents, aptitudes, and areas of expertise present among colleagues and establish an assessment team to work closely with the leader and also with other faculty or staff.

Step 3: Develop an internal capacity-building strategy that provides staff and faculty with accurate information and introduces them to key concepts of student learning, student development, and assessment practice. Decide what elements of this strategy will be addressed by formal, intentional professional development and training and what components will require either hands-on practice within the structure of existing positions and roles or self-study.

Stage 2: During this stage, which includes steps 4 and 5, an infrastructure emerges. The creation of a glossary will result in a common language. But, more importantly, the process of developing the glossary allows time and resources to be devoted to asking important questions and engaging in discourse to bring clarity and rationale to assessment activities. Step 5 brings common concerns to the table and should include candid conversations about perceptions and realities of who on campus "owns" assessment; how assessment differs from institutional research; and the roles of faculty, staff, and administrators as well as their respective strengths and weaknesses.

Step 4: Create a glossary of terms that brings clarity and common understanding to pertinent concepts so as to make that glossary easily accessible. It is more important to have consistency within the institution than to make the institution's terms exactly the same as those of some other institution or professional organization.

Step 5: Consider and respond to potential barriers, impediments, and challenges, including power dynamics, internal departmental or institutional politics, and various manifestations of change resistance.

Stage 3: This stage includes the next three steps, 6 through 8, which are the processes of inquiry and assessment with which to inform the assessment plan. Important questions to ask during this stage include the following:

"Where do students naturally learn on our campus and in our community? What are the sociographics of our students? What is important to them? How do they learn? Why did they choose our institution? How can we best serve and educate them? What programs, student organizations, professional honoraries, and services are already in place to promote student learning and development? What programs and services could be enhanced? With what members of the faculty and staff should we develop partnerships?"

Step 6: Map existing campus and community resources—an institutional topography of learning.

Step 7: Determine learning and developmental needs of students in relation to the institution's overall desired student learning outcomes.

Step 8: Determine program strengths and areas for improvement—that is, define what programs address what areas of students' learning and developmental needs and then study the effectiveness of each of those programs in addressing those needs.

Stage 4: This stage incorporates the final two steps, 9 and 10, which synthesize much of the information gathered in the previous steps. Data about program and personnel talent can be arranged in a matrix that illustrates program names, departmental objectives, leadership, and professional development needs. In some ways, this stage is the culmination of all the planning. At this point, the stage is set for developing and assessing student learning outcomes.

Step 9: Develop an assessment curriculum, including a scope and sequence that describes and illustrates who will lead what program; what the learning outcomes are for each program; when and how learning will be assessed; and when and how data will be gathered, analyzed, and disseminated.

Step 10: Based on sound assessment data, evaluate the quality or effectiveness of programs and institute processes of sustainability or improvement.

For institutions that do not already have a structure in place, this provides a framework with which to implement a strategic assessment process. Yousey-Elsener (2013) has also described an assessment cycle (p. 11) (see Figure 3.2). The center of the cycle contains the institutional, divisional, or departmental mission that serves as the foundation for all activities. The cycle includes identifying outcomes, determining methods, planning assessment

Figure 3.2 The Yousey-Elsener assessment cycle.

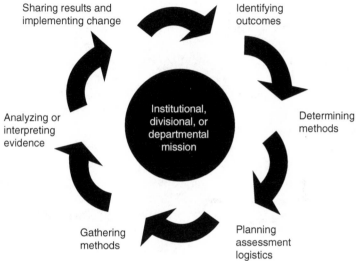

logistics, gathering methods, analyzing or interpreting evidence, and sharing results and implementing change. The outcomes should be derived from the program goals. Program outcomes describe what the program, process, or service will achieve. Alternatively, learning outcomes describe what the participant will know or be able to do at the end of an intervention. The established outcomes will guide the methods used to collect data (covered later in the book) and the rigor needed to answer the assessment question/purpose. The logistics include who, what, when, where, why, and how of the project. Gathering evidence is the actual collection of data needed. Once that occurs, the data are analyzed and interpreted in the context of the assessment question. The last step of the cycle is sharing information and making improvements in the program. The cycle then begins again, which is especially important if significant changes have been implemented.

Suskie (2009) has also provided a simple, continuous four-step cycle to assess student learning: (a) establish learning goals, (b) provide learning opportunities, (c) assess student learning, and (d) use the results. Suskie stresses that assessment must be integrated into the learning experiences so as to create a seamless environment. In addition, the use of results should lead back to adapting the learning goals.

Most recently, Fulcher, Good, Coleman, and Smith (2014) proposed an assessment model particularly related to providing evidence of student learning called program learning assessment, intervention, and re-assessment

(PLAIR). In other words, they described it as "weigh pig, feed pig, weigh pig." In collecting examples of PLAIR, they found that many programs completed only two of the three steps. Although student learning might have occurred, the programs could not provide evidence that student learning improved because of specific interventions. In their model, these investigators suggest several steps. First, staff identify targeted objectives, indicating why each is important and what specific direct assessment results would lead to the conclusion that it needed to be improved. Second, staff investigate current efforts to know what the program or process is doing right now to address the objective. A curriculum map can illustrate where and how the objectives are or are not addressed. Third, staff propose learning modifications and interventions. Fourth, staff create an improvement timetable. They concluded that student affairs staff need training in how to improve learning, not just in the mechanics of assessment. As members of institutions of higher education, we have a responsibility to provide evidence of student learning in a coordinated manner.

Having a model for the assessment process helps staff understand the expectations and the process. Divisions, departments, or units can choose an assessment cycle that fits their particular needs. The cycles described here do have commonalities, but adapting a cycle that works with the assessment priorities and culture of the division increases the likelihood of a smooth transition.

Assessment Priorities

Division leadership provides the charge and expectations of the assessment priorities. They communicate, through their words and actions, the importance of assessment and provide an assessment agenda for staff to follow. SSAO know (or should know) what their presidents need and want to know. If they do not, they should ask. Department heads know (or should know) what their vice presidents need and want to know. Department staff know (or should know) what their department heads need and want to know. Some institutions are focused on the retention, persistence, and graduation rates of students. Others are more focused on the institution's stated learning domains or outcomes. Still others focus on career preparation or social justice. Some institutions focus on all of these issues at the same time. Those priorities and contexts should inform and impact the student affairs assessment efforts in addition to program-specific goals and outcomes.

In order for assessment to take hold, divisional leadership must ensure that sufficient resources are devoted to the process (Banta, Jones, & Black,

2009). These would include human (who is coordinating the process, who has specific expertise, who is preparing any reports or publications), financial (investment in technology, support for training and development, hiring of staff if needed), expertise (online and in-person training, assessment teams), and time (how much time individual staff are expected to devote to different steps in the assessment process) resources. In times of "do more with less," divisions of student affairs have to decide where to allocate resources that create a manageable and meaningful process for all staff. Conducting a staff needs assessment can identify professional development topics, attitudes, and resources needed. As assessment becomes ingrained in the work of a division, the processes and resources should be reviewed and improved on a regular basis to make sure that the momentum continues and new staff are educated in the assessment culture. A review of the assessment process may reveal that individual assessments need improvement or that a different assessment method needs to be used (Banta et al., 2009).

As assessment planning initiatives and specific assessment plans are developed, staff may be concerned about the level of precision involved and the amount of time that may take. Keeling et al. (2008) recognize the issue:

> A common concern in the development and implementation of assessment plans and their accompanying activities is ensuring *rigor*. Rigor describes the processes put in place so that the educational processes for supporting and accompanying student learning, defining desired learning outcomes, identifying and collecting data and determining and analyzing results are each and all credible. Common terms associated with rigor are: reliability, validity, objectivity, generalizability, trustworthiness, transferability, dependability, and confirmability. (p. 34)

These terms are discussed in more detail in later chapters in the context of student affairs assessment and specific assessment projects.

Student affairs practitioners may be uncomfortable with the terminology without a guide of what it means for them on a regular basis. Realistically what student affairs staff need to know to improve programs, services, and learning does not always lend itself to an intensive research protocol. They may be under a time constraint or may not have the resources to get a 90% response rate to a survey. At times they have to accept that the information they have is more information than they had before. Obviously the more important the decision, the more rigor should be incorporated into the assessment. For example, residence life could seek feedback from residents about chairs in one study lounge, a new paint color for individual rooms in one building, or desired amenities for a newly constructed residence hall.

Each one of those areas varies in cost, permanence, and complexity. Formality and rigor would vary for each assessment.

This can also be considered the "doable–ideal" continuum. Any assessment project can be placed on a continuum of rigor from doable to ideal. A doable assessment project may simply use personal experience and anecdote, whereas an ideal assessment project may employ validated collection tools and the triangulation of data from multiple sources. Decisions on where any project should be on this continuum should be made based on the importance of the inferences. For example, deciding what social activity to have in a residence hall on a Saturday night may be toward the "doable" end of the continuum. There does not need to be a random sample survey sent to residents requiring a 95% response rate. The hall director could simply ask the first 10 or 15 students she sees earlier that day. The implications for failure are low. The worst that might happen is that pizza is ordered for watchers of a movie in the lounge and no one shows up. On the other hand, designing a new multimillion-dollar residence hall needs a bit more rigor than asking 10 or 15 students if faculty offices, a snack bar, a dining hall, and an activity room should be included in this new building. This assessment project would be closer to the "ideal" end of the continuum, requiring multiple, more sophisticated methods of assessment.

Keeling et al. (2008) have proposed that assessment practice should be transparent, as this builds trust with stakeholders. The purpose and values underpinning the assessment should be very clear and shared. The position or stance of the assessor should be articulated to avoid any conflict of interest or confusion. Practitioners should be clear about their biases and relationship to the assessment project. The intended use and commitment to use should be expressed. In addition, Keeling et al. have noted that assessment should engage stakeholders as something that is done *with* them and not *to* them. The chosen method should reflect the purpose and context of the assessment. A qualitative focus group is more appropriate in some situations than a quantitative survey. On the other hand, a reflective essay or a pre-/posttest might be the best method. Staff should also adhere to the standards for that method as practicable to maintain quality. Assessment should follow ethical guidelines related to assessment, research, and functional area associations (see Chapter 15). Finally, assessment should promote the public good in relation to larger social and democratic goals (Keeling et al., 2008).

Divisional leadership also empowers others to take leadership roles in the assessment process through assessment teams, staff learning communities, partnering with faculty on research projects, and coordinating their units' assessments. Staff needs to take ownership of such assessments. Banta et al. (2009) recognized the role of the student affairs staff in the process in stating that "student affairs professionals and advisors are the experts in setting student learning outcomes for campus activities and advising" (p. 12).

Overall, staff need to understand the process and expectations of assessment and align them with the institutional and divisional priorities. Particularly if assessment planning is new, the process must be manageable and simple. There must be support from the institutions in terms of training, technical support, processes, and language. Concrete information must be distributed, including training dates, timelines, review processes, and report structure. Sufficient resources to implement assessment must be provided.

At the program level, staff who are expected to lead the assessment process need to reflect on the purpose of their program, its goals and outcomes, and the performance expectations. Those considerations will guide the assessment planning process. In addition, they need to consider the budget impact, the environment, and current research in the functional area.

Creating an overall planning calendar for all assessment in an area is also helpful. Units that have more than one assessment project in a year need to have a plan to ensure that their projects are timed correctly. These plans should be integrated into a divisional or campus calendar, so that populations of interest are not overassessed and that topics are not needlessly repeated. This also helps to ensure that useful information is collected before a decision has to be made.

Overcoming Barriers and Challenges

Realistically, there are barriers to staff being fully engaged in an outcomes assessment process. Bresciani, Moore Gardner, and Hickmott (2009) have identified several common barriers described by faculty, administrators, and student affairs staff: lack of time, lack of resources, lack of assessment knowledge, lack of understanding of student learning and development, lack of collaboration within student affairs and with faculty, and a disconnect between what student affairs professionals expect students to do and the intervention that will lead to the expected outcome. These are realistic barriers in today's environment of limited resources, increasingly complex student needs and external expectations, and student affairs preparation and training.

Kuh and Banta (2000) have described obstacles that impeded collaboration between faculty and student affairs administrators in the assessment processes. First, the cultural-historical obstacles include lack of trust and respect, suspicion, competition, and differing value of in-class and out-of-class learning. Second, the institution creates bureaucratic-structural barriers that include governance structure, schedules, and salary differences. Third, leadership issues can be obstacles: sending mixed messages, no clear role modeling, and no benefits for collaboration.

Wehlburg (2008) has identified additional institutional obstacles. Faculty may prioritize their discipline over the university, so they do not value any collaboration that takes away from their job of creating and disseminating knowledge. In addition, many campuses succumb to the "silo mentality," which inhibits communication and collaboration.

Fortunately, these barriers can be addressed. Training, education, and professional development can increase staff knowledge and skills and thus confidence. The cost and time commitment can vary with resources that include webinars, online training, conferences, institutes, consultants, and academic courses. Ideally, student affairs staff could collaborate within the division and with faculty who have specific skills, knowledge, and interests. Division leadership can set reasonable expectations and provide resources to coordinate and streamline efforts. Bresciani et al. (2009) encourage celebration, flexibility, and simplicity. By making the process easy and pleasant, more staff will be willing and able to successfully assess programs and services.

Banta and Kuh (1998) have provided six themes to integrate student affairs and academic affairs assessment to foster cross-divisional teamwork. First, administrators need to serve as role models in their commitment to gathering and using data in the decision-making process. Second, faculty and student affairs staff have a responsibility to plan and assess the curriculum (think of the programs and activities as being part of the curriculum). Third, collaboration is easier when there is a common view of student learning outcomes and priorities. Fourth, student learning experiences and their assessment should be coordinated across the campus, both within and outside the classroom walls. Fifth, faculty and student affairs staff need to recognize, promote, and assess institution-specific outcomes, regardless of who gathers the information. Sixth, assessment results should be used to improve the holistic student experience.

Another resource for student affairs staff is the institutional research or institutional effectiveness office. The staff in these areas have technical skills as well as broad campus knowledge to assist student affairs staff. They may actually have information already collected that can assist staff. For example, many campuses participate in national surveys, which are usually coordinated through the institutional research office. The residence life department can request the results for specific questions for students who live on campus (the survey may ask a residence question or the department can provide student identification numbers if that was part of the implementation process) or an analysis comparing residential and commuter students. By working together, student affairs and academic affairs create a more accurate picture of students and their experiences.

Assessing Assessment

Regardless of methods, models, time frames, and outcomes, student affairs staff should take time to review their assessment process and products on a regular basis. It is important to be sure that assessment practices are still useful and relevant. As institutional, divisional, and departmental priorities change, the assessment priorities may change as well. As an accreditation visit approaches, the institution may be more vocal about specific data needs and deadlines. It may create earlier deadlines for reporting outcomes assessment data. A new institution or division leader could articulate a different set of priorities and expectations. For example, the priority could shift from an emphasis on service-learning and social responsibility to global competence when a new president or vice president arrives on campus. While these areas are not mutually exclusive, they may shift resources and assessment measures.

Technology also impacts the assessment process. New products are developed all the time. Adopting a new technology could greatly improve efficiency of staff reporting their assessment results. Someone—whether the information technology department, the divisional assessment director, or the department assessment coordinator—should be paying attention to technological developments. The changes do not have to be major; it could be as simple as changing the Word or Excel template, or it could be as complex as adopting a new web-based survey and analysis software requiring significant training.

In order for assessment to be adopted and integrated into day-to-day practice, it has to be as simple and easy as possible. In order to understand barriers, frustrations, and potential solutions, the entire process must be evaluated. This could be done through a survey, a focus group, or benchmarking with other institutions for best practices. The person or team involved in making those changes can then begin to make improvements to the process and products.

Assessing the assessment process includes determining if, when, and how units are using their assessment data. If staff are not using assessment to improve programs and services, there is a problem. The person responsible for the overall assessment process has to determine why staff are not using it. Are they assessing the "wrong" areas, collecting nonmeaningful data, assessing for assessment's sake, or unable to make any necessary changes? Any of these are frustrating and need to be addressed in different ways.

There are several concrete measures staff can implement to improve the assessment process. If there is an assessment committee (or an interested group of staff), they may be responsible for reviewing assessment reports, annual assessment plans, or other material and providing suggestions. They may find commonalities across the division that would not be apparent without a broader review. Staff can also serve as peer consultants for assistance as well as gather feedback about what is effective and what might be frustrating to other staff. The Council for the Advancement of Standards in Higher Education (CAS) (2012a) also provides guidance for assessing individual functional areas to perform a simple or in-depth self-study. The most important piece of assessing assessment is to engage staff in meaningful work and dialogue that makes a difference in their practice.

Conclusion

In beginning an assessment endeavor in student affairs, it is important to understand the big picture, including your stakeholders; institution, division, and unit priorities; and resources. The overall assessment program should be transparent, structured, and manageable in order for staff to buy into the process. Because the environment always changes, the assessment process and products should be assessed on a regular basis. In the end, student affairs assessment should lead to program and service improvement as well as accountability to various stakeholders.

Key Points

- Assessment efforts should follow a structure and cycle that makes sense for those involved.
- Institutions and/or divisions need to determine a common language around assessment.
- An assessment champion (or champions) can increase the likelihood of buy-in while also supporting the people, processes, and products surrounding student affairs assessment.

Discussion Questions and Activities

- Describe the main steps in an assessment cycle.
- What processes are currently in place at your institution to promote student affairs assessment? What needs to be improved?

- Describe the resources available to you with which to implement assessment.
- What challenges and barriers have you observed? What steps have been or can be implemented to ensure success?
- What processes are in place to review the assessment process and provide support for staff?

4

PLANNING AND DESIGNING INDIVIDUAL ASSESSMENT PROJECTS

Classroom assessment follows specific guidelines to help faculty assess student learning. In student affairs work, staff may not have the same structured environment: Student experiences may last more or less than one semester, students may enter and leave experiences at different times, and the learning content may be less controlled and tested. Those challenges should not prevent student affairs professionals from assessing. Student affairs staff can follow a similar assessment process to gather data and use information to improve specific programs and services. Wehlburg (2008) has correlated the out-of-class assessment with the in-class assessment process:

> The same basic process will work in the development of embedded assessment activities within non-classroom-based programs. Identifying the overall goals and outcomes is a first and necessary step. Following this, a process similar to curriculum mapping can take place. . . . Student leadership plans, student work with specific cocurricular organizations, and even programming done within residence halls are all potential sources of student learning data. (p. 149)

Curricular mapping (Maki, 2010) is simply the process of visually aligning the outcomes of an experience with the specific activities that develop or enhance the outcomes over time. The maps can illuminate any gaps or redundancies in the learning. Maki (2010) has described the following main mapping purposes in building a commitment to assessment: (a) to stimulate discussion on learning priorities, (b) to illustrate how expectations align with educational practices, (c) to visually represent contexts for learning, and (d) to hold students accountable for their own learning. For complex or longer-term experiences, the activities can be designated as introducing an outcome, reinforcing an outcome, or emphasizing an outcome. This also helps identify the appropriate assessment methods at particular times. See Appendix 4.1 for an example of a cocurricular map.

Assessment that does not address student learning can follow a general process that includes similar key steps. By following a general set of guidelines (see Chapter 3 for assessment cycles), staff will have an easier time implementing an assessment project aimed at one particular topic or assessment question. Although individual projects have their own nuances and challenges, there is a common path that helps ensure success. Appendix 4.2 provides an example of a template for assessment planning. This chapter will highlight common steps in the assessment process.

Develop a Purpose Statement

Staff new to assessment may have a naïve enthusiasm that prompts them to just jump in and start when in reality having a thoughtful process will help to ensure success. Others eagerly want to assess everything all the time. Still others have no idea of where to start, which leaves them with a fair amount of anxiety. Even before thinking about the process, it is important to fully develop the purpose of the individual assessment project. What does the program coordinator/service provider really *need* to know (versus what they *want* to know)? What is the plan for using the information collected? Who needs to know the results? The purpose could be for program improvement, to assess student learning at the end of an event, to gather student feedback about the quality of services, to support the university's accreditation and accountability requirements, and so on. The assessor must maintain a focused, narrow, and well-articulated purpose statement that is consulted on a regular basis to keep the assessment project manageable and on track. This statement should provide a continual foundation for the direction. It is easy to stray from the original purpose as interesting ideas begin to surface, but the reality is that assessment projects require practical parameters.

Identify Stakeholders

Once the purpose of the assessment has been articulated, the assessor must also consider the stakeholders of the project. Who else will be interested in or impacted by the results? What do they need to know or do based on the results of the assessment? Once stakeholders have been identified, the assessor has to decide how to include them in the process. Will they be part of the planning team? Will they assist in getting participants? Are they only interested in the results?

Stakeholders can include external parties, such as legislators, donors, administrators, and parents, and internal parties, such as the senior student affairs officer, faculty, administrators, supervisors, colleagues, and students. Granted, legislators will probably not be providing hands-on support and expertise to a small project about a single program, but students and colleagues could easily be involved in the details of planning and implementation. Depending on the topic, a legislator may be interested in the results, so it is important to consider all of the lenses through which the project could be interpreted.

Examine Existing Data

The next step is to determine what information may already exist; data may not even have to be collected. Good practice suggests that literature should be reviewed to understand any recent trends, research, theories, or models. The question still remains: Does the specific population of interest align with the literature? The assessor also determines what information is already available on campus. Other departments may have collected information in recent years that is relevant. The institutional research office may have relevant assessment data from other studies or national surveys. Before jumping into data collection, determine if, in fact, the data must be collected from current constituents.

Determine What Data to Collect

If the needed information cannot be garnered from a national survey or other available data, a locally developed data-collection tool may be the best option. Advantages are that the questions are tailored to the interest area at hand and the process can be flexible (Sternberg, Penn, & Hawkins, 2011). Unfortunately, locally developed tools usually do not have the same validity and reliability measures as a standardized assessment, and they may not allow benchmarking comparison between institutions. At the same time, national or standardized instruments may not focus on the specific information needed and can be costly to implement. Before choosing or creating a locally designed option, review all the data that might already be available, so that time and energy do not have to be devoted to creating a new assessment.

Decide From Whom Data Should Be Collected

Other key questions to answer relate to the participants. Who has the information? What are their characteristics of interest? How large is the pool of potential participants? Of the pool, how many people will have to participate to provide useful information? For example, is the audience of interest all graduate students or female students pursuing a master's in chemistry. Being as specific as possible will provide a better chance to get the most useful information from the audience of interest. That will also provide guidance about the appropriate assessment method and how many people will be needed in the sample.

Collecting Data

The data-collection methodology can be determined only after the following questions are answered: What is the purpose of the assessment? What other information is available? Who has the information yet to be gathered? Cooper (2009) has stated that "a clearly defined purpose helps identify the data collection methods appropriate for the inquiry" (p. 51). There are many options from which to choose; one size does not fit all. Most novice assessment staff gravitate to a survey, but that may not be the most appropriate method. Other common methods include focus groups, observations, rubrics, portfolios, reflections/journals, standardized tests, and more. These options will be covered in other chapters. The assessor also has to think about whether the potential participants will be willing to provide the information and the ease with which the data can be collected. Is the audience already oversurveyed? Does the purpose indicate the need for deeper or unstructured information that does not fit into a survey format? Is there a captive audience, or should the data be collected from an audience that cannot be accessed at one time? Data-analysis skills should also be considered before the data-collection process begins. Kaufman and Guerra-López (2013) have summarized the importance of selecting the best assessment instrument for each project:

> A useful assessment instrument allows us to answer important questions, and answer them based on research and evidence. An assessment method could be well implemented, but if it was poorly designed, it amounts to nothing useful, and perhaps could even be harmful, as it may render

unreliable or inaccurate information. . . . Other important factors to consider when selecting data collection instruments are the relative costs, time, and expertise required to develop and/or obtain them. (p. 129)

Time Frame for Data Collection and Analysis

The time frame of the assessment can have a tremendous impact on the success of the project. As part of the process, it is better to overestimate the amount of time each step will take. For some people, backward planning helps clarify what needs to be done. The end of a particular project could include making a decision to be implemented in the new fiscal year or a report that needs to be shared with constituents by a specific date. If there are fiscal resources needed to implement the decision, those need to be calculated into the timeline. Writing reports or making presentations will take time, but that will depend on the complexity and variety of the information being presented. Student affairs staff new to sharing assessment information should plan extra time to prepare, as several drafts may be needed and feedback will have to be solicited. Before information is shared, data analysis must be completed. This step intimidates many student affairs professionals. If the assessor does not have the skills to use quantitative or qualitative analysis technology, plan extra time for this step as well. Seek people with those skills to assist in the process. Although statistical analysis is as quick as clicking on the options in software packages such as Statistical Package for Social Sciences (SPSS), Statistical Analysis System (SAS), or Qualtrics, it is useless to proceed without knowing correct statistical analysis. Similarly, qualitative analysis tools can help code the data, but, once again, the professional has to make the ultimate decision about how to interpret the data. Some staff still prefer a relatively low-tech qualitative analysis, which might include a group of staff deciding on the codes and categories. Faculty and graduate students in the social sciences can be valuable resources when data are being analyzed.

In collecting data, the time frame also depends on the methodology. For example, a random sample electronic survey is not the same as conducting focus groups or making observations. The survey may be open for responses for two weeks, whereas two focus groups could be held in two days and take 90 minutes each time, with more time needed to organize and/or transcribe notes. Observations could be made at one student organization meeting that lasts an hour. Reminders might need to be sent for the electronic survey if the expected response rate has not been achieved. For focus groups, additional meetings might be planned to increase perspectives. On the longer side, students may be journaling all semester about their service-learning experiences.

If the project is considered "human subjects research" by the institutional review board (IRB), that process can increase the timeline by a few days to several months. It is always prudent to understand the IRB process on a particular campus before collecting data. A few studies may go to full review, which may take several months, depending on the IRB process at a specific institution. On the other hand, exempt protocols may be approved in a few days. Other projects may not be considered human subjects research if they are program evaluations or general assessments of learning. Every campus interprets federal policy differently. Projects that are submitted to the IRB need their approval before any data collection takes place. If there is any question regarding this process, the IRB should be consulted. More information about the IRB process is included in Chapter 15, on ethics.

Developing the Data-Collection Tool

Determining the actual questions to ask participants in the assessment project tends to take more time, energy, and expertise than would be expected by the novice student affairs professional. A national instrument has an advantage because the questions are already developed, but it can be expensive and not as timely. Locally developed questions are created for a very specific topic and audience. Expect several revisions after referring back to the purpose statement and getting feedback from others. It is important to include content experts as well as process experts in this step. Conducting a pilot test with a few people who fit the profile of end respondents can provide very valuable feedback regarding how participants interpret the questions, the amount of time it might take for a respondent to participate, questions that might be repetitive, or questions that should be added. Piloting the tool ensures collecting the most meaningful information in the best format. Good surveys, for example, are as short as possible while still providing the needed information; it is harder to narrow down than to include every question brainstormed. A good heuristic is to consider how the data from each item will be used. If a sound rationale cannot be provided for a question, it should probably be omitted. When thinking about the questions consider the respondents. The questions should be written using easily understood language (e.g., avoiding jargon) in a sequence that makes sense. Overall, the survey should be interesting and short enough for the respondents to complete quickly.

Demographics

As the questions are created, consider what demographics need to be collected. Frequently used demographics include major or academic college (at large universities), sex/gender, class standing, ethnicity, and residence. Others that might be important are first-generation status, age, international status, grade point average, socioeconomic status, credit hours completed, organization involvement, transfer status, and so on. Some institutions have all of this information in one location, while others keep the information in separate databases and yet others may not collect a specific type of information at all. The institutional research office, the registrar, and financial aid office may have data but they may not release the data because of Family Educational Rights and Privacy Act (FERPA) regulations or because they may need memorandums of understanding to allow release of information. If the data collection includes a confidential web-based survey, preload the demographics, if possible, to avoid adding additional questions to the survey. If the assessment is an anonymous paper-based or electronic assessment, demographic questions will have to be included. If a focus group/interview process is used, there could be a separate form for respondents to complete coded to the respondent. Be sure to consider what demographics are useful—collect only what is needed, but know that if demographics are not collected at the time of implementation, they probably cannot be collected later.

Sample

Determining and selecting the participants could also take unexpected time. In sending an electronic survey to a random sample, the institutional research office may gather the sample and email addresses and/or the information technology office may send out the email messages. Keep in mind the logistics of when the survey will launch. Consider when students are likely to check email (e.g., early in the day, early in the week); when course breaks are; and when students may be occupied by other events such as finals, homecoming, or the rival basketball game. For focus groups or interviews, choose and contact the sample with enough time for them to plan time in their schedules. Specific sampling choices are discussed in future chapters. In either case, the communication to recruit the sample from the population must be carefully planned and constructed. Before the intended audience takes part in data collection, they need motivation to participate. Communication may come in the form of an invitation from a person in authority, but the invitation may also call on them to help a department and explain how previous assessment results contributed to an improvement. Obviously, the communication should be professional (e.g., no typographical errors, delivered early enough for students to participate, and specific about the purpose and use of the assessment) and personal when possible.

Incentives

Staff new to assessment typically wonder about the use of incentives to increase the response rate or participation. There are several decisions to be made before using incentives. They must be offered in terms of something that the audience values. Will every respondent get something at fairly low cost (a slice of pizza from dining services) or will only one or a few people receive something more expensive (a new tablet, a $500 gift card)? If respondents feel that they do not have a likely chance to win the high-value prize, they do not have incentive to respond. At the same time a very small or not desirable incentive may also not motivate people to respond. In the pizza example, students may not actually like the pizza from dining services, or the location/operating hours may not be convenient for them.

Furthermore, the assessor has to determine whether the incentive implementation process is worth the effort. Institutions typically have policies about using incentives in research projects; these govern limits, record keeping, and reporting requirements. There may be reporting procedures if the recipient is an employee of the institution and the value of the incentive exceeds a certain dollar amount. Some incentives may be taxed depending on their dollar value. In the assessment implementation process, there must be a way for the respondents to be identified (which can be a challenge if the assessment is supposed to be anonymous or the respondents do not want their names associated with their responses). If not everyone gets the incentive, there must also be a process with which to choose a winner or winners while still maintaining the confidentiality of their assessment responses (if confidentiality was guaranteed). Once recipients are notified, there has to be a process for them to accept the incentive. Students may need to sign a release form before their names or pictures can be used in further marketing. Some students never claim their incentives, even after several notifications. What is the deadline for students to pick up their incentives? What happens with the unclaimed prizes?

If the assessment method is an interview, a focus group, or an in-person survey, the incentive can be provided at that time; implementing the focus group during a regular mealtime may be beneficial so that the participants do not see any additional time costs (they must eat a meal anyway). When participants complete a survey in person, they can receive their rewards at that time. Some of the previously listed processes are still in place here; there may be additional paperwork if the participants are also employees and/or the assessor wants to use their likeness in ads.

Survey research shows mixed results about the use of incentives, and there is limited research specifically regarding college students (Porter & Whitcomb, 2004). Some research has concluded that the number of contacts increases the response rate more than a monetary incentive would. With college students, that can be a balancing act, because they tend to be over-surveyed, especially if there are no campus policies about survey research. Students may also not check their college email on a regular basis. They may become annoyed by repeated contacts, which can influence their decisions to respond to additional surveys. In most electronic survey software used to send surveys to a preselected group, there is typically a way to note who has responded so that they do not receive reminders. There may also be an option for students to click on an "opt out" link if they do not want to participate and do not want to receive reminders.

Analysis

Once the data have been collected, the analysis phase begins. Early on in the planning cycle, though, the expected analysis process should be determined and described in detail based on the overall assessment purpose and need. This helps ensure that the format of the collected data is appropriate for the intended analysis. Many student affairs professionals do not have advanced expertise in quantitative and qualitative analysis methods and may require additional assistance. Sometimes the analysis can be fairly basic in terms of means and frequencies for quantitative data or theming for qualitative responses. Inexperienced student affairs professionals should plan for additional time; experienced professionals will have a more accurate perspective about time needed for analysis. Initial analysis may lead to additional questions that require further analysis; be sure to refer back to the original purpose statement to provide the structure and parameters of analysis for each project. Chapters 9 and 11 address analysis for different forms of data. As a part of the analysis phase, staff need to take time to interpret those results in the specific context and make judgments about the information. The literature should also be consulted to assist in interpretation. Reflection is a key part of the assessment process.

Sharing Results

Once the analysis is completed, the sharing begins. As with the analysis phase, determining how the information will be shared should be identified early on in the planning cycle. New skills or resources may have to be garnered if information is shared in a new or unfamiliar way. Consider who wants the information, their knowledge level, and what decisions they need to make. Also, determine the appropriate methods of sharing. Information may be shared in written form, orally, graphically, and so on, and different audiences may have distinct preferences. Chapter 13 focuses on how to share information for a variety of audiences and purposes.

Closing the Loop: Using the Assessment Data

Using the assessment information is one of the most important steps in the process. If there is no plan to use the information for improvement, there is no reason to do an assessment. The purpose statement and early planning should include a tentative plan of how the information will be used to implement change, including an accountability plan that addresses responsible units and timelines. Not knowing what the data will actually show can make creating an accountability plan challenging, but a plan must be in place. The Education Advisory Board (2011) concluded:

> Research revealed that the greatest barrier to systematic use of assessment data is the lack of accountability. While a unit might outline services and program changes in its annual report, senior leaders do not regularly check in to see whether those changes are implemented and the subsequent impact on student learning. (p. 135)

Making a change can be difficult, so it is important to have commitment, support, accountability, and continual attention to the assessment cycle to ensure that needed changes are made and those changes are reassessed to demonstrate their success. "Gathering data is far less risky and complicated than acting on the evidence in the data. . . . Another stumbling block to using assessment results is getting caught up in creating the 'perfect' research design" (Kinzie, Hutchings, & Jankowski, 2015, p. 58). All of the barriers have to be removed along the way in order to make the use of results as smooth and positive as possible, while also remembering that assessment's purpose is to make improvements rather than to just gather information for generalizable knowledge. Using assessment results will be discussed in more detail in Chapter 14.

Addressing Poor Results

There are times when the results do not yield useful information. The Education Advisory Board (2011) found several causes of poor assessment results. In terms of the instrument selected, examples included poorly worded questions, nonspecific rubrics, and incorrect scales, which made the results inaccurate or not helpful. In addition, small samples were easier to manage but provided distorted data that were not representative of the population; therefore, the results provided an inaccurate picture. The researchers also found that staff chose the wrong methods for the type of assessment they were implementing (e.g., time-intensive methods with large groups of students and long reflections with programs with sporadic student contact). Staff also struggled with outcomes by measuring the wrong goal, developing unclear outcomes, and asking too many irrelevant questions. All of these issues will result in assessment findings that are not helpful, making the assessment process a waste of resources.

Conclusion

More staff engage in the assessment process as higher education expects more assessment from student affairs to demonstrate effectiveness. Most of the time, staff are assessing for program improvement or student learning. One of the most important decisions in the assessment process is to determine the purpose of the specific assessment. Although it may be exciting to consider all of the possible assessment opportunities, staff do not have the time and resources to assess everything all the time. No assessment is perfect, but staff have the responsibility to create and use the best assessment that is relevant, manageable, and timed to their environment. Staff need to have clear, useful processes that involve the people who have the needed expertise, information, and interest.

Key Points

- Following a structured assessment process improves the likelihood of success in implementation.
- The purpose of the assessment should drive the data collection and analysis process rather than vice versa.
- Including colleagues and stakeholders in the process can ensure multiple perspectives, generate a higher-quality product, and increase the likelihood that results will be used.
- Allow for plenty of time for the entire process.

Discussion Questions and Activities

- What part of the assessment process is the most difficult for you?
- How can you overcome any identified barriers to assessment?
- Describe the key stakeholders for your assessment projects and what their interest is.
- What resources do you need that you do not currently have?
- What existing data may be available to you?

APPENDIX 4.1

Cocurricular Map Example for a Leadership Certificate

Activity	Intro to Leadership Course	Strengths Quest Workshop	Student Leader Experience	Service-Learning Project	Leadership Senior Seminar	Capstone Project
Leadership theories	I				R	
Self-awareness	I	R				
Teamwork			I	R		E
Delegation			I	R		
Oral communication			I			R
Understanding difference		I		R	E	
Critical thinking	I		R	E		

I = Introduce; R = Reinforce; E = Emphasize

APPENDIX 4.2
Assessment Planning Worksheet

Project title:

Purpose statement:

Related goals and/or outcomes:

Stakeholders:

Related theory/model/literature:

Is approval from the IRB needed?

Improvements made from previous assessment(s) (if applicable):

Population of interest:

    Sample:

    Demographics needed:

Data-collection method:

Dates for instrument creation:

Dates for data collection:

Data-analysis method:

Dates for data analysis:

Methods to share results:

Dates for dissemination of results:

Planned use of results:

5

TYPES OF ASSESSMENT

Assessment should not be one dimensional. In order to get a valuable, well-rounded picture of organizational effectiveness, it is important to vary the type of assessment to meet the evaluation need. The assessment can address the effectiveness of a program, service, unit, department, or division as well as any learning that occurs in any of these venues. In order to be manageable, the various types of assessment should be planned and implemented over time rather than being done all at the same time or even in the same year.

Assessment can be described as summative or formative. *Summative assessment* occurs at the end of the program or time period that includes the overall perspective. *Formative assessment*, however, provides continuous or frequent feedback to a program or time period, so changes can be made before its conclusion (Kaufman & Guerra-López, 2013). In higher education, most students have the opportunity to evaluate a course and faculty member at the end of the semester/quarter, which is considered a summative assessment. During the semester, some faculty members implement an informal formative assessment to make sure that their teaching methods are effective and students understand the content. In student affairs, residence life might survey students who attend programs in the fall semester to determine any changes that should be made during the rest of the year, and it might assess student opinion at the end of the spring semester to get an overall perspective about programming in the residence halls.

Another distinction in assessment is between quantitative assessment and qualitative measures. As its name implies, *quantitative assessment* uses numbers for analysis and interpretation. For example, it can be as straightforward as age or number of hours completed toward a degree, but it can also be used to assign numbers to a logical sequence of words (e.g., 4 = strongly agree, 3 =

agree, 2 = disagree, 1 = strongly disagree). The numbers have meaning based on the statistical analysis. Alternatively, *qualitative measures* include words, pictures, or other descriptors that sometimes defy a number. Open-ended questions in a focus group or reflective journals are examples of qualitative measures. Depending on the use of the assessment, the measures can overlap. Surveys, usually thought of in the quantitative realm, can include open-ended questions. Focus group analysis can quantify the number of times a specific response was provided. Rubrics can apply quantitative ratings to qualitative work, such as a paper or presentation. More detail on the methods will be provided in later chapters.

Assessment can also be defined as direct or indirect, particularly in relation to student learning. *Direct assessment* is the actual demonstration of knowledge or skill that can be observed or measured. Suskie (2009) describes direct evidence of student learning as "tangible, visible, self-explanatory, and compelling" (p. 25). Direct assessment is seen as a stronger measure than *indirect assessment,* which typically focuses on students' perception of their learning or other measures that are tangentially related to the learning. As an example in student affairs, one might be conducting a leadership workshop. A direct measure would ask students to describe the components of a specific leadership theory and an example of how they have applied that theory in their own lives. An indirect measure might ask students to respond to statements such as "I can describe a leadership theory" and "I can apply a leadership theory to my own experiences" using a strongly agree to a strongly disagree scale. Another indirect measure might also be reporting the number of students who participate in the workshop.

Student affairs assessment encompasses a myriad of purposes and topics. This chapter will highlight several common types of assessment that student affairs professionals commonly use. Although they are not all used for all units each year, they do provide a holistic view of programs and services as they are systematically implemented over time.

Types of assessment discussed in this chapter are the following:

- Tracking usage
- Needs
- Satisfaction
- Outcomes
- Campus climate
- Program review
- Benchmarking

- Resource effectiveness
- Accreditation
- National instruments

Tracking Usage

Simply put, tracking usage counts the number of people or things. This can indicate to what extent programs and services are used. If the assessor has a way to access related information, the demographics of people engaging in the programs and services can be determined. That describes not only who uses the programs, but also who is not interacting with the unit. Are certain types of students attending programs? Not attending programs? Is that the intended audience? Are there audiences that should be served but are not?

Some campuses have the ability to have students swipe their ID cards, so additional information can be easily collected. Programs can then track the students' frequency of attending particular programs or services. In addition, the time stamps can determine busy days and times. Tracking may be more than counting people. Relatively passive methods of tracking include hits to a website, forms submitted, applications received, and so on. Departments that get frequent phone calls with questions might keep a simple tally of the types of questions so as to put more information on their websites.

For example, student unions that plan campuswide programs may find card swipe systems particularly useful. Although all students are probably invited, there may be specific groups that do not attend in the percentage represented at the institution. Several years ago, late-night programming was a popular strategy as an alternative to students consuming alcohol on Friday nights. What if the union discovered that international graduate students and their families attended such functions more frequently than did undergraduate students of the traditional age? The union could regroup and think about how to get more of their intended population to attend, gear more activities to families, or do something completely different. Without tracking the use of the program, the union would not know whom it was attracting.

Needs

In order to best serve stakeholders, stakeholder needs should be determined. Part of the responsibility of student affairs professionals is to meet the needs of students so that they can be successful in their college careers. A comprehensive needs assessment plan can identify gaps, the causes of those gaps, potential solutions, an implementation plan, and evaluation of the change (Kaufman & Guerra-López, 2013). It can compare the current state with the desired state. Needs of students today differ from what they were 10 years ago, or even 5 years ago, although there are probably some areas that remain consistent over time. Institutions serve different types of students, which may also change over time (e.g., student veterans are returning to higher education in increasing numbers and may have specific needs as compared with those of more traditional students). Therefore, professional judgment and knowledge are necessary to know constituents' needs. Keeping up with the professional literature will provide additional guidance about student needs. Student affairs professionals do not have to conduct a needs assessment every year, but they cannot rely on "we've always done it that way" as a reason not to do it.

Needs differ from wants. For example, first-year students need education about alcohol abuse and sexual assault, but they probably would not indicate those topics as a want. Because students may not be able to identify or know their needs, the questions must be carefully crafted based on the audience. At the same time, for practical purposes, needs and wants can frequently be combined in one assessment.

Examples of needs/wants assessment questions include the following:

Check the hall programs you are interested in attending (followed by a list of sample programs the resident assistants might provide).
What do you need to be successful in this program? (open-ended)
What do you wish you had known prior to attending _____ (e.g., orientation, conduct meeting, leadership retreat, study abroad)?
Which of your leadership skills need further development? (open-ended, or a list of skills that can be addressed in the leadership program)

Satisfaction

Student affairs professionals want stakeholders to be happy. If customers/clients/stakeholders are not satisfied with what student affairs is providing, they may not use important services, they might tell others about their poor experience, or they might even leave the institution. Satisfaction assessment is a common place at which to start assessment because it is something familiar. Most people probably have been invited to take a satisfaction survey at some point (e.g., after eating at a restaurant, purchasing a product, staying in a hotel, or attending a conference). They may have been asked about the quality or quantity of some attribute, service, or staff knowledge or friendliness. They might have been asked if they would recommend a particular experience or product to their friends.

In student affairs, common areas for satisfaction assessment are residence life, dining services, recreational sports, and any experiences that rely on students using nonmandatory services, for example. Whereas students may have a first-year mandatory freshman housing requirement, residence life may want returning students to fill the rest of the beds. Satisfied students will be more likely than dissatisfied students to renew their contracts. Satisfaction can include amenities, timeliness, quality, friendliness and/or knowledge of the staff, cost, and so on.

Although satisfaction is a fairly easy and useful area of assessment, student affairs staff should challenge themselves to also assess other areas of their programs and services. In some assessments, asking about needs also makes sense in a satisfaction survey. Using residence life as an example again, they will want to know how satisfied students are with various aspects of their program: rental rate, study space, Internet connection, application process, interaction with their resident assistant, and so on. In addition, they might want to know what additional amenities students need to be successful or to continue to live on campus: This could include access to tutoring in the hall, ability to cook in their rooms, or changes in policies. Alternatively, there are times when satisfaction is not particularly useful. A student who has just been suspended for a conduct violation will probably not express satisfaction with the outcomes, although the conduct office may want to know if the student felt listened to, understood the process, and so forth.

The following are examples of satisfaction-type questions:

How satisfied are you with _____ (e.g., variety of exercise equipment, options to get involved, ease of making an appointment)? (Very satisfied, satisfied, dissatisfied, very dissatisfied)

Would you recommend _____ (e.g., this leadership conference, living on campus, health services) to your friends? (Yes, no)

How likely are you to participate in _____ (e.g., intramurals, this volunteer experience, a diversity workshop) again? (Very likely, likely, neither likely nor unlikely, unlikely, very unlikely)

How would you rate _____ (e.g., quality of the food, knowledge of the staff, ease of registration)? (Excellent, above average, average, below average, poor)

What were you most satisfied with? (open-ended)

What were you least satisfied with? (open-ended)

Outcomes

An outcome is the end result of an experience. Although covered more thoroughly in the next chapter, a brief description is provided here. Student learning outcomes describe what students know or are able to do as a result of some activity or intervention. In comparison, program/process/performance outcomes address what the program will accomplish but do not describe any level of learning. Higher education is particularly concerned with what students are gaining from their college experiences both inside and outside the classroom. Before learning experiences are measured, student affairs staff should articulate the outcomes and identify which activities support those outcomes. The outcomes could be used to market the benefits of participating in a particular program or could be used to provide a link from a particular program to a larger context, such as an institution's learning outcomes. With more attention being focused on the value of the cocurricular area, student affairs must be able to provide evidence of the positive impact they have on student success.

Examples of outcomes questions include the following:

Because of this workshop, I can compare and contrast three leadership models. (Strongly agree, agree, neutral, disagree, strongly disagree)

Describe how you have applied communication skills in your leadership experience. (open-ended)

What did you learn from this program? (open-ended)

Campus Climate

People experience their environments differently based on their own characteristics, expectations, past and current interactions, and group norms and history. Hart and Fellabaum (2008) concluded that campus climate definitions were vague, study designs varied widely, and not all models were fully developed. They therefore suggested that discussion of campus climate should include "the historical legacy of diversity; the social structural or demographic diversity of the campus; the perceptions of campus climate by all campus constituencies; and the lived experiences and behaviors of the members of the campus community" (p. 233). Assessing how different groups perceive the climate provides an important picture to the accepted culture at an institution. Because of the complexity of climate, assessing it is also complex. This is not a beginner's assessment method.

Campus climate studies can focus on one demographic characteristic or they can address several areas. Frequent topics include race/ethnicity, gender, and sexual orientation, but they could also address veteran status, disability, religion, socioeconomic status, parental status, citizenship, or just about any other factor with identified characteristics. In recent years, climate surveys regarding sexual assault have been developed (White House Task Force to Protect Students From Sexual Assault, 2014) to better understand the issue so that campuses can take action to prevent and address it through policies, education, and response. Because people comprise many identities, it may also be difficult to address only one area and for respondents to focus on only one characteristic.

Because of the sensitivity of the topics, this type of assessment requires the staff to be knowledgeable about the area of interest. They need to know the current literature and research, but they should also be familiar with the variety of assessment methods that may be appropriate. Surveys provide a sense of anonymity, but focus groups can more easily delve into people's experiences and reactions. Either way, students must feel a sense of trust if they are to provide honest answers with an expectation that action will be taken to address any areas that need attention. It is helpful to have a diverse group of staff (and students) in order to develop, implement, analyze, and make recommendations about the assessment.

Examples of climate questions include the following:

I am respected on this campus. (Strongly agree, agree, neutral, disagree, strongly disagree)

_____ (e.g., female, atheist, LGBT) students are respected on this campus. (Strongly agree, agree, neutral, disagree, strongly disagree)

In the last year, how frequently did you hear derogatory remarks about _____ (e.g., female, atheist, LGBT) students? (Never, once, 2 to 6 times, 7 to 11 times, monthly, weekly, daily)

Describe an experience where you felt included. (open-ended)

Program Review

Standards-Based Program Review

Student affairs has the opportunity to compare functional areas against set published standards. These reviews are very beneficial in ensuring that organizations do not get caught in the "we've always done it that way" mind-set. Reviews provide a fresh perspective, structured and consistent expectations, and a direction for the future. While this assessment method is very enlightening, it is not one that is fully undertaken frequently because of the potential commitment of time and resources.

The Council for the Advancement of Standards in Higher Education (CAS) (2012a) has created a set of evaluation principles for over 40 functional areas related to student affairs. As student affairs further develops in the complex higher education environment, new standards are developed or significantly modified to meet the needs of these many areas. Nearly 40 professional organizations are represented in the development of the standards and process for self-assessment. The purpose of the CAS standards is to identify not only what a program *must* do as a foundation, but also what a program *should* do to enhance its practice. The areas are mission; program; organization and leadership; human resources; ethics; law, policy, and governance; diversity, equity, and access; institutional and external relations; financial resources; technology; facilities and equipment; and assessment and evaluation. Self-assessment guides (SAGs) are worksheets that provide guidance for the review of each standard. The rating scale for the specific criteria includes exceeds, meets, partly meets, does not meet, and insufficient evidence/unable to rate. There is also a "does not apply" rating that can be used in the event that the rating question is not applicable (M. D. Sharp, personal communication, June 30, 2015). As part of the review, staff are expected to collect supporting evidence of their ratings. The evaluation process can be used as an internal self-study or to support an external review with experts who determine if the unit is truly meeting standards and what the unit can do to improve.

Examples of questions included in CAS standards are as follows:

The [functional area's] mission statement references learning and development.
The [functional area] has clearly stated goals.
The [functional area] reviews relevant professional ethical standards and implements appropriate statements of ethical practice.

Locally Developed Program Review

Program reviews are used for a variety of purposes. They can identify areas of internal strength and areas for improvement, they can meet the requirements imposed by external agencies, and they can be the foundation for improvement (Bresciani, 2006). Some institutions develop their own program reviews to meet their unique needs or characteristics. They can combine resources from campus academic program reviews, CAS, or even the Baldrige Excellence Framework (National Institute of Standards and Technology, 2015) for educational settings. Although locally developed program reviews can address the distinctiveness of the campus, division, or department, they can also be time consuming to develop and norm across units. Program reviews provide a systematic process for a unit to examine their work on a broader scale, and a typical review can take many months to complete. They do not need to be done on an annual basis; there should be several years between reviews to allow the unit to implement strategic plans and make recommended changes. Division leadership, such as the vice president for student affairs, should support the process and provide the needed resources for a program review and resulting action to be useful.

Questions include the following:

Describe your unit's learning outcomes and methods to assess those outcomes.

Provide strengths and areas of improvement related to your unit's facilities.

How are staff trained on relevant legal issues facing your department, division, or institution?

Benchmarking

In order to determine how programs or services relate to current peers or aspirational peers, it is beneficial to benchmark against similar organizations. Benchmarking allows units to systematically compare themselves to other entities that perform a similar function. Benchmarking collects data about best/promising practices (i.e., how and how well do others perform), so that a unit can use those practices to improve. In student affairs, a residence life department could identify other departments of a similar size and scope to compare and contrast the budget, the staffing model, programmatic efforts, facilities, the assignment process, partnerships with academic units, and so forth. Those departments could be identified by Association of College and University Housing Officers–International (ACUHO-I) region, peer institutions identified in the institution's strategic plan, Carnegie classification, sports conference, or a mixture of characteristics. But the comparison does not have to be within higher education or functional area. If the student health center was reviewing its appointment process to become more efficient, it could not only look at peer health centers but also review the processes of the local clinic or the student counseling center. As with all assessment methods, benchmarking requires systematic planning to develop useful questions, a manageable process, and a plan to use the information for improvement.

Example questions include the following:

Describe your process for _____ (e.g., scheduling students/groups/teams, recognizing student organizations, updating the website). (open-ended)

What is your timeline/promptness for _____ (e.g., scheduling students, processing appeals, approving programs)? (open-ended)

Resource Effectiveness

In recent years, higher education and student affairs have been subject to increased scrutiny about resources, including budgets, human resources, and the value added of cocurricular experiences. Student affairs staff should pay attention to the cost-benefit analysis of their programs and services as well as how their programs promote retention, persistence, academic success, and time to graduation.

Several student affairs examples may be helpful to illustrate this. The campus programming board pays a nationally recognized speaker $20,000 for a two-hour presentation. Ten people attend. Is that a good return on investment? In very simple terms, that's $2,000 per person just for the speaker fee (that does not include any marketing, facility rental, travel cost, etc.). What if 100 people attend? The cost per person drops to $200. Is that a good return on investment?

At a large campus student counseling center, two psychologists want to implement an academic success program to retain students who are struggling badly in their classes and personal lives. The program costs $20,000 for the materials, their time, and the software for diagnostic testing. They expect the program to reach 100 students per year with a 90% retention rate to the following term and an 80% graduation rate (i.e., 90 students will continue their studies, and 80 of those students will make it to graduation). The time per week the two psychologists spend on the program would take away the time they spend in individual client treatment, which could be five appointments a week per psychologist. Once again, the cost per participating student is $200, but there are long-term benefits to the student and the institution. Is it worth implementing the program?

One more example. The multicultural affairs department offers a 10-day international excursion to South Africa to study the country's culture, history/politics, economy, and educational system. The trip is open to all but is especially marketed to students who have not studied abroad or had international experience. The department allocates $20,000 to offset the travel costs for the 10 students who can attend ($2,000 per person). Participants are expected to pay part of their expenses. Multicultural affairs has agreements with the departments of political science, history, economics, and education to send faculty on the trip as well as to offer several briefings before the trip to provide context. Because of recent budget cuts, the multicultural affairs office is considering eliminating the program because of the logistics and the small number of students who can attend. Should the program be discontinued?

There are no right or wrong answers to these questions, but it is important to calculate the answer in light of various other factors. Decisions about resource effectiveness are impacted by current and expected budgets, relationship to institution priorities, politics, unit mission, number of students served, effectiveness of the program, and much more.

Here are some examples of questions to ask:

How much does this program or service cost in terms of human resources, physical materials, or facilities?

How many students are reached in these efforts?

Does this align with department, division, or institutional goals and priorities?

What are the measures of effectiveness of the program or service?

Accreditation

The vast majority of institutions undergo accreditation at least every 10 years. The purpose is to create more accountability and transparency, particularly in the areas of assessment of student learning outcomes, institutional effectiveness, and ongoing strategic planning (Middaugh, 2010). Accreditors are not there to tell an institution what to do, but are there to ensure that institutions are doing what they say they do. The Council for Higher Education Accreditation (2015) advocates on behalf of institutions and accrediting agencies for self-regulation and quality, especially to the federal government. The six regional accreditation agencies perform the actual institutional reviews, and they vary somewhat across the country in their expectations and standards. Institutions complete a comprehensive report based on the accrediting agency criteria. Following a review of the written material, an on-site team of experts visits the campus for interviews and other data collection. The accrediting agency issues a decision about the reaccreditation. If all goes well, institutions get commendations or at least approval. If there are areas that do not meet standards, the institutions may be given a warning and given a chance to correct any deficiencies. All institutions that receive federal funding must be accredited by one of the accrediting agencies. International institutions can also receive regional accreditation.

As part of the accreditation review, student affairs professionals are often asked to contribute information related to student learning, institutional and unit effectiveness, and use of assessment to improve effectiveness and efficiency. For example, the New England Association of Colleges and Schools Commission on Institutions of Higher Education expects a systematic assessment of student learning with an understanding of "what and how students are learning through their academic program and, as appropriate, through experience outside the classroom" (Middaugh, 2010, pp. 11–12). Accreditors are no longer satisfied that assessment is being done; they are requiring evidence that results are being used for improvement. This is an opportunity for student affairs professionals to demonstrate their value to the institution and students.

Some functional areas typically found in student affairs also have accrediting bodies. The American Psychological Association Commission on Accreditation (APA CoA, 2015) reviews doctoral programs, internship programs, and postdoctoral residency programs. Counseling programs submit a self-study. Once that is reviewed and approved, the CoA sends an on-site review team to the campus. That team submits a report to the CoA, which then decides whether accreditation should be granted. Health services can also receive accreditation. The Accreditation Association for Ambulatory Health Care (2015), for example, has specific standards for high-quality patient care. The process includes an application, evidence of continuous evaluation of services, a self-study, and an on-site visit. The College of American Pathologists (2015) has a laboratory accreditation program that ensures compliance with best practices, accuracy of test results, and value to the organization.

Although not all student affairs functional areas have their own accreditation processes, those that do should evaluate the benefits of receiving accreditation. The cost and commitment of resources may be worth the quality endorsement both internally for staff and externally for students and parents. In addition, not all student affairs professionals will be engaged in the regional accreditation process, but as they develop a systematic assessment cycle, they should be knowledgeable about the accreditation expectations.

National Instruments

Many institutions participate in national survey instruments. Although in-depth analysis of each instrument is beyond the scope of this text, some similarities and examples are useful in the student affairs context. Whereas some assessments address the entire student experience, others focus on specific topics, such as health, leadership, and living on campus. They also allow a large number of students to reply, which gives institutions and units the ability to usually make generalizations based on student self-report. Not all of the national instruments emphasize the out-of-classroom experience, but student affairs staff can extract important information. Most institutions do not participate in national assessments every year because it takes time to receive the results, implement changes, and gather information about the success of changes. In addition, students do not typically change drastically from one year to the next, so trends are more evident when institutions allow several years between data collection. Before subscribing to a national instrument, the campus needs to fully understand the purpose and use of the instrument as well its appropriateness to the students' characteristics.

Logistically, national assessments have various options or requirements. Some are distributed to a captive audience using paper and pencil, whereas others are distributed electronically. Depending on the survey, the institution can choose the method. Generally the implementation needs campus coordination to determine the sample (unless the assessment requires the whole population), how the assessment will be distributed (If using an email invitation and web link, who will coordinate that, so it is not considered spam by the campus email system?), and when the assessment will be distributed (How long will data collection take? What other assessments might interfere with the response rate?). Depending on institutional policies, the survey may also need to be approved by the campus institutional review board (IRB), which ensures that participants are protected from harm. That time frame needs to be considered since data collection cannot begin until the IRB approves the study, if applicable.

National surveys have several advantages. One of the main advantages is the ability to benchmark against peer institutions. This helps institutions know where they excel and where they need to improve if peer comparison is important. Another advantage is that the instrument usually has been psychometrically reviewed for validity and reliability to provide confidence that the survey measures what it purports to measure and is consistent over time and locations. Because the instrument has been created by another entity, the unit does not have to take the time and resources to develop a local instrument. Many of the national instruments do allow for additional local questions to be inserted at the end of the survey. The surveys do not change drastically from year to year, so institutions can also use the data longitudinally to measure change over time. The summary reports typically include the campus results, a comparable group, and potentially comparisons of campus subgroups (e.g., gender or academic classification).

Of course, the national instruments also have disadvantages. They tend to be fairly costly, which is a deterrent for using them. Some instruments require all students to be surveyed, while others will use a sample of the population of interest. Because the surveys are developed by another organization, the content may not exactly fit your unique institution and priorities. The amount of data can be overwhelming, because most instruments are lengthy and may include statistical analyses unfamiliar to student affairs professionals. The length of many of the surveys may also be a deterrent to a high response rate unless students are engaged and have a commitment to the survey. Depending on the analysis that the survey company does, it may take numerous months after data collection ends to receive the summary/

comparison report and the data file. In addition, as student diversity increases, the results may not be as consistent and relevant as they had been in the past.

National Survey of Student Engagement

The National Survey of Student Engagement (NSSE) (Center for Postsecondary Research, 2015), through Indiana University, surveys first-year students and seniors in the spring semester. In measuring engagement, the survey asks students about the time and effort they put into academic and other purposeful activities as well as what the institution does to engage them in their learning. Institutions receive an institution-specific report, comparisons with peer institutions, and comparisons with all participating institutions. NSSE publishes its validity and reliability measures as well as reviews the survey questions on a regular basis. In 2014, over 700 four-year institutions participated.

The NSSE organization also sponsors the Faculty Survey of Student Engagement (which looks at engagement from the faculty perspective, their interactions with students, and how they spend their time) and the Beginning College Survey of Student Engagement (which examines precollege experiences and college expectations). The surveys can be used to complement each other (Center for Postsecondary Research, 2015). NSSE sparked other assessments: Community College Survey of Student Engagement (CCSSE), Community College Faculty Survey of Student Engagement (CCFSSE), Survey of Entering Student Engagement (SENSE), and Community College Institutional Survey (CCIS), all hosted at the University of Texas' Center for Community College Student Engagement (2015). The Law School Survey of Student Engagement (Center for Postsecondary Research, 2015) at Indiana University focuses specifically on the law school experience.

Higher Education Research Institute

The Higher Education Research Institute (HERI) at UCLA sponsors a series of assessment instruments under the Cooperative Institutional Research Program (CIRP). The Freshman Survey (TFS) is administered to incoming students at orientation or registration, before they have had collegiate experiences. The instrument collects student characteristics and demographics, high school experiences, college expectations, career plans, and values and beliefs. As a follow-up, the Your First College Year (YFCY) survey builds upon TFS by asking about academic and personal development, adjustment to college, engagement in cocurricular experiences, first-year programs, and student change. YFCY can be used as a stand-alone assessment, but pairs well with TFS. TFS and YFCY are available in both paper and web formats, and institutions can add locally developed questions.

The Diverse Learning Environments (DLE) survey focuses on climate (discrimination, positive and negative cross-racial interaction, sense of belonging, academic validation, etc.), practices (curriculum of inclusion, cocurricular diversity activities, support services, etc.), and outcomes (habits of mind, pluralistic orientation, social action, civic engagement, etc.). The web-based instrument can be administered to community college students with 24 or more hours or second- and third-year students at four-year institutions. Institutions can choose up to five additional modules above the core set of questions and include locally developed questions.

The College Senior Survey (CSS) addresses outcomes related to academic, civic, and diversity experiences. The survey asks about faculty-student interaction, academic engagement, cognitive development, students' goals, career plans, and overall satisfaction. The web or paper posttest survey can be used in conjunction with TFS, YFCY, and DLE, or it can be used as a stand-alone assessment.

All of the HERI questionnaires include an institutional summary report, a comparison with similar-type institutions, statistical measures, and construct reports. All surveys have a base cost, cost per response, and optional costs (e.g., local questions, HERI-managed email messages). TFS has been in existence since 1965; the other surveys are newer. All of the instruments are reviewed on an annual basis for changes and examined for validity and reliability.

Multi-Institutional Study of Leadership

The Multi-Institutional Study of Leadership (MSL) (n.d.) focuses on leadership development and involvement of college students to address gaps in the theory-research-practice cycle. First administered in 2006, the design is now on a three-year data-collection cycle (2015, 2018, etc.). The design is based on Astin's (1993) input-environment-outcomes model, asking students about their experiences and characteristics before college (parental education, involvement, etc.) and during college (mentoring, civic engagement, etc.) that impact their outcomes (leadership capacity, behaviors, and efficacy; resilience; sense of belonging; etc.). The theoretical framework is a fairly recent social change model (Higher Education Research Institute, 1996) that includes individual values, group values, and societal/community values, but it continues to evolve and include more leadership and development theories.

Implementation, which occurs online in the spring during a three-week time span decided by the institution, allows campuses to identify a random sample (4,000 undergraduates) and an optional comparative sample that can be used for additional statistical analysis to compare groups. The institution can include some demographics in the data file provided to the MSL as well as the student identification numbers if the campus wants to perform additional analysis and/or connect these data to other survey results. In addition, campuses are provided peer institution comparisons and national norms for benchmarking.

National College Health Assessment

The National College Health Assessment (NCHA) is sponsored by the American College Health Association (2014). This survey collects information about student behaviors and perceptions based on topics such as alcohol, tobacco, drugs, sexual health, exercise, nutrition, mental health, and personal safety. Institutions use the data to plan interventions to address health concerns, compare perceptions of social norms to actual behavior, and guide resource allocation. The survey can be administered to a sample or the whole population, at any time of the year, and on paper or the Internet. It is estimated that the survey takes 30 minutes to complete. The results include comparisons with other participating institutions and can be used longitudinally.

Student Learning

With the national focus on what students are learning on campus, there are instruments that provide a standardized measure of student learning. The advantages of student learning tests include national norming with large, diverse populations, psychometrically sophisticated yet easily explained results, and comparisons with other institutions (Sternberg, Penn, & Hawkins 2011). The disadvantage is that a standardized test does not account for the diversity of student majors and relevant learning outcomes priorities. As Sternberg et al. (2011) remark,

> An overemphasis on standardized tests . . . risks focusing our institutions on a narrow set of analytical and written communication skills that, while important, represent only a small subset of the skills and abilities we need to help our students develop in order to prepare them fully for later life. (p. 6)

Although these tests do not necessarily focus on out-of-class experiences, they can provide useful knowledge about what skills and abilities students need to improve. For example, advisors and supervisors can provide opportunities to write and provide feedback, and they can engage students in conversation about decision making, gathering information, ethics, and consequences to develop students' critical thinking skills.

As examples, some institutions use standardized tests to measure proficiency in critical thinking (e.g., Collegiate Learning Assessment [CLA], Collegiate Assessment of Academic Proficiency [CAAP], Educational Testing Service Proficiency Profile [ETS-PP]) and other areas such as written communication, mathematics, and reading (e.g., CAAP and ETS-PP) (Sternberg et al., 2011). The Critical Thinking Assessment Test (CAT), developed by Tennessee Technological University (Stein & Haynes, 2011), assesses the skills of evaluating information, creative thinking, learning and problem solving, and communication. It provides a real-world scenario with increasingly deeper essay questions to which students respond. Following training, campus faculty evaluate the essays using predesigned and tested rubrics. The creators of the assessment have tested the validity as well as the correlation with other tests, such as the ACT, SAT, California Critical Thinking Skills Test, and NSSE. Student affairs professionals know that students learn critical thinking skills through their involvement in cocurricular experiences. Staff can work with the campus institutional research office in recruiting student leaders to take the test. Their scores can be compared with those of the other students in the general population who took the test.

Conclusion

Divisions, departments, and programs should undertake assessment on a regular basis, using various types of methods. The assessments should be planned over several years to provide the clearest and broadest picture of student learning and program performance. Staff do not have the time and resources to assess every aspect of a program all the time, so a manageable assessment plan will provide direction and scope. Student affairs staff should work with institutional partners to get assessment results and other data that would be helpful in planning for improvement.

Key Points

- Student affairs professionals have a wide variety of options in choosing assessment methods, and they have to decide on priorities for implementation.
- These methods vary in complexity, purposes, and resources needed.

Discussion Questions and Activities

- Describe at least five different types of assessment.
- Which methods do you see most often? Which ones do you see least often?
- What methods have you seen implemented? How were the results shared and used?
- What methods need to be implemented more frequently at your institution?

6

OUTCOMES

Outcomes are critical components of any assessment program. When they are derived from goals based on a mission statement, they provide the concrete embodiment of the mission, demonstrating its achievement. They provide direction in the planning of programs and services and dictate what should be assessed. *Outcomes* can be defined as participant-centered, desired effects of a program, a service, or an intervention (Henning, 2007). In other words, an outcome is the end result you want to achieve following a given activity. The activity could be a learning exercise, a one-on-one meeting with a staff member, or a more complex experience such as participating in a student organization. Ideally, these activities are planned interventions that result in intentional outcomes.

Benefits of Outcomes

There are a number of benefits of using outcomes in both program development and assessment. The following is a description of a few of the major benefits.

Outcomes help determine what should be assessed. An example may be a reduction in the alcohol binge rate by 5% within one academic year. With this example it is easy to determine how to assess a reduction in the alcohol rate on campus. Many colleges implement annual or semiannual health surveys that have items regarding alcohol use that match the definition of *binge rate*. Assessment would be comparing the items on each survey that address binge rate and determining if there has been a 5% reduction over a period of time.

Outcomes are not only helpful for assessment, but also beneficial in planning. Outcomes provide "destination postcards" or pictures of what actualized goals look like. This concrete, forward-thinking vision helps staff intentionally consider the best strategies to reach the final destination.

Outcomes provide direction in developing strategies for their achievement. This is similar to planning a trip. The vacationer needs to decide where to go, perhaps California. But to actually go on the trip, a more specific location must be identified, maybe the Hotel del Coronado in San Diego. After the specific location is determined the way to get there can be decided. Similarly to achieving outcomes, there may be multiple options—driving (which could include a number of routes to choose from), flying, going by train, or a combination.

Consider this analogy with a campus example. If the destination is a 5% reduction in the binge rate, staff can then cull the literature, review conference programs, and talk to colleagues to pinpoint evidence-based strategies that have been used to reduce binge rates on other campuses. The strategies could include more education at orientation, early interventions with students violating policy, increasing training for resident assistants, developing a video campaign using respected student leaders, and so on. With a clear destination, the best route for reaching it can be mapped.

Initiatives require resources such as money, staff time, technology, or intellectual skills. Once the strategies for addressing an outcome have been determined, then requisite resources can be identified. If educational programs and policy enforcement are proven approaches to decreasing alcohol use rates, then details of these approaches can be defined and resources attached to each strategy. Staff may need to be hired to increase educational outreach into residence halls, fraternities and sororities, and other student organizations. Alcohol prevention programs such as AlcoholEdu may need to be purchased or funding for staff training in Brief Alcohol Screening and Intervention for College Students (BASICS) (U.S. Department of Health and Human Services, 2015) may have to be secured. Student staff may need to be hired to monitor violations of alcohol policy in the residence halls. If resources are not available for intended strategies to address outcomes, those strategies may have to be revised to ensure that outcomes can be achieved.

Because outcomes provide the destination postcards, they can also keep staff on track during the implementation of the activity or activities. Similar to how a map helps keep drivers en route to their destination once the route has been determined, outcomes can play the same role. Assessments can be done along the way (e.g., formative assessment) to ensure that the strategies being used are successful. Consistent policy enforcement has been one way to help reduce binge rates. Formative assessment can be implemented to determine the impact on individual alcohol use for students involved in policy violations. If that assessment demonstrates that alcohol usage decreases as a result of students being held accountable for alcohol policy violations, then staff are on the right track for reducing the campuswide binge rate. Similar formative assessment can be done with other proven measures such as alcohol education initiatives.

In addition to providing direction for planning and assessment, outcomes can help students know what they are learning and make connections to their curricular programs, involvement, and work experiences. Although students find it easy to list all of the activities on their résumés, many find it challenging to describe what they have learned through those experiences, especially in interviewing for jobs or graduate programs. Outcomes provide language that enables students to connect learning with their involvement. Many institutions provide leadership training to organization leaders. During that training students may learn how to collaborate, communicate, and manage conflict, among other skills that they will use as student leaders. With these outcomes, students can clearly articulate to future employers and graduate school admission counselors the knowledge they have acquired and skills they have developed by their involvement on campus.

While outcomes help students articulate what they are learning, outcomes also help staff to communicate to stakeholders what they are doing and the impact they are having. In the planning phase, outcomes help staff describe the intent of a given office or activity. This description is useful in developing partnerships and also communicating direction to those who are implementing strategies designed to achieve outcomes. From the assessment perspective, proven outcomes communicate the impact a unit has on the student experience, student learning, or the academic mission of the institution. Staff can demonstrate the return on investment of resources given and can also advocate for additional resources to expand the impact of their programs and services.

Outcomes have numerous advantages for both program development and assessment, but they also carry challenges that must be overcome.

Challenges of Outcomes

Although there are many benefits to using outcomes in student affairs work, there are also several challenges to implementing them. If staff are unfamiliar with the process of developing and assessing outcomes, there could be resistance. This could stem from a fear of change ("We've always done the program this way"), fear of failure ("I am not competent writing, implementing, or assessing outcomes"), or fear of punishment ("If the students don't reach the outcomes set, I will be fired"). Another challenge is that student affairs staff are busy (as are faculty and other administrators), so if this is a new initiative, staff may balk at the amount of time it takes to implement a new process. Although initial training and application can take time, these steps should also save time in the long run by providing direction for programs and services. In today's higher education environment, it is more important than ever for staff to be able to demonstrate how their program or service supports the institution's outcomes and provides added value to students' education.

Students may also resist outcomes language related to cocurricular experiences. Whereas they are used to being assessed in the classroom through tests, projects, and rubrics, for example, they may be taken aback when an advisor or supervisor also wants to develop a more formalized "curriculum" for their leadership or employment experience. At worst, students may claim they do not learn in the cocurricular area, but they may also respond negatively to being assessed in a different environment that they perceive to be fun and a release from academic stress. Advisors and supervisors must be able to articulate how these experiences can improve students' experiences and ability to translate skills to a variety of situations and create an expectation for continuous improvement and growth.

Types of Outcomes

There are primarily three different types of outcomes that provide the benefits discussed. These outcomes are operational, learning and development, and program. The focus for each is a little different, and all three are critical to student affairs work.

Operational outcomes—also called administrative outcomes, service outcomes, or outputs—are metrics that document how well the operational aspects of a program or an activity are functioning; however, they do not document learning, development, or the overall impact of a program or service (Henning, 2009). They can also be referred to as process or performance indicators. Examples of operational outcomes include number of programs in the residence halls, average attendance at events on campus, the wait time in the counseling center, the speed in which work orders are addressed, and so on. While these outcomes are useful, impact cannot be equated with number of students served or number of programs held as the service could be poor or the programs could be devoid of learning. However, they do provide a context for impact.

Learning and development outcomes are desired learning and development effects of a program, a service, or an intervention, but are more specific than goals and are result-focused and participant-centered (Henning, 2009). In other words, "learning and development outcomes are the knowledge, skills, attitudes, and habits of mind that students take with them from a learning experience" (Suskie, 2009, p. 117). They are what students are expected to know or do. Examples of learning and development outcomes may include increased résumé writing (skill), development of conflict resolution skills (skill), identification of academic resources on campus (knowledge), increased confidence (attitude), or persistence (habit of mind).

Finally, program outcomes describe the desired aggregate impact of a program, a service, or an intervention but are more specific than a goal. Examples include a decrease in the binge drinking rate on campus, an increase in first- to second-year retention in the residence halls, and an increase in the number of students incorporating wellness into their lives. Basically, they are what the program is expected to accomplish.

Not all programs, services, and interventions have all three types of outcomes. For example, some activities may have just operational outcomes, or some may have operational and program outcomes but no learning outcomes. However, when developing programs and services all three types of outcomes should be explored prior to and during program development in order to maximize the impact of the activity.

Language of Outcomes

To better understand outcomes, it may be helpful to view them in their larger context, which can be called the language of outcomes. Figure 6.1 represents the alignment of key concepts centered on outcomes.

The mission of the institution, division, department, or program forms the base of the pyramid. The mission is the foundation on which a division or department is set. Bryson (2011) states that a mission "clarifies an organization's purpose, or why it should be doing what it does" (p. 127). All of the activities of that unit should support the mission. Program missions should support the department missions. Department missions should support a division mission, and division missions should support an institutional mission. Using the mission as a base, goals are developed to operationalize the mission. A goal is an end result written in broad terms (Henning, 2007). Inputs are the resources or raw materials that are available to develop a program or an intervention, which can include faculty, staff, budget, facilities, technology, and so on (Henning, 2009). It is critical to consider the inputs prior to assessment as the program developer needs to be aware of the resources available for implementation. Once outcomes are developed, strategies to implement those outcomes are developed. Each strategy is then broken down into smaller action steps.

Figure 6.1 Outcome language pyramid.

The following example may be useful to see how all of the pieces fit together:

> Institutional mission: Graduates have the skills and knowledge to transform themselves and the world.
>
> Division mission: The Division of Student Success facilitates programs, services, and experiences that help students develop into leaders who think critically, ethically, and reflectively.
>
> Office mission: The Office of Student Involvement engages students through campus involvement, leadership development, and college transitions.

Readers will note that there is explicit alignment between the three mission statements. The division mission supports the institution mission while the office mission supports the division mission. This alignment is critical. In times of diminishing resources, funding is dependent upon initiatives that support the institutional mission. This alignment through the organizational hierarchy helps departments directly and indirectly support the educational mission of the institution.

> Goal: As a result of participating in the Emerging Leaders Program, students will increase their leadership skills.

This goal related to a leadership program is aligned with the department mission.

Operational outcome: Two hundred students will participate in the Emerging Leaders Program by the end of the 2016–2017 academic year.

Learning outcome: As a result of participating in the Emerging Leaders Program, students will be able to effectively facilitate a meeting.

Program outcome: Sixty percent of students will lead a student organization during their college career.

Each type of outcome addresses a different type of component of the program. The operational outcome addresses participation, while the learning outcome addresses a skill learned by students. The program outcome addresses the aggregate impact of the program itself. There can be multiple operational, learning, and program outcomes per program. It is important to note that not all student affairs interventions will have all three types of outcomes. However, it is useful to at least consider each type of outcome for each intervention. The length and depth of the experience will also have an impact on how the outcomes are written and accomplished.

Strategy: In order for students to be able to effecively run a meeting, they will identify and describe three best practices in meeting facilitation.

Action steps: To identify and describe three best practices in meeting facilitation, action steps might include identifying meetings to attend, developing an opportunity for reflection, developing a framework for that reflection, evaluating the experience, planning and implementing a meeting, getting feedback from peers, and so on.

Action steps are component parts of a strategy. It is essential to consider and document the action steps, as failure to achieve an outcome may not be the result of the strategy itself but instead the manner in which the strategy was implemented. Documenting the action steps used for implementation will provide a record that can be reviewed and revised if a strategy is unsuccessfully implemented.

The language of outcomes closely mirrors the assessment cycle presented by Suskie (2009). She depicts assessment as a four-step process. The first step is establishing learning goals rooted in the institutional mission and purpose. Step two is developing learning opportunities to help students achieve the learning goals. The third step is assessing student learning to determine if the goals are achieved. In the fourth step, results are used to make change. While Suskie's cycle focuses on learning, it can be applied to nonlearning initiatives as well. Goals are established. Strategies are developed to achieve the goals. The strategies and goals are assessed and that information is used to close the loop by making changes. To effectively implement this cycle, clear outcome statements are needed. This was discussed at greater length in Chapter 3.

Writing Outcome Statements

Whereas outcomes are concepts that guide the development and assessment of programs and services, the concepts need to be operationalized into statements that can be communicated to others. Beginning with learning outcome statements and moving to operational and program outcome statements, this section will discuss several processes that can be used to develop outcome statements.

Using Existing Outcome Frameworks

Before beginning to develop learning outcomes from scratch, it may be worthwhile to explore existing frameworks for outcomes. There are many sets of learning outcomes that may be used as is or with minor adaptation.

One such framework is the Council for the Advancement of Standards in Higher Education's (CAS) Learning Domains and Dimensions (2012b). In 2003, CAS created a set of 16 domains of learning outcomes. In 2008, after the publication of *Learning Reconsidered* (Keeling, 2004), CAS combined the outcomes from the original set of 16 with those included in *Learning Reconsidered*. The result was a set of six domains: knowledge acquisition, construction, integration, and application; cognitive complexity; intrapersonal development; interpersonal competence; humanitarianism and civic engagement; and practical competence. Each domain has more specific outcome dimensions. Practical competence has eight dimensions, while the other five domains have four dimensions each.

Another useful resource is the list of the Essential Learning Outcomes developed by the Association of American Colleges and Universities (AAC&U, n.d.). AAC&U has identified four domains: knowledge of human cultures and the physical and natural world, intellectual and practical skills, personal and social responsibility, and integrative and applied learning. Within these four domains are 12 outcomes. Although the astute reader will note different learning domains for the CAS and AAC&U learning outcomes, further exploration reveals significant similarities between the dimensions of learning outcomes across both documents.

Formulas for Writing Learning Outcome Statements

The acronym ABCD is a useful approach to writing outcomes statements. The letters stand for audience, behavior, condition, and degree. Although the acronym is ABCD, the actual order can be slightly different. The formula for ABCD is

$$Condition + Audience + Behavior + Degree$$

In most cases in student affairs, the audience is students or a specific group of students such as students attending orientation, students in the leadership class, or student athletes. It is always better to be as specific as possible when describing the audience as this provides for clearer communication regarding the outcome statement to others.

Behavior is what the audience is expected to do as a result of the intervention. Students attending orientation may need to be able to describe academic resources on campus. Students in the leadership class may have to be able to compare and contrast the leadership styles of people they know. Student athletes may need to be able to resolve conflict between teammates. The behavior is what is being measured.

The condition is the program, service, or intervention that should foster the behavior. For students attending orientation, the condition could be a panel of staff from the academic support offices. For the leadership students, there may be an activity where they learn about leadership styles. For student athletes, the condition may be having to collaborate with people different from themselves.

Finally, degree is the level at which you expect the behavior to be displayed. This provides a threshold to determine if the outcome has actually been achieved. It describes how much or how frequently something is to be done. The following outcome statements provide examples of the ABCD formula:

> As a result of the panel presentation, students attending orientation will describe at least four offices on campus that provide academic support.
> As a result of the leadership syles inventory activity, students in the leadership class will be able to compare and contrast the leadership styles of two people they know.
> As a result of playing on an athletic team, student athletes will effectively resolve at least two conflicts between teammates.

Like ABCD, SWiBAT is another formula for creating learning outcome statements. SWiBAT stands for *students will be able to*. The benefit of this approach is the SWiBAT antecedent enables an easy way to begin writing outcome statements. The general idea is to start with "Students will be able to . . ." and then add an action verb followed by a condition. The formula is

SWiBAT + action verb + condition

The outcomes created by using ABCD can be adapted to the SWiBAT formula. For example,

> Students attending orientation will be able to describe at least four offices on campus that provide academic support as a result of the panel presentation.

Students in the leadership class will be able to compare and contrast the leadership styles of two people they know as a result of the leadership styles inventory activity.

Student athletes will be able to effectively resolve at least two conflicts between teammates as a result of playing on an athletic team.

As can be seen from the SWiBAT and ABCD examples, the same information is included but in a different order. Thus, either process can be used, the choice being a matter of personal preference.

Suskie (2014) offered additional recommendations for developing learning outcomes. The point is to describe outcomes, not learning products or activities. There should be a focus on the destination. Suskie (2014) also suggests that fuzzy terms be avoided. "The clearer and more explicit your students' destinations, the clearer the path you and your students will take to get there, and the easier to confirm that they have arrived" (p. 125). Her final recommendation is to use observable action verbs, which will be discussed later in this chapter.

Writing Operational and Program Outcome Statements

Writing operational and program outcome statements is similar to drafting learning outcomes statements. With these types of outcomes, there may not be an audience, but the statement must include some type of change and the intervention that should facilitate the change. Here are some examples of operational outcome statements:

Two hundred students will attend the sexual assault prevention workshop.
Health services will facilitate 25 alcohol education courses during the academic year.
The average caseload per advisor will be 250 students.

Examples of program outcome statements include the following:

As a result of the new alcohol use policy, the number of alcohol violations in the residence halls will decrease by 10% in the 2016–2017 academic year.
As a result of the new anonymous reporting process, the number of sexual assaults reported on campus will increase by 25% in the 2016–2017 academic year.
As a result of financial aid training at orientation, the number of student questions to the finanial aid office will decrease by 50% during the first week of classes.

Characteristics of Well-Written Outcomes

After outcome statements are drafted, especially learning outcome statements, it is helpful to evaluate those statements to ensure they will be useful. An acronym that is helpful in evaluating outcome statements is SMARRT (specific, measurable, ambitious but attainable, results-oriented, relevant, and time-bound). This is an adaption of SMART as used by the University of Central Florida (2004).

The outcome statement must be specific in that the audience, behavior, condition, and degree are all clearly identified. Without a clear definition of each component of the outcome statement there may be a challenge in developing the intervention to foster the outcome and/or in assessing achievement of the outcome.

If the outcome statement is not specific it will be difficult to measure. Some assessment professionals believe that the measurement should be included in the outcome statement itself. While this does provide a clear connection between the behavior to be measured and the measurement, developing the outcome statement should not include the measurement tool. The outcome statement can be a guide for both development and assessment. Additionally, you have more flexibility to choose an appropriate assessment tool once the outcome has been implemented. The tool may change over time, even if the outcome stays the same.

The outcome statement should also be ambitious but attainable. The behavior should not be so easy to achieve that all students can achieve it all of the time. If that happens, you might consider a differently worded outcome or desired result. However, it should not be so aggressive that only a few students can achieve it. The behavior students must demonstrate should be a stretch allowing them to increase their learning and development.

Outcome statements should also be results-oriented. The focus of the outcome should be on what the audience can or should be doing. Often, statements are developed but focus on a department or staff. Statements such as "Staff will provide" and "The office will implement" place the focus on strategies, not on end results. The implementation of strategies, no matter how well implemented, does not necessarily ensure results. Moving the focus to the behavior increases intentionality around strategies to achieve the results.

Relevance is an important characteristic relating to outcome statements. If an outcome statement is inappropriate given a department's or program's mission or purpose, stakeholders will wonder why the department is engaging in this activity. Using the language of outcomes and aligning outcomes with goals that are consistent with mission statements ensures the relevance of those outcomes.

There should also be a time frame connected to the outcome statement. Often the time frame is the completion of an activity such as a program or service. But, there may be other outcomes, especially program outcomes, that have a different time frame. Take these examples:

As a result of campus efforts, the alcohol binge rate on campus will decrease by 5% by the end of the 2016–2017 academic year.
Students will demonstrate ethical decision making by the time they graduate college.

The time frame is important, as it provides an indication when the change is expected to take place and directs when the measurement of the outcome should be done.

Like SMARRT, the 3 Ms provide guidance for well-developed outcome statements. The *Ms* stand for *meaningful, manageable,* and *measurable* (Bresciani, Zelna, & Anderson, 2004). When considering how *meaningful* outcomes are, staff should ensure that the outcome is aligned with division and department mission and goals. This is very smiliar to *relevance* in SMARRT. *Manageable* relates to how achievable the outcome is for students and how practical it is for staff to implement. Finally, the outcome should be *measurable* (i.e., countable, observable). However, just because an outcome is not easily measured does not mean that it should be dismissed. Outcome statements do provide direction for implementation even if they cannot be assessed easily.

Considerations for Learning Outcomes

Suskie (2014) provided considerations for learning outcomes. First, she stated that they should be relevant and in response to student needs; that is, they should be student-centered. Learning outcomes also should reflect the college's values and distinctive traits. Second, she suggested limiting learning outcomes to between three and six for each program; otherwise the focus becomes diffused with too many outcomes, making it difficult to achieve any of the outcomes. In student affairs, think about the hour-long programs offered, several-hour workshops or trainings provided, the semester-long courses such as transitioning to college, and the year-long (or more) student leadership or employment opportunities. Each of these would have a different quantity and depth of learning outcomes and assessment measures.

Action Verbs

One of the most difficult components of writing an outcome statement is choosing the appropriate action verb. Bresciani (2013b) identified the reasons action verbs play a vital role in the outcome development and assessment processes. Action verbs clearly identify for students what type of behavior is expected. Knowing the behavior expected influences the assessment method used. Action verbs can also describe the level of learning expected.

One thing to keep in mind is that action verbs vary in their meaning and interpretation. *Identify* is not the same as *describe*. *Describe* is not the same as *implement*. *Implement* is not the same as *create*. Each one of these terms is aligned with different types of behavior, requiring different methods of assessment. It is helpful to have a list of action verbs handy in writing outcome statements. These lists are readily available by doing a simple Internet search.

It is best to use action verbs that represent observable behavior, as this makes the outome easier to measure. However, this may not be possible with affective outcomes. To be able to measure if someone knows something, that person must demonstrate his or her knowledge in some way.

Learning Taxonomies

Bloom's Taxonomy

Benjamin Bloom and his colleagues met at the American Psychological Association Convention in 1948. The goal of their gathering was the creation of a classification method for behaviors believed to be important to learning (Forehand, 2005). The group identified three different types of learning: cognitive, affective, and psychomotor. Each type had different levels, going from least to more complex types of learning. These taxonomies can provide guidance in learning outcome development to ensure that learning at multiple levels is considered. A simple Internet search produces lists of action verbs for each level that are helpful when writing learning outcome statements. Taxonomies are also useful for assessment purposes, as knowing the level of learning that is supposed to take place will influence the assessment strategies used to measure outcome achievement at each level. Different levels of outcomes require different types of assessment methods.

Cognitive Taxonomy

The cognitive domain was originally developed in 1956 and included the following levels: knowledge, comprehension, application, analysis, synthesis, and evaluation. This domain was revised in 2001 to have the following levels: remembering, understanding, applying, analyzing, evaluating, and creating (Forehand, 2005). Remembering is simply the ability to recall information, whereas understanding requires the construction of meaninig from instruction or guidance. With applying, the individual must perform some action or procedure given by the information that has been acquired. When people are analyzing they are deconstructing information into component parts and determining how these are related to one another.

Evaluating requires making judgments based on a set of criteria or standards, and creating requires combining components into a new functional whole (Anderson et al., 2000).

The following are outcomes for each level. Students participating in the Emerging Leaders Program will

- Identify three leadership theories (remembering)
- Explain three key elements of two leadership theories (understanding)
- Effectively facilitate a meeting (applying)
- Differentiate the leadership styles of two leaders (analyzing)
- Evaluate the meeting facilitation of a peer (evaluating)
- Develop an action plan for improving their conflict resolutions skills (creating) (Henning, 2009)

Affective Taxonomy

The affective domain was developed by Krathwohl, Bloom, and Masia (1964) and includes the manner in which people process things emotionally, involving feelings, values, appreciation, enthusiasms, motivations, and attitudes. The levels are: receives phenomena, responds to phenomena, values, organizes, and internalizes values. An individual who receives phenomena is aware of a phenomenon and is willing to attend to it. Responding to a phenomenon requires active participation with the phenomenon rather than passive awareness. At the values level, the individual attaches a worth to a particular object, phenomenon, or behavior, which can range from acceptance to commitment. Organizing takes this worth to a higher level where the individual prioritizes this worth by contrasting it with different levels, resolving conflicts between them, and creating a unique value system. At the final level, the individual internalizes the values toward the phenomenon, and this new value system controls behavior. It is challenging to assess appreciation for something such as art or diversity. Being able to better define those concepts can lead to more concrete behaviors that could be observed and measured.

Outcome statements for this domain may include the following. As a result of participating in Intergroup Dialogue, students will

- Describe how the stories of other students have impacted them (receives phenomenon)
- Ask questions of others during discussions (responds to phenomenon)
- Explain in a weekly journal entry what they are learning about diversity (values)
- Compare their experiences with those of other students (organizes)
- Confront others when derogatory terms are used (internalizes values) (Henning, 2009)

Psychomotor Taxonomy

Bloom was not involved in the development of psychomotor taxonomies but others were (Dave, 1967; Harrow, 1972; Simpson, 1966). The taxonomy developed by Dave (1967) will be discussed. Although this domain originally focused on physical movement, coordination, and use of motor-skill areas, it can be applied to college students around skills in general. The five levels are imitation, manipulation, precision, articulation, and naturalization. At the imitation level, the student simply copies the action of another person, whereas in manipulation the student reproduces activity from instruction or memory. With precision, the student executes a skill reliably and independent of assistance. Articulation is the adaptation and integration of expertise to satisfy a different situation. At naturalization, there is an automated, unconscious mastery of activity and related skills at strategic levels.

Outcomes for this domain could include those in the following list. After participating in setup-crew training, student staff will

- Set up a room using the instructions in the manual (imitation)
- Prepare a room without using instructions in the manual (manipulation)
- Supervise other staff during room setup (precision)
- Solve technology problem during a presentation (articulation)
- Develop the training manual for tech crew (naturalization) (Henning, 2009)

Taxonomy of Significant Learning

To facilitate classroom learning, Fink (2013) reviewed descriptions of quality teaching and learning to create the taxonomy of significant learning. His goal was to build on other taxonomies such as Bloom's but to create one that was broader and that would take into account different types of learning. According to Fink (2013), there must be some type of change in the learner for learning to occur. Significant learning then requires some kind of important, lasting change.

Fink's (2013) taxonomy has six kinds of learning, called domains here, that are related to one another, but yet distinct. Each domain has specific elements or dimensions as illustrated in Figure 6.2. These areas are as follows:

- *Foundational knowledge* is the basic understanding of topics such as science, history, literature, geography, and so on. Foundational knowledge provides the basic understanding needed for other types of learning.

- *Application* is putting the knowledge to use in some way. Application learning enables learning to become useful.
- *Integration* is the connection between different things such as ideas or experiences. Integration provides learners with intellectual power.
- The *human dimension* relates to what people learn about themselves or others allowing them to interact more effectively. This area of learning informs people about the human significance of what is learned.
- *Caring* occurs when a learning experience changes for them to pay more attention to something. This care may be reflected in new feelings, interests, or values. When people care about something they want to learn more about it and make it a part of their lives.
- In *learning how to learn*, also known as metacognition, people learn about the process of learning. This enables them to continue to learn and develop in the future.

Figure 6.2 Taxonomy of significant learning.

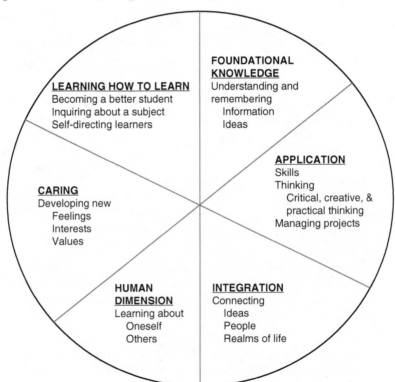

Figure 6.3 The interactive nature of significant learning.

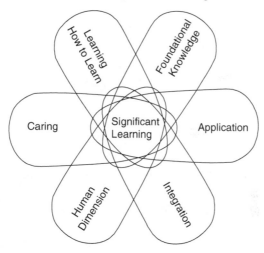

Bloom's and similar taxonomies reflect the fact that that learning is hierarchical. Fink's (2013) taxonomy is not hierarchicial but relational and interactive. One form of learning and its impact on other forms is shown in Figure 6.3. The application of knowledge to different settings can lead to understanding connections, which is integration. Caring about something may lead individuals to learn more about themselves, which is the human dimension.

The taxonomy of significant learning provides a useful set of domains to consider in the development of outcomes and the creation of learning experiences. The power of this taxonomy is the theorized interrelation between the different domains that suggests that one type of learning can impact other types of learning. In addition, there may be interaction effects between different types of learning if educational activities are developed to intentionally address outcomes in each domain.

Hints

In writing outcome statements there are a few hints that may be helpful. First, writing outcome statements is similar to writing a paper in college. The process is an iterative one that requires multiple drafts. In the first draft, simply get the basic elements down. In the subsequent drafts, the statements are fine-tuned with particular attention to the action verb being used.

Second, it is helpful for outcomes to be reviewed using SMARRT or the 3 Ms as a checklist. Each outcome statement should be read to be sure it meets each characteristic of a well-written outcome and revised as appropriate. In addition, the broader documents, such as the institution or department mission statement, should be referred back to frequently to ensure alignment.

Third, reviewers can provide useful feedback on outcomes. It is helpful to have reviewers from different departments as they bring new and fresh perspectives. Reviewers can use the SMARRT and 3 Ms characteristics to provide a framework for review. Students also provide insightful feedback about the outcomes associated with their experiences.

Conclusion

In student affairs and higher education, college student educators want students to gain skills and knowledge that will help them succeed in a variety of situations and environments during and after college. Defining outcomes provides staff a road map for structuring programs and services, as well as determining appropriate assessment methods. Although developing outcomes takes practice, it is something that student affairs staff need to do in order to align with the larger organizational contexts and priorities.

Key Points

- Types of outcomes include the following:
    - Operational (also called objectives or administrative outcomes)—metrics that document how well operational aspects are functioning
    - Learning and development—describe the desired learning and development effects of a program, a service, or an activity
    - Program—describe the desired aggregate impact of a program, a service, or an activity
- Existing frameworks can be used to develop outcomes.
- Learning taxonomies that can be used for outcome development include the cognitive, affective, and psychomotor taxonomies and the taxonomy of significant learning.
- The formulas for writing outcomes include ABCD and SWiBAT.

Discussion Questions and Activities

- Develop two examples of each type of outcome: operational, learning and development, and program.
- Develop two strategies to achieve each type of outcome.
- Break each strategy down into at least two component parts.

- If you were developing a study skills program for traditional-aged first-year students, which taxonomy would be most useful in developing outcomes? Why?
- If you were developing a study skills program for adult first-year students, which taxonomy would be most useful in developing outcomes? Why?

7

QUANTITATIVE DESIGNS

As noted earlier, traditional educational research approaches are often employed in implementing assessment. As such, it is useful to understand the various types of designs that can be used so that the appropriate assessment approach can be employed. This chapter will focus on descriptive, correlational, causal-comparative, and experimental designs.

Descriptive Designs

Descriptive studies are just what the name suggests: studies that attempt to describe educational phenomena. The goal of these designs is to understand what is happening but not necessarily to try to determine causality or associations between variables. Both qualitative and quantitative designs can be used to describe phenomena, but the focus of this chapter is the use of quantitative descriptive designs. Topics of descriptive assessment studies include issues such as student satisfaction living in the residence halls, health behaviors of students, and attitudes regarding the climate on campus.

Descriptive studies attempt to capture one moment in time or may be longitudinal capturing attitudes, behaviors, and so forth over a period of time. Both approaches use similar data-collection methods, often surveys.

Longitudinal Designs

There are four types of longitudinal designs: trend studies, cohort studies, panel studies, and cross-sectional studies. Trend studies "describe change by selecting a different sample at each data-collection point from a population that does not remain constant" (Gall, Gall, & Borg, 2007, p. 303). A campus health service could utilize a trend study to understand health behaviors of college students over a 10-year period. The population would be all the students, who change yearly, as students enter and others leave. During each data-collection point, perhaps biennially, a sample of students would be surveyed regarding their behaviors. Those behaviors would be summarized over time.

Like a trend study, a cohort study uses different samples over time. However, unlike trend studies, the population is the same during that time period (Gall et al., 2007). This design may be used to track the employment status of students who graduated from a particular college between 1990 and 1999. Information gathered from these alumni may include type of job, career field, salary, and so on. The population remains the same (graduates from 1990 to 1999), but for each data collection the sample changes—a new group of people participate in the data-collection process. For example, a sample would be selected for each year and be surveyed in 2000, 2005, 2010, and then again in 2015.

The challenge with both the trend and cohort studies is that the differences seen over time may result from the different samples selected. And in the case of the trend study, the changing population from which the sample is drawn may also complicate inferences made from the results, since it is continually changing. Panel studies help to address these challenges.

In a panel study, the sample is selected at the beginning of the study, and data are collected from that same sample across time (Gall et al., 2007). A panel study would be an advantageous format for understanding the experience of veterans on campus. A set of veterans could be selected before the study began, and data could be collected via survey at various points during the panel's college career. One challenge of longitudinal studies is the amount of time needed to gather data. In the example regarding veterans, data collection would take place during the students' college career, which would range from four to six or more years. Another challenge is mortality, which means that some participants may leave the panel before the end of the study.

One solution addressing this disadvantage is the use of a cross-sectional design. In this design, the data are obtained at one point in time (rather than across a larger time frame) but from participants of different ages or different stages of development (Gall et al., 2007). Revisiting the example of understanding health behaviors, a cross-sectional study could be used to gather data from a college population and reported behaviors could be examined for each class to see if there are changes over time. Rather than surveying a sample at different points in time, the data are collected just once.

The benefit of descriptive designs is that they can provide detailed information regarding a specific phenomenon. They also provide insight into how a phenomenon changes over time that is specifically helpful in student affairs assessment as it explains student development and the impact of interventions on student growth. This strength is also a weakness. If the point of the assessment project was to understand the change in behavior resulting from an intervention, the observed change in behavior may be the result of student maturation rather than intervention. For example, an increase in the moral development of traditional-aged college students may be due to brain development rather than experiences on campus.

Descriptive studies are useful because they shed light on various educational phenomena. However, they do not provide insight regarding causality. Because the student experience does not exist in a vacuum, it is difficult to ascribe changes to one intervention.

Correlational Designs

In some cases, it is important to know that two (or more) variables are related. These studies use correlational design and uncover relationships through the use of specific statistics (Gall et al., 2007). Correlational designs may be used to understand the relationship between students' average hours of sleep per night and their grade point averages (GPAs), the relationship between alcohol use and the use of other drugs, or the relationship between age and moral development.

Before discussing correlational designs, a little background on the concept of correlation may be useful. A correlation is a linear relationship between two or more variables. The focus in this chapter will be on the relationship between two variables rather than the relationship between multiple variables. A positive, or direct, correlation is one where both variables change in the same direction: As one variable increases, the other variable increases, and as one variable decreases, the other variable decreases. For example, there is a positive relationship between age and height. As children grow older, they generally grow taller. A negative or indirect correlation suggests that as one variable increases, the other decreases (Salkind, 2013). A negative correlation exists between the average amount of snow a region gets per year and the average temperature for that region. The higher the average temperature, the lower the average amount of snow. In higher education, there is a negative correlation between alcohol use and GPA.

The relationship between two variables is measured by the correlation coefficient, denoted as r. Correlation coefficients provide two types of information. First, correlation coefficients are positive or negative. The sign dictates the direction of the relationship, with a positive sign noting a positive correlation and a negative sign noting a negative correlation. The second piece of information conveyed in the correlation coefficient is the magnitude of the relationship.

It is easy to make the faulty interpretation that if two variables are correlated, one causes the other. However, this interpretation is not always correct. Just because two variables are associated does not mean that one causes the other. There may be another variable that is the causal factor, or another reason for the association of the two variables. Height and mathematical ability have a positive correlation. Just because there is a relationship between these two variables does not mean that height causes mathematical ability or math ability causes height. Although one variable may certainly cause another, only experimental designs can be used to determine causation. It is important to be careful in drawing conclusions about causation.

In designing correlational studies, it is critical to consider how the data are going to be collected. Except in unique circumstances, both independent and dependent variables must be continuous in order to calculate the correlation coefficient. Dependent variables are those that will change if something is influencing them. An example of a dependent variable would be participation at a campus program. Independent variables are those that are thought to have an impact on the dependent variable. If participation at a campus program is the dependent variable, independent variables would include marketing, date/time of the event, incentives such as pizza, and anything else that might affect attendance. If surveys are used to collect data in correlational studies, the questions must be worded in such a way that the data represent intervals or ratios (see Chapter 9 for details).

One of the advantages of correlational designs is that they allow for the analysis of a larger number of variables in a single study (Gall et al., 2007). Another advantage was alluded to earlier—the fact that a correlation coefficient offers information on both the direction and magnitude of the relationship, thus providing evidence to assess both the statistical and practical significance of the data.

Limitations of correlational studies include the issue that correlation is not causation. Whereas correlational studies allow for the exploration of causation, only an experiment can confirm causation. Additionally, it is possible that a third variable is actually causing the relationship between the two variables under study. The failure to consider alternative explanations for correlations may result in faulty inferences between variables. Another criticism of these types of studies is that they reduce complex human behavior to a bivariate relationship (Gall et al., 2007).

Correlational designs can be used to clarify the relationship between the amount of sleep students get each night and their academic success. Another use of correlation may be to elucidate the connection between involvement on campus and graduation rate. Yet another example might be the relationship between age and level of engagement in extracurricular activities.

Causal-Comparative Designs

Causality, or the impact of one variable on another, is useful in assessment, as this provides evidence that can inform programs, practices, and policies. For example, on college campuses it may be important to know that students with chronic diseases are less engaged on campus than students without chronic diseases. It may also be helpful to know that students working on campus feel more connected than students working off campus or that students who build relationships with faculty are more academically successful than students who do not. Perhaps a staff member might also want to know that students who are members of student organizations achieve better outcomes and at higher levels in a leadership class than those who are not. In each of these examples, the independent variable is already present or absent (e.g., having a chronic disease versus not having a chronic disease, working on campus versus off campus, being in a student organization versus not a member). This is the hallmark of causal-comparative studies, which comprise a type of nonexperimental design where investigators seek to identify cause-and-effect relationships (Gall et al., 2007).

Causal-comparative designs have similarities to and differences from correlational designs. Both are examples of associational designs and attempt to explore causation, although neither can definitively determine causation. The focus of correlational designs is usually multiple continuous variables, whereas causal-comparative designs include a categorical variable. Categorical variables are variables that have discrete groups. *Residence hall* is a categorical variable, as a student lives in one or another hall. Another categorical variable would be *students' majors*. Another difference is that correlational designs utilize correlation coefficients, whereas causal-comparative designs use other statistics for analysis (Fraenkel, Wallen, Hyun, 2014).

Selecting appropriate groups for the study is critical in planning a causal-comparative design. In the example of leadership skills, it is clear who is a member of a student organization and who is not. However, every instance may not be as clear. For a causal-comparative design, there must be a group of students who do not have a chronic disease. It is important to select comparison groups that are as similar to each other as possible except for the independent variable being examined.

Once the data are collected, the appropriate analysis must be selected. When response means or averages on an instrument, such as a test or survey, between the two groups are being assessed, a *t*-test would be the appropriate analysis method. A *t*-tests is a statistical method that helps determine if the difference between two means is statistically significant. If more than two groups are used in the causal-comparative design (e.g., students from different race/ethnic groups), then analysis of variance (ANOVA) would be used to compare their means. If the ANOVA results are statistically significant, then post-hoc tests would be needed to determine which pairs of means are different. ANOVA is just like a *t*-test; a *t*-test compares the means of two groups, and ANOVA tests the difference between means of three or more groups. Post-hoc tests then determine which means between which groups are statistically different. If the dependent variable is not continuous or the variances are not assumed to be equal, then a nonparametric test must be used. Nonparametric tests are statistical tests that are used when statistical assumptions for other tests are not met. The chi-square (χ^2) test is one of the most popular. See Chapter 9 for more detail on these statistics.

The benefit of causal-comparative studies is that they allow for examination of cause and effect without manipulating variables. This design uses differences that already exist rather than ones that are created. However, with preexisting differences, it is difficult to determine what other differences may exist between comparison groups beyond the independent variable being studied. In addition, one must still be very careful about claiming causation in assessment work unless the necessary requirements discussed in this section are met.

Experimental Designs

One of the most useful quantitative designs in student affairs assessment is experimental design. Experimental design is unique in two ways. First, it is the only design that directly attempts to influence a particular variable. Second, it is the best design for understanding cause-and-effect relationships (Fraenkel et al., 2014). These designs can validate the impact of interventions and allow for cause and effect between variables to be determined. In an experimental design, a variable is manipulated to understand the impact of that intervention on one or more dependent variables.

The most frequent experimental design in student affairs assessment is the pretest/posttest design. In this design a pretest is given, then an intervention is introduced with two or more types of levels or formats, and then a posttest is given. For an experiment to assess the effectiveness of two leadership development programs, different levels or formats may be *no intervention, homegrown leadership training program*, and *nationally recognized leadership training program*. The changes in scores on the pretest and posttest for individuals in each treatment group are compared. One intervention may be no treatment at all. Thus, an intervention may be compared with no intervention. An example can be the use of a matching survey to assign residence hall roommates. In this experimental design, one group of students could be assigned roommates based on their matching survey scores, while another group is assigned randomly. The happiness of the roommate assignments could be measured at the end of the semester to determine which approach was more effective. Another example could be the use of an educational intervention for alcohol use. One set of students could be assigned to participate in a homegrown educational intervention while another set of students could be assigned to participate in Brief Alcohol Screening and Intervention for College Students (BASICS) (U.S. Department of Health and Human Services, 2015). The alcohol use of both groups could be measured at a later point to determine which intervention was most effective in reducing alcohol use.

There is an adaptation of the pretest/posttest called a "posttest then pretest." This design is used if there is a belief that the pretest may influence performance on the posttest. This design includes a "reflective pretest." An intervention is given and afterward participants are asked about their attitudes, behaviors, and so on as a result of the intervention. They are then asked about the same attitudes and behaviors before the intervention. Important features of this design include clear instructions, reflective order, and presentation style (Klatt & Taylor-Powell, 2005). This design includes concise instructions that clearly tell the respondent what to do. The reflective order allows the participants to use the same frame of reference for both responses.

At this point, it is important to distinguish between experiments and quasi-experiments. In experiments, participants are randomly assigned to a group whereas this does not happen in quasi-experiments (Fraenkel et al., 2014). Consider the alcohol intervention example. That could be set up as either an experiment or a quasi-experiment. In the experimental format, students required to participate in an alcohol intervention would be randomly assigned to either the homegrown or BASICS group. In the quasi-experimental version of this study all students required to participate in an alcohol intervention during fall term would take part in the homegrown activity; then, during the second semester, all students required to participate in an intervention would participate in BASICS. Random assignment is intended to reduce or eliminate the impact from extraneous variables (Fraenkel et al., 2014). In this example, there may be a difference between students required to participate in an intervention in the fall semester compared with the spring semester. This difference may be what causes any change in alcohol use instead of the intervention itself.

Validity Issues

Internal Validity

Since the focus of an experiment is to determine the effect of an intervention on the dependent variable, it is crucial to isolate any extraneous variables that can also impact the dependent variable. However, there are a number of issues that can influence the internal validity of the study. Some of these issues include maturity, differential selection, instrumentation, and mortality.

Current brain research suggests that the part of the human brain that controls decision making does not develop fully until the mid- to late-twenties (Giedd et al., 2009). Thus, if a program was developed to assist students' ethical decision making, a change observed over time may be as much a result of the development of students' brains, or maturity, as the intervention itself. Maturity can confound experimental results.

Another issue to consider is differential selection. For example, reconsider the alcohol intervention discussed previously. Students who participated in the intervention in the fall may differ from those who participated in the spring. This difference could then impact ongoing alcohol use, which is the dependent variable being measured to study the impact of each intervention. The differential selection could have as much impact on the dependent variable as the intervention did.

A threat to internal validity may also happen as a result of instrumentation. Ratings by hall directors could be used to measure the change in the group facilitation skills of resident assistants. The skills could be measured by observations by the hall director. It could be possible that the observations taken at the end of the school year may differ from those taken at the start of the school year, since the hall director would have gained more skill and accuracy in observation. Therefore, the gain that was observed may be as much a result of different observations by the hall director as actual skill development. In this case the hall director is the instrument.

Another issue relates to mortality. For experiments that take place over time, it is possible that some participants will drop out. Emerging leaders programs are found on many campuses. These programs are often for first- or second-year students and take place over a semester with weekly or biweekly meetings. To assess the knowledge and skills developed over the course of the program, pre- and posttests could be used. Since the program occurs over a semester, some students who start may not finish the program. Students may leave because they are no longer interested, because they cannot attend the meetings, or because of some other reason. If the students who leave the program differ from those who stay, the differential results of the posttest could depend on the differences in those students who left more than on the intervention itself.

These are just a few of the threats to internal validity that could occur in student affairs assessment projects. A full list of these threats is covered in most educational research texts.

External Validity
In addition to threats to internal validity, there can be threats to external validity in experimental designs. External validity is the "extent to which the findings of an experiment can be applied to individuals and settings beyond those that were studied" (Gall et al., 2007, p. 388). This threat can occur when the sample participating in the experiment is different from the population to which the results are to be generalized.

Threats to external validity occur when the results of a study cannot be generalized to other settings. This happens when more than one treatment is used on some participants (Gall et al., 2007). Thus, it is not clear what is actually having the impact. Another threat is called the Hawthorne effect. This occurs when participants change their behavior because they are aware that they are part of a study. Another threat to external validity may occur for novel situations. Simply being exposed to something different from normal can produce changes in behavior. Thus, the novelty facilitates the change, not the intervention itself (Gall et al., 2007). The experimenter can also impact the results. Someone implementing an intervention the first time may not do it well; thus, there may not be any resulting change.

These are just a few threats to external validity. The designs described address many of these threats. Research methods texts will provide further in-depth discussion.

Designs

There are six basic experimental designs that can be used to assess the impact of a treatment or intervention. They can be divided into three major categories: single-group designs and control-group designs with random assignment.

Single-Group Designs
The most basic single-group design is the one-shot case study. This includes a treatment and then an observation. There is no pretest. This design is improved upon in the one-group pretest/posttest design that comprises the pretest, then the treatment, followed by the posttest. The design gathers baseline data that are compared against the posttest to determine if there is a change from the pretest. The final single-group design is the time-series design that has a number of observations, then the treatment, and then a number of posttreatment observations. The benefit of this design is that multiple observations before and after the treatment can help isolate the impact

of the intervention while clarifying any change that would normally occur over time.

Control-Group Designs With Random Assignment
The first control-group design includes two groups, with participants being randomly assigned to each. Both groups are given a pretest. One of the groups receives the intervention and then both groups receive a posttest. The change from pretest to posttest can be measured for both groups to determine the impact of the intervention. A simpler design is the posttest-only design. This design also involves two groups whose participants have been randomly assigned. However, in this case, there is no pretest. One group receives an intervention and both groups receive the posttest. The changes in each group cannot be compared. Only the posttests for each are compared. The most complex experimental design is the Solomon four-group design, which is a combination of the pretest/posttest control design and the posttest-only control design. It includes four groups to which participants are randomly assigned. Group 1 receives a pretest, treatment, and then a posttest. Group 2 receives the pretest and posttest but no treatment. Group 3 receives no pretest but does receive a treatment and posttest, while group 4 simply receives the posttest. Although this design is more complex and more resource-intensive to employ, it aims to address all threats to internal and external validity. Table 7.1 offers details on each of the designs.

Posttest-Then-Pretest Designs
Another survey style option is to use a "post-then" method (Umble, Upshaw, Orton, & Matthews, 2000). At the end of an experience, participants are asked what they knew before the experience and also what they know now. Before the activity, participants may not know what they do not know. After the experience, they have a more accurate view of what they learned, although this is still their perception and not necessarily a demonstration of learning. For student affairs, these types of questions are particularly relevant for educational sessions or training. An example of a post-then structure is as follows:

> *After* the workshop, I can create and maintain a budget (strongly agree, agree, neutral, disagree, strongly disagree).
> *Before* the workshop, I can create and maintain a budget (strongly agree, agree, neutral, disagree, strongly disagree).

Although this method does rely on self-report and retrospection, which can be faulty, it can be convenient for estimating change.

TABLE 7.1

Experimental Designs and Their Potential Sources of Invalidity

Design	Sources of Invalidity	
	Internal	External
Single-group designs		
1. One-shot case study X O	History, maturation, sample selection, and mortality	Interaction of sample selection and X
2. One-group pretest/posttest design O X O	History, maturation, pretesting, instrumentation, interaction of sample selection and other factors	Interaction of testing and X, interaction of sample selection and X
3. Time-series design O O O O X O O O O	History	Interaction of pretesting and X
Control-group designs with random assignment		
4. Pretest/posttest control-group design R O X O R O O	None	Interaction of pretesting and X
5. Posttest-only control-group design R X O R O	Mortality	None
6. Solomon four-group design R O X O R O O R X O R O	None	None

Key: R = Random assignment
    X = Experiment treatment
    O = Observation, either a pretest or posttest of the dependent variable		

Source: Adapted from Gall, M., Gall, J., & Borg, W. (2007). *Educational research: An introduction* (8th ed., p. 398). Boston, MA: Pearson.

Quantitative Assessment Design: An Example

Many institutions have emerging leaders programs or something similar. A familiar design is a semester-long program where students meet weekly to develop leadership skills. Such a program will serve as an example of a quantitative assessment design.

The director of student engagement oversees the program. Given the amount of human and financial resources expended on this program each semester, the director wanted to discover what students were learning as a result of the program. Believing that reality is observable and facts would be isolated, the director chose a quantitative approach. After considering multiple quantitative designs, the director decided to use a pretest/posttest control-group design. This approach would measure learning over time and perhaps would demonstrate causation. A correlational design was not the best design because uncovering a relationship between variables was not the goal. Since the director had access to the students before and after the next program cycle, a causal-comparative design was not needed.

After the director received approval from the institutional review board for the assessment, the control group was selected. The director asked the institutional research office to pull a random sample of 30 students who matched the demographics of the 20 students enrolled in the program. The director oversampled, assuming that two thirds of the control group would agree to participate.

The director had identified a leadership assessment instrument that matched the curriculum being used for the course. This instrument-curriculum alignment provided confidence in the validity of the instrument. The instrument was administered to both groups prior to the start of the leadership program.

Knowing that results would not be known until after the program, the director met with the program instructors to discuss two assessment methods that would be used at the end of each session to help them understand if the program was on track and help identify what students were learning. Using index cards, students were asked at the end of each session to write down three to five things they had learned in that session. This is a version of the one-minute paper. On the other side of the index card, they were asked to write something that was confusing—a version of a "muddiest point" assessment. At the end of each session, the instructors collected the cards and read them to see whether students' reports regarding what they had learned matched the outcomes for that session. They also identified confusing points and could revisit those at the next session. After the cards were reviewed and notes made, a rubber band was placed around each session's cards and a sticky note marking the date was attached.

At the end of the program, both groups received the posttest, and composite scores were calculated. Once the surveys were collected, the pretest and posttest scores for each student were put into a spreadsheet. Gain scores were then computed by subtracting the pretest score from the posttest score. The *t*-tests were run in Excel to determine if the gain scores of the experimental group differed from those of the control group.

The director wrote a report outlining the findings, which included the statistical analysis of the pretests and posttests as well as summaries of the one-minute papers and muddiest points. An appendix to the report included detailed steps of the assessment process, providing directions in the event that another person should want to do a similar assessment. The findings were used to identify recommendations for improvement based on the three different assessment tools used.

In addition to this comprehensive report, an executive summary was created for senior divisional leadership, and an infographic was created to share with students. The director also presented the findings at a divisional meeting. Participants were given access to any of the reporting formats they might wish to see.

When the following program cycle approached, the director worked with the instructors to identify the changes that were made to the program based on the assessment. Those revisions were added to the comprehensive report to document improvements made.

Conclusion

Although student affairs staff do not frequently venture in deep educational research, they still have the responsibility to understand quantitative research design. There are a variety of methods from which to choose. Some are more suitable for the environment in which we operate, while others require a high degree of complexity and control that takes planning and time. Staff must be cautious about making claims of causation and correlation when, in fact, there might not be a relationship.

Key Points

- Quantitative designs include descriptive, correlational, causal-comparative, and experimental designs.
- Types of experimental designs include single-group, control-group, and posttest-then-pretest, and there are variations of each of these.
- Types of validity in experiments include internal validity and external validity.

Discussion Questions and Activities

- What are the advantages and disadvantages of each type of quantitative design?
- Give examples of when each design would be used for assessment.
- What are five threats to internal validity of a study?
- What would impact the extent to which a study would be generalizable?
- Think of two different issues to be assessed. For each one, identify which quantitative design you would use and your rationale for employing it.
- Imagine you are an assistant director of student involvement and want to assess training for student organization executive board members put on by your office. Describe how you would design that assessment using a quantitative approach.
- Each year, your office spends $10,000 to bring in the same speaker to talk with students during orientation about sexual violence. With budget cuts, you have been asked to design an assessment to determine if the office should continue to hire this speaker. Describe how you would design this assessment.

8

SURVEY DESIGN

Many people erroneously assume that the survey is the only/best/ easiest way to collect data. Questionnaires are ubiquitous: Almost everyone has received surveys after dining at a restaurant, buying a product, or using a company's customer service staff. Higher education and student affairs are no different. Students evaluate their instructors, provide feedback about their academic learning environments, and express their satisfaction or dissatisfaction about their parking situation, their residence halls, and their dining options. That does not even include any surveys distributed for graduate student research, student organization questionnaires, or institutional participation in national studies. Because of their frequent use, surveys should be thoughtfully designed to meet the desired needs of the organization.

When to Use a Survey

Even when it is the appropriate method, there is an art and a science to constructing the best survey that will yield the most valuable results. Cooper (2009) has identified questions to consider in using a survey:

- What do you want to measure by using a survey data-collection method?
- Are the population and method identified for selecting a sample? Will it be a random or convenience sample?
- What is the size of the sample? Or is it a census survey?
- Will this survey be used at more than one point in time and over the course of time (e.g., longitudinal)?
- What type of instrument will be used? A published instrument or an instrument developed locally?
- How will the survey be pilot tested?
- What is the time line for collecting data?

- How will the survey be implemented (e.g., web-based or paper and pencil)?
- Will the participants be compensated? (p. 54)

Advantages

Surveys do have certain advantages. They are particularly useful in sampling a group of respondents in a large population to determine attitudes and behaviors (Dillman et al., 2009). In addition, they are cost-effective methods for collecting large amounts of data, especially for Internet surveys (Dillman, Smyth, & Christian, 2009). With the resources of the Internet, people around the world can respond to questions at any time from anywhere. This is particularly useful with today's college students, who seem to be continuously connected to the Internet and are awake at all hours of the day and night. Surveys are also useful with a "captive" population where data are collected from a group of people in the same room at the same time. Large groups of people can answer numerous questions. Depending on the questions asked and the data-collection method, the data analysis can be straightforward. Cooper (2009) included an important advantage in using surveys to collect data:

> One advantage to using a survey method is the confidentiality (i.e., participant identifiers are kept and could be linked with the data, but the data are secured securely) or anonymity (i.e., no potential connections between the participant and the data collected) afforded to participants. As a result, participants are often more likely to be open (that is, candid, sincere) in their responses. (pp. 53–54)

Overall, surveys can be an efficient way to receive feedback that can be reflective of the population of interest from a large number of people in a short period of time. The data can then be used to make decisions about programs, resources, and policies, especially if paired with other data that have been collected.

Disadvantages

Of course, surveys have some disadvantages. Most of the time this method can yield only a finite amount of information because the assessor typically cannot follow up for clarification or elaboration. For surveys completed using the Internet, the respondent's identity may or may not be verifiable.

Recipients of an electronic survey invitation also may not trust the identity of the survey sponsor, especially if recipients cannot verify the sponsor's identity (Dillman et al., 2009). In addition, to draw the most accurate conclusions, the assessor should have at least some knowledge of statistics (or partner with someone who does), which has not traditionally been a strong skill set of student affairs practitioners.

One of the main disadvantages of surveys today is that students (and staff!) suffer from survey fatigue. With the increase in the number of survey software programs available to the public, people are oversurveyed (Dillman et al., 2009). The effect of that is a decrease in the response rate. Many institutions participate in national surveys, most of which are now administered online. Those surveys may overlap with the locally developed surveys. Porter, Whitcomb, and Weitzer (2004) cautioned that multiple surveys, nonsalient surveys, and participation in a coordinated series of surveys (i.e., a panel) may lead respondents to feel that they have done their fair share already and stop participating. Although a high response rate is desirable, it is important to determine if the respondents represent the sample and/or population of interest before making generalizations.

Sources of Error

No survey is perfect; there will always be potential error. Pulliam Phillips, Phillips, and Aaron (2013) have highlighted four types of error. Coverage error happens "when you have selected the wrong respondent group and when all members of the targeted group do not have an equal opportunity to participate" (p. 16). For example, in student affairs assessment, this could occur if a survey about the use of the counseling center was sent only to undergraduate students, leaving out graduate students who also have access to the services. Sampling error, or selection bias, is another issue. This naturally occurs when a sample rather than the whole population is surveyed (Pulliam Phillips et al., 2013). For large populations, though, assessing everyone can produce survey fatigue, so sample selection is a strategic process. Nonresponse error occurs "when people selected for the survey who do not respond are different from those who do in a way that is important to the survey project" (Pulliam Phillips et al., 2013, p. 17). In student affairs, this might appear if women responded to a survey in much greater numbers than men when the sample sizes were the same. Other examples could be academic classification (freshman, sophomore, junior, senior) or users and nonusers of a particular service, such as the health center. There can also be important differences between people who respond quickly to the survey compared with those who respond only after several reminders or not at all.

The final type, measurement error, occurs when "wrong questions are asked or when the right questions are asked in the wrong way" (Pulliam Phillips et al., 2013, p. 17) and is more common in surveys designed by novices. Examples of this could include asking multiple questions within one question or the scale not matching the question.

When student affairs staff undertake the survey methodology, they must pay attention to possible error and take efforts to reduce or eliminate error. If error cannot be eliminated, it should be considered and explained when the results are shared, rather than making incorrect generalizations or leaving the reader wondering about limitations. Student affairs staff should seek out resources, such as the institutional research office, for assistance in addressing the types of error and developing a systematic process designed to decrease the error.

Delivery Methods

Data for surveys can be collected over the phone or in person; they can be paper-based or web-based. Technology has had a profound effect on data collection. Before the advent of the cell phone, companies and institutions used to call people on their home (or residence hall room) phones. As more students got cell phones with different area codes and institutions had a harder time keeping track of students' phone numbers, the phone survey method fell out of favor. People can still be asked several questions in person under certain circumstances, but the surveys must be short and relevant. Paper-based and Internet surveys are much more common these days.

Paper-based surveys are particularly useful for a captive audience. The response rate can be at or near 100%. On the other hand, branching questions, if used, require very clear instructions (e.g., "If you answered 'no' to question 1, please skip to question 14."). There are technologies that allow the paper responses to be scanned into a spreadsheet or database, although some people enter data by hand. Being able to use technology to enter data saves time (thus money) and reduces data entry errors. Depending on how the survey was created, respondents have the ability to check or circle answers and provide qualitative responses. Respondents are able to see the length and content of the survey from the beginning, so they can make decisions about responding.

Web-based surveys have become pervasive in assessment. These surveys are created to be accessed and collect data through the Internet, transferring the data to some form of digital data file. These surveys have more flexibility than paper-based surveys. For example, the questions can be designed to use branching, also called *skip logic*, which shows only relevant questions to the respondents. In addition, respondents have flexibility to respond on a device at a convenient time. Some web-based surveys allow respondents to return to an unfinished survey at a later time. Right now, some institutions are using survey technology through text messaging or clickers, for example. As a result, data can be collected in real time and incorporated into presentations. It is also important to use survey software that is accessible to students with visual impairments. As technology changes, survey technology changes as well. But the response rate is typically lower with electronic surveys because there is no immediate time constraint or social pressure to respond.

Survey Design

Before designing a survey, it is important to review the steps in the assessment process. The purpose and the information needed guide the questions to be asked. Each question should match the purpose of the survey to ensure that the survey is as short as possible while providing the most relevant information. If the responses to a particular question will not be used, consider eliminating that question. Always keep the focus on how the respondents are going to engage with the survey and what they are expected to do.

There are several considerations in creating questions. It is important to make it as simple as possible for respondents to provide information, so the visual presentation of the survey is also important. Font, color, size, graphics, and other visual properties should be considered (Dillman et al., 2009). Obviously all spelling, grammar, and punctuation should be correct. In addition, questions should be written with consideration for education level, native language, and local terms. If possible, avoid using jargon and acronyms that may confuse respondents. Questions should easily and clearly specify what is being asked and should usually be written as complete sentences (Dillman et al., 2009). It is extremely important to consider the respondents' perspectives as questions are developed.

The flow of the questions should make some logical sense but should also engage respondents at the beginning. Questions should move from simple to more complex, so respondents are not overwhelmed or challenged in the beginning. If that happens, there is an increased likelihood that respondents will stop answering. The first question should "hook" each individual into the rest of the survey. Beginning with quantitative questions will ease respondents into the survey and build their commitment level. If and when qualitative questions follow, respondents will already be engaged and thinking about the topic. If the survey covers several different topics, address each topic as a segment so respondents will not get confused.

Next, in asking chronological questions, think about how accurate the respondents will be. The farther back, the less accurate the memory. For example, asking how many hours the respondent worked last week is very different from asking today how many hours the respondent worked two years ago. Even when chronological questions are being asked, think about the unit of measure—hours, days, weeks, months, or years. Once again, the questions should be easy for respondents to answer with accuracy. Precise quantifiers such as hours versus months may be more accurate; however, in reality, the results could be less accurate because there could be more error in responses when more precise answers are required.

Questions (especially in web-based surveys) should not require the respondent to answer unless an answer is needed to move through the survey (e.g., when an answer to one question branches to different questions depending on the first answer). Respondents will be frustrated if they are required to answer each question, especially if they do not know the answer, they do not understand the question, their response is not available in the options, or they do not care about a particular question. It is better to get more surveys with some missing data than fewer surveys, because individuals tend to become frustrated and quit. In electronic surveys, it is easy for respondents to close their browsers. For paper-based surveys, it is easy for respondents to skip questions and not provide valuable information. Paper-based surveys should also have very clear instructions about branching if needed ("If you answered 'no' to this question, skip to question 10") and checking more than one option ("Check the top *three* reasons. . . .") if respondents should not check all that apply.

Dillman et al. (2009) have also identified several considerations applicable to student affairs assessment for developing good survey questions. They include the following:

- Make sure the question applies to the respondent.
- Make sure the question is technically accurate.
- Ask one question at a time (avoid using "and" or "or").
- Use concrete and specific words (e.g., units of measure, definitions).

In addition, the respondent should have the information needed to answer the question.

Demographic Questions

Demographic information usually refers to the respondent's characteristics, such as gender, age, and ethnicity, but it could also include the number of hours worked in a typical week or membership and leadership positions held in student organizations. As questions are created, think about the demographic questions of interest in the analysis phase. Depending on survey implementation and the question, the respondent will be asked to provide demographics (paper survey or anonymous web-based survey) or the assessor will match known demographics to the respondent (as in a web-based survey where respondents get an individual link and demographics are uploaded from the student information system). The advantage to preloading information is that it reduces the number of questions respondents have to answer, and therefore the answers might be more accurate (Do students accurately know their GPAs or their parents' income?). In implementing a paper survey or a web-based survey with an unknown sample, demographic questions must be included. Keep in mind that if the surveys are anonymous, demographics cannot be added in later. Before adding many demographic questions, really think about what sort of analysis will be conducted. Demographics add length to the survey, and the more that are identified, the more likely it will be that a respondent could be individually identified. If there are no plans to analyze results by a particular demographic, leave it off. Put demographics at the end of the survey so as to gather important information first and get respondents engaged in the survey with more interesting questions. Then, if respondents do not answer the demographic questions at the end, the responses about the purpose of the survey will still be included. Putting demographics first could also influence how respondents answer; they might think about their multiple identities and how the assessor will use their responses. As with all questions, demographic questions must be crafted carefully. What are the differences between gender and sex? Race and ethnicity? What are the current common descriptors in the LGBT community? The institutional research office, campus and federal guidelines, and current literature will be assets in defining the terms, collecting data, and analyzing responses.

Question Types

There are a myriad of options in creating survey questions. This section will provide a brief overview and examples for yes/no, choose all that apply, rankings, ratings, choose one, and open-ended questions. Knowing how best to use these questions will improve the quality of the responses.

Yes/No

The simplest question form yields a yes/no response. The condition either exists or it does not exist. This could also be considered a true/false question.

Such questions are commonly used when there are follow-up (branching) questions to divide respondents into particular groups (living on or off campus, attending a campus program or not). In creating the question, determine whether or not a "maybe" or "don't know" response should be included. Although it may seem simple, the wording is nonetheless important in ensuring that respondents will be able to answer the questions based on the parameters. Be sure that *yes* means yes and *no* means no; the use of double negatives can be confusing to respondents (Dillman et al., 2009).

In terms of data analysis, two groups can be compared. The data are typically dichotomous (if there are truly *yes* and *no* answers), so the data are scaled and can be included in parametric analysis (Suskie, 1996). If there is a "don't know" or "unsure" type of answer, determine how to code that as a third category or as missing data because that is not a group of interest.

The following examples provide slightly different meanings. Even for yes/no responses, the questions should be crafted with the specificity desired.

> Are you enrolled in college?
> Are you enrolled in North College this semester?
> Are you enrolled as a full-time undergraduate student (12 or more hours) at North College this semester?

Novice survey developers often use many yes/no questions. However, such questions provide limited data. By reframing a question you may obtain additional data that can be analyzed in a way to create yes/no categories. If someone is interested in comparing alcohol issues for people of legal drinking age and those who are not, the yes/no format would be "Are you 21 years of age or older?" However, this question can be asked in a different way to gather more information. A revised version would be "How old are you?" This way, respondents can be divided into those of legal drinking age and those below that age. This format allows for additional types of analyses including correlation between age and alcohol use.

Choose All That Apply

At times there are questions that can have multiple "correct" answers. The responses are considered nominal or categorical data in the analysis phase. Respondents may be given instructions to select all options that apply to them, or they can be given instructions to choose up to a set number of responses that apply ("Choose up to three. . . ."). This really is another way to structure a yes/no question for each option. This type of question can give a rough order of popularity of responses but without a rating that would show how close they were to each other in value. If there is a long list of items, consider the order of the responses. They could be put in a random order, alphabetically, by the predicted popularity of each item, by categories, or some other way. If it is something factual, such as intramural sports played in the last year, it is easier and quicker for the respondent to skim an alphabetical order list to choose the answers than to have to read a randomly ordered list to find the answers. On the other hand, if the question asks about the reasons people attended a particular program, the response options could be in random order, so respondents do not just pick the first several options. Although the response list should be extensive, be careful about the length of the list: Too many questions will frustrate the respondents. The responses could include an "other" option, enabling respondents to write in their answers if they are not in the list. The "other" option is also a good safety net if a possible response is omitted from the response option list by mistake or is not considered.

The advantage to the "choose all that apply" question is that it gives a sense of popularity to the answers. Respondents do not have to be forced into one response. As Suskie (1996) has stated, the advantage is that these lists are quick and easy to answer. On the other hand, "choose all that apply" questions do have disadvantages. If there is a long list, for example, and respondents are told to check only three items, the assessor does not know whether a fourth option would have made the selection. This type of question does not indicate the relative priority of the items chosen. In a paper format, respondents can choose as many options as they want (regardless of instructions), even if they are told to choose a certain number. In web-based surveys, the design can allow a certain number of responses (a minimum and maximum) to avoid the problem that paper surveys have. Web-based surveys also allow the responses to be randomized if there is concern that respondents will gravitate to the first responses. Data analysis is limited and does not explain the relative importance of the choices.

The following examples illustrate "choose all that apply" options.

How did you find out about the program? (Choose all that apply)
Newspaper ad
Television ad
Radio ad
Word of mouth
Email
Social media (Facebook, Twitter, etc.)
Flyer
Other (please specify): _____

Which residence hall programs would you attend? (Choose all that apply)
Study skills
Easy meals to make in your room
Preparing to run a 5K
Sexual health
Alcohol awareness
Dinner in the dining hall
Other (please specify): _____

Rankings

In some cases, it may be appropriate to have respondents put the possible answers in a priority order. Most respondents will find the process easy to understand. These types of questions are considered ordinal because there is no set difference between response options. In the data-collection and analysis phases, think of this as a horse race: The difference between the first and second horses crossing the finish line does not matter in determining the winner.

Depending on the number of response options, respondents can be instructed to rank all of them or only the top few answers, depending on the length of the list. If the list is longer than about seven items, the respondents should be asked to rank the top five or so. Too many options will frustrate respondents. This type of question is more difficult on a paper-based survey because respondents must understand the difference between ranking and rating and must be able to visually understand the instructions. Web-based surveys are a little easier because respondents might be able to move responses on the page or get an error message if they try to rank two different items with the same value.

One of the disadvantages is that ranking does not show the distance between the answers provided. (A rating scale is more useful to determine the relative value between each question.) For example, a respondent may be very passionate about the top three or four answers and not care about the rest of the answers. Depending on how many responses there are, that may frustrate the respondents.

The following are examples of ranking questions:

Please rank the following recreational sports classes from most favorite (1) to least favorite (5):
_____ Zumba
_____ Pilates
_____ Yoga
_____ Spin/cycle
_____ Kickboxing

Please rank the top *four* residence hall programs that interest you (1 = most interested, 4 = fourth most interested):

_____ Study skills
_____ Easy meals to make in your room
_____ Preparing to run a 5K
_____ Sexual health
_____ Alcohol awareness
_____ Dinner in the dining hall
_____ Community service project

Rating Scale

A popular question type is set up as a scale rather than in categories. This typically means that the answers are in some order that describes more or less (or positive or negative) of some construct. For example, common scales include the following:

strongly agree/agree/neutral/disagree/strongly disagree
excellent/above average/average/below average/poor
never/rarely/sometimes/frequently/always
very satisfied/somewhat satisfied/neither satisfied nor dissatisfied/some-
    what dissatisfied/very dissatisfied

Dillman et al. (2009) have stated that answers should be in order of some variable that has positive and negative responses and, for most assessments, respondents can assume that the scale values are relatively equidistant (i.e., the values placed on them for analysis are 5, 4, 3, 2, and 1).

There is debate about whether to have the positive response first or last (Dillman et al., 2009) because of response bias (a respondent may be more likely to choose the first visual response or the last oral response, regardless of what it is). There is no absolute answer to that. In reviewing research on scale order, Dillman et al. (2009) did conclude that respondents answered faster when the most positive response was first. For most assessments, whichever order is chosen, use that order consistently to avoid confusing the respondents. Because words are easier to interpret most of the time, each response option should have a word descriptor rather than just the number. In other words, providing a five-point scale of "strongly agree" to "strongly disagree" is easier to interpret than saying, "On a scale of 1–5, please rate your agreement with the following statements." Dillman et al. (2009) concluded that including numerical responses with the words adds "significantly to response time" (p. 144).

Decisions must be made on how the responses will be coded in the analysis stage—does a golf score (lower is better) make more sense or does a grade point average (higher is better) make more sense? In asking a negative in a question stem, be sure that the respondents will see that (use bold, italics, or all capital letters) and, in analyzing the data, recognize how to interpret that (or recode it to make sense).

In formulating the response set with a scale, make sure that answers are not omitted. In the "strongly agree" to "strongly disagree" scale example, it would be inappropriate to exclude the "disagree" response. The scale must balance to avoid bias, meaning that there should be the same number of positive responses as negative responses (Dillman et al., 2009).

How many response options should there be in a scale? To some extent, that is personal preference, but the survey design should always consider potential respondents. It depends on question wording and how much specificity is needed in the analysis. More than likely, respondents will tolerate a five-point scale easily. Once the scale goes above 10 or so response options, respondents will have a harder time deciding on one option and differences in the options become meaningless (Dillman et al., 2009).

Should the scale have an odd number of responses so as to allow for a neutral/average response or should there be an even number of response options? Some survey researchers debate whether respondents can be truly neutral about an issue, and some assessment professionals do not want people to straddle the fence of indecision. The final decision rests with the survey designer. If being neutral about an issue is an important piece of information, it makes sense to include it. If the respondent must pick a side, then leave it off. Once again, using words, not just numbers, will help the respondent see the nuances. If there is a middle option on a "strongly agree"/"strongly disagree" scale, for example, and the responses are labeled only with numbers, the middle option could represent neutral, but some respondents might interpret that as "not sure" or "don't know." If those are viable response options, they can be placed on the right side of the scale, as can a "not applicable" response (Dillman et al., 2009).

Some scales are actually numbers or ranges of numbers. For example, the question, "How many student organizations are you a member of?" could have a response set of 0, 1, 2, 3, and 4 or more. Alternatively, the response to that same question could be 0, 1-2, 3-4, 5-6, and 7 or more. The choice of responses depends on the specificity needed, and it is still important to create responses that do not overlap.

Choose One

Questions can be created for respondents to choose one "correct" answer. It could be categorical data (In what state do you currently reside?) or a range (annual salary categories such as $0-$20,000, $20,001-$40,000, $40,001-$60,000, etc.).

The length of the list is an important element to consider. Too many options will confuse and frustrate respondents, whereas too few may not provide enough differentiation. In most cases, do not use more than about seven options. Using an open-ended text box labeled "other" will allow a respondent to contribute even if the answer is not one in the prechosen list.

Answers to "choose one" questions should be provided in a logical order. For numerical answers, the numbers increase in the order they are given. A list of factual items (state of residence, academic college) should be in alphabetical order. Chronological lists should appear in sequential order (e.g., January through December, Sunday through Saturday). There are times when the list of the options should be in random order (some online survey software allows that option, with each respondent seeing the order differently) to avoid respondent bias of picking the first option.

In using numerical ranges for the responses, be sure that the numbers at the ends of the ranges do not overlap. In addition, the ranges should be the same amount unless there is a strong reason to do otherwise. For example, if the campus includes mostly traditional-aged college students, an age question could include these choices: under 18, 18, 19, 20, 21, 22, 23–25, 26–30, 31–35, and 36 and above.

Examples of "choose one" questions include the following:

Which *one* residence hall program would you most likely attend?
_____ Study skills
_____ Easy meals to make in your room
_____ Preparing to run a 5K
_____ Sexual health
_____ Alcohol awareness
_____ Dinner in the dining hall
_____ Community service project

For how many hours do you study in an average week?
_____ 0–5 hours
_____ 6–10 hours
_____ 11–15 hours
_____ 16 or more hours

Open-Ended Questions

Some questions are best suited for respondents to answer in their own words. They result in qualitative data that can be analyzed using qualitative analysis techniques. Novice survey developers sometimes make the mistake of asking open-ended questions that would be easier to answer as scale questions (e.g., What is your academic classification?), because it is often easier to draft an open-ended question than a closed-ended one. Once they begin the analysis, they realize that a closed-ended question would provide more accurate data and require less time to analyze. Open-ended questions are useful as stand-alone questions (e.g., What did you learn from this workshop?), but they are also good as follow-up questions after quantitative ones (e.g., If you answered yes to the previous question, please explain your response). The advantage of open-ended questions is that they allow respondents to answer in their own words, which can be useful if there is no known set of responses. On the other hand, the disadvantage is that such questions require the respondent to do more work to respond and take more time to analyze.

Pilot Testing

Before launching the survey, a short period of pilot testing can save time and frustration. Ask people similar to those who will actually take the survey to respond to the questions, keep track of how long it takes them to respond, and note any questions or confusion they have about the survey. Colton and Covert (2007) have also suggested getting feedback about the directions, response alternatives, flow, and length. Of course, proofread all of the written material associated with the survey for spelling, grammar, punctuation, clarity, and biased language. For web-based surveys, check the survey on multiple browsers and versions to be sure the formatting works; for paper-based surveys, be sure the format and instructions are clear. Many web-based programs use time stamps to determine how long people are taking to complete their surveys. Make any necessary changes before implementing the survey, keeping in mind that conflicting feedback is a possibility during the pilot-testing phase. Planning time in this phase will increase the quality of the assessment.

Dillman (2007) has summarized four steps in the pilot-testing process. The first step is to have colleagues review. They will be able to identify problems to remedy. The second step is to have potential participants review. These individuals will be able to spot issues that others may not, especially concerning wording or phrasing. A focus group is a good model to use for this step. The third step is a small pilot study. In addition to getting feedback regarding the question wording, length, and so on, data are actually collected and reviewed for irregularities that might suggest revisions. In the fourth and final step, there is one more review by the survey developers just to make sure that nothing was missed.

Electronic Cover Letters and Reminders

With the proliferation of Internet survey invitations sent through email, it is extremely important to pay attention to the details of the communication with potential participants. College students in particular get many emails on a daily basis, so these emails must stand out from the very beginning. It is easy for them to hit the delete button before even opening the email, especially if email is not the primary communication medium used. Students may not even check their campus email on a regular/daily basis.

As part of the email, think about what the "From" and "Subject" lines say. If possible, the "From" line should come from someone in authority or from a department, an organization, or a person having legitimacy with the audience. With the number of scams that come through email, students are reluctant to open email and click on a link that could be detrimental. The more students recognize the sender (in some survey software programs, the "From" line and the actual sender can be different), the more likely they are to open the email. Although today very few surveys are actually mailed through the postal system, if that is the choice, be sure the cover letter is on organizational letterhead, again with someone in authority signing it. For example, if a student organization wants to get feedback from its members about their satisfaction with meetings and events, the president of the organization has the name recognition to be in the "From" line. On the other hand, if the institution is participating in a national survey, the "From" line might be from the university president to emphasize the significance of participation. If the student government association needs to get feedback from students about a campus policy or current event, the "From" line might be the student body president.

Similarly, the words in the subject line can motivate a potential respondent to open the email or hit the delete button. In particular, for random sample surveys where respondents have no affiliation with the topic or the person, they should be engaged from the very beginning. The word *survey* should not be used in the subject line, which can cause students to disregard the email before understanding the topic. Even slight differences in wording (e.g., "We Need *Your* Feedback!" versus "Customer Service Survey") can make a difference in the importance given to the email.

In the body of the email, the potential respondent's attention must be captured. Dillman et al. (2009) have suggested personalizing the contact as much as possible to create a connection with the potential respondents. Students are more likely to engage if they feel like they are more than just numbers. Rather than starting with a generic "Dear Student," survey developers should personalize the email with a first name if possible. Most survey programs have the option to not only embed the name but can also insert other personalized information. Programs might be able to insert specific information such as "Thank you for attending your career advising session with Kara on January 15." Dillman et al. (2009) have reported that personalizing the email increases response rate; in one study, they found an 8% increase over nonpersonalized email.

The language should be clear, concise, and meaningful to the respondents. Jargon and acronyms are to be avoided, but language that connects to the audience should be used. If *engagement, involvement,* or *services* are important to the population, use those terms in the cover letter. Keep the communication short but long enough to explain the purpose and the importance of their participation.

Response Rates

Most staff new to assessment stress about survey response rates, which have consistently declined over the past decade, especially with web-based surveys. Although that is not the only measure of survey success, it is helpful to have responses from people who represent the population of interest. Cooper (2009) found that a low response rate could affect the generalizability of the respondents' results to the larger population. Researchers should be concerned about the reliability of the data collected beyond the basic response rate, which could include comparing demographic variables of respondents, the sample, and the population (if known). Although response rates will vary by survey, there are ways to improve overall response rates.

Umbach (2004) and Dillman et al. (2009) have proposed that multiple contacts with the sample increase the response rate. Because web-based surveys are relatively low-cost, sending additional emails is easy. The first notification will result in the highest percentage response rate, with each additional notification providing an additional spike in the response rate. However, sending too many reminders to nonrespondents may have a detrimental effect overall, especially with students who become frustrated by so many emails. Depending on the importance of the survey, an organization may choose to send a prenotification so that respondents will be less likely to delete a future email without reading it. An effective approach is to send an invitation with two reminders.

In sending reminders, it is important to vary the content and maybe even the sender's name, so respondents do not feel spammed. Dillman et al. (2009) have suggested that each additional contact be shorter and more direct with the potential respondent. Providing a deadline for participation may motivate potential respondents to complete the survey in a timely fashion. The deadline should not be so soon that potential respondents do not receive the invitation in time to take action. The deadline should not be too far away either because potential respondents may procrastinate, forget, and miss the deadline. The "just right" time depends on the population, but seven days to two weeks is usually a reasonable amount of time for most respondents. Umbach (2004) has suggested several additional strategies to increase response rates in electronic surveys: Keep email invitations brief, keep the survey short, and do not offer incentives without the ability to manage that process and cost.

One popular idea to increase response rates is to provide incentives. Porter and Whitcomb (2004) concluded that lottery incentives, those provided after the survey is completed, had little or no impact on response rate, although they noted that at the time of their study no research had been done using college students. The authors' experience suggests that lottery incentives are not effective in boosting response rates. Prepayment, provided with the survey, can increase response rate, although the relationship between size of incentive and increase in response is unclear (Porter & Whitcomb, 2004). For web-based surveys, incentives may also be challenging to implement and control unless the prize is also something respondents can access online. Incentives can be sent through the mail, but that also increases cost. Porter and Whitcomb (2004) found that increasing the size of the prize did not linearly increase the response rate. They also questioned the cost versus benefit of incentives: The cost of the prize, whether a small token that everyone gets or a large prize only a few receive, may be too high when other, more effective and efficient means can be used, such as reminders.

Dillman et al. (2009) have proposed increasing the benefits of participation by using social exchange theory. Those strategies included providing information about how the results will be used, asking for help or advice, saying thank you, supporting group values, making the assessment interesting, providing social validation (others like them have responded), and informing potential respondents that the opportunities to respond are limited. Most people want to feel respected, to help others, and to feel that their participation matters. If possible, share how past results have been used to make improvements on campus.

Alternatively, Dillman et al. (2009) have identified ways to decrease the respondents' cost of participation. Strategies included making it easy to respond, asking for help in a respectful manner, keeping the survey short and easy, minimizing requests for sensitive information or explaining why it is needed, and emphasizing the survey's similarity to other tasks in which the respondent has already participated. Potential respondents will not participate if they perceive this as being too difficult or inconvenient. It takes careful planning and attention to increase benefits and decrease costs.

Dillman et al. (2009) have also suggested methods to increase the trust of potential respondents: The request should come from a legitimate authority, a small token of appreciation in advance can create a social exchange, respondents' participation should appear to be important, and their confidentiality and information security should be respected. Overall, in using a survey as a data-collection method, it is important to show respect for the respondents so as to create a positive relationship, even for the short time it takes to complete the survey.

Conclusion

Student affairs professionals frequently use a survey as a data-collection methodology. This approach requires assessors be detail-oriented and organized in order to appropriately manage the process. In order to get the most benefit from questionnaires, staff must understand the process of developing, implementing, and analyzing survey data. Question development, timing, invitation, and more need to be addressed as part of the process to make sure that the responses provide useful, relevant information.

Key Points

- The survey is a flexible and useful data-collection method, but it can be overused.
- Question creation takes practice if useful information is to be gathered.
- The process of implementing a survey needs attention to encourage participants to respond.

Discussion Questions and Activities

- Describe situations in which a survey would be an advantageous data-collection method.
- What topics are appropriate for survey work on your campus?
- What topics are best suited for other data-collection methods?
- What strategies on your campus can you use to increase response rates?
- What resources are available to you in using surveys as an assessment method?

9

STATISTICAL OVERVIEW
FOR ASSESSMENT

Quantitative methods are often used in assessment because numbers are compelling to decision makers and statistics are a valuable component to these methods. Statistics comprise methods for making sense of quantitative data, making sure that analyses and interpretations are valid and understood. Used in conjunction with quantitative methods, statistics help student affairs professionals better understand the students and their needs; challenge assumptions; and provide evidence about needs, processes, and outcomes. Inferences are more easily and accurately made with statistics. Statistics are a powerful tool for assessment.

Levels of Data

When using statistics it is important to understand that there are different levels of data that exist in a hierarchy of complexity. There are four levels of measurement of data: nominal, ordinal, interval, and ratio (Keller, 2005, p. 13). Nominal is the most basic measure of data and ratio is the most multifaceted. Salkind (2013) has described data at each level. Nominal data are often called *categorical* and identify an outcome that fits into a specific category such as race/ethnicity (e.g., White or African American). One category is not more or less than another category; they are just different. Ordinal data are data that are measured on a ranked scale such as a Likert scale. An agree-disagree scale is a common form of a Likert scale. Technically a Likert scale will have an odd number of response options. Although there is a hierarchy to the responses, the distance between the ranks may not be the same. It is not known whether the difference between "agree" and "strongly agree" is the same for one person as it is for another person. However, some do assume that the distance between each of these is equal. In a horse race, bettors do not care if the first horse won by a nose or several lengths. All that matters to them is which horse passed the finish line first and which horses finished second and third. With interval data, the distance between each interval is the same. The benefit of this level is that you can apply mathematical formulas. For example, 10 correct answers on a test are twice as many as five correct answers. However, there is no zero point on an interval scale. A ratio scale, on the other hand, is the same as an interval scale, but it does have a zero point. Examples could include household income or grade point average (GPA). Interval and ratio data together are also considered continuous data.

As described, each level of data has certain properties that affect the type of statistics that can be used with each. What is the mean or average of a set of college majors such as engineering, psychology, business, and education? Thus, the ability to perform accurate statistical analyses depends on choosing statistics that will help to answer the assessment question and that are appropriate for the level of data collected. The statistical analyses are described next.

Descriptive Statistics

There are essentially two broad types of statistics: descriptive statistics and inferential statistics. "Descriptive statistics are mathematical techniques for organizing and summarizing data" (Gall, Gall, & Borg, 2007, p. 132). Inferential statistics comprise a set of mathematical procedures using probabilities and information about a sample to draw conclusions about a population (Gall et al., 2007, p. 137). Urdan (2010) states that descriptive statistics apply only to the data that are collected, whereas inferential statistics use sample data to draw conclusions about the population from which the sample has been drawn.

Frequencies

Frequencies are the most basic way to describe data. The responses are simply totaled. Percentages are also computed, as in Table 9.1. Cross-tabulations, also called cross-tabs, are frequencies broken down by grouping, as demonstrated in Table 9.2. Cross-tabs are useful for making comparisons between groups. Because groups rarely have the same number of responses, percentages are widely used in cross-tabs. In Table 9.2, there are 891 women and 803 men. Comparisons of the raw numbers do not make the differences between the groups as clear as do the percentages.

TABLE 9.1
Frequencies of Responses to "Like Living in the Residence Halls"

Response	n	Percentage
Strongly disagree	126	7.3
Disagree	134	7.9
Neutral	325	19.2
Agree	436	25.7
Strongly agree	673	39.7

TABLE 9.2
Frequencies of Responses to "Like Living in the Residence Halls" by Gender

	Women		Men	
Response	n	Percentage	n	Percentage
Strongly disagree	74	8.3	52	6.5
Disagree	51	5.7	83	10.3
Neutral	116	13.0	209	26.0
Agree	217	24.4	219	27.2
Strongly agree	433	48.6	240	29.9

Measures of Central Tendency

Measures of central tendency provide simple summary measures for sets of data where counts and frequencies are not enough. Gall et al. (2007) define a *measure of central tendency* as one number that describes an entire set of scores. The three measures of central tendency most often used in student affairs assessment are mean, median, and mode.

Mean
The mean is the average of a set of scores and is calculated by adding all of the scores and dividing by the number of scores. In journal articles, mean is usually represented by "M." The average is helpful as it takes into account every score. However, the mean is also sensitive to extremely high and extremely low scores. Income is not often measured by the mean because very high income scores skew the average.

> List A: 18, 18, 18, 19, 19, 21, 22, 21, 19, 18, 18, 23
> List B: 18, 18, 18, 19, 19, 21, 22, 21, 19, 18, 18, 61

In List A of students' ages, the average (mean) is 19.5, which is the sum of all the numbers then divided by the number of scores (235/12 = 19.5). In

List B, the last number (23) is changed to 61. The average for List B is 22.7, although only one number was changed. One way to interpret the data using the mean is in relation to something such as the legal drinking age of 21. The first group has an average age below the legal drinking age of 21, while the second group is above the legal drinking age. In a small sample, one number can have a dramatic effect.

Median

The median is the middle number in a list of numbers. In a list of scores ranked from high to low, if the list has an odd number of scores, the median is the center score. If the total number of scores is even, then the median is computed by averaging the two center scores. Although extremely high or low scores do not affect the median, the focus is only the center of a distribution. As such, the median provides less information than the mean regarding a set of scores.

Using the previous lists of numbers can help demonstrate the stability of the median with high and low numbers impacting the mean. First, we need to take List A and put it into numerical order: 18, 18, 18, 18, 18, 19, 19, 19, 21, 21, 22, 23. Since there is an even number of responses, the median is calculated by the average of the two middle numbers: 19 and 19 = 19. Using List B (also put into numerical order)—18, 18, 18, 18, 18, 19, 19, 19, 21, 21, 22, 61—the median is computed the same way and is, again, 19. As can be seen, with high or low numbers, a median can be a stable measure of central tendency.

Mode

Different from the mean and median, the mode is the most frequent score in a distribution. Since the focus is only the most frequent score and no other scores are taken into account, the mode provides the least amount of data of these three measures of central tendency. The mode for both List A and List B is 18, as it is listed five times. In some cases, a set of scores can have multiple modes if two multiple numbers occur at the same frequency.

Each measure of central tendency serves a different purpose. A mode is used to highlight common scores and for nominal data. A median is used to get a sense of the midpoint in a set of scores, particularly when high and low scores could throw off the average. It is often used for ordinal data or when the data are skewed. A mean is an average; it is commonly used in many settings, so audiences have a general sense of what it means. It is particularly good for interval and ratio data if the data are not skewed.

Variability

Variability describes the dispersion of scores about the mean score or other measure of central tendency (Gall et al., 2007, p. 135). Urdan (2010) described variability as the variety of data. Central tendency measures tell us about the middle or common scores of a set, but we use variability measures (most often, range, variance, and standard deviation) to examine the extent to which the scores are similar or varied.

Range

Range describes the distance between the smallest and the largest number (Fraenkel, Wallen, & Hyun, 2014, p. 198). It is computed by subtracting the smallest number from the largest. Range provides an indication of how far apart the scores can get. The range takes into account only the highest and lowest scores and thus provides a simplistic picture of the variability of scores.

Using List A, the range is 5 (23 minus 18), while the range of List B is 43 (61 minus 18). Similar to the mean, the range is highly affected by large or small numbers.

Variance

Variance provides a statistical average of the amount of dispersion in a distribution of scores. It is used to compute standard deviation, the more commonly used measure. Using Microsoft Excel to calculate the variance of each list, List A has a variance of 3.18, while the variance for List B is 147.7.

Standard Deviation

Standard deviation is the square root of variance and is a measure of the extent to which scores are distributed around the mean (Gall et al., 2007, p. 135). A small standard deviation denotes that the scores are tightly clustered around the mean. This statistic can be used to compare sets of data with different scales, such as comparing college aptitude between two students—one who has taken the ACT and one who has taken the SAT. In journal articles, it is usually signified as "SD." Using Excel to calculate the standard deviation of each list, List A has a standard deviation of 1.78; the standard deviation for List B is 12.2. A more complex discussion of both variance and standard deviation may be found in a statistics textbook.

Correlation

Assessment questions frequesntly regard the association between two or more variables. It may be important to know if age is related to alcohol use or if number of hours spent studying is related to GPA. The goal of correlation is to understand what happens to one variable when another one varies in some way. *Correlation* describes the relationship between variables, and the correlation coefficient, noted as *r*, is the number representing the linear relationship between two variables (Salkind, 2013). The important characteristic of correlation is that it provides two types of information. As discussed in Chapter

7, it provides the direction of the relationship and then the magnitude of the relationship. If variables vary in the same direction, the correlation is a positive or direct correlation. Thus, as one variable increases, the other variable increases. Or as one variable decreases, the other variable decreases. If the variables vary in opposing directions, the relationship is negative or indirect. In this case, as one variable increases, the other decreases.

Correlation coefficients range from −1.0 to +1.0 (Fraenkel et al., 2014, p. 341) and the closer to 1 or −1 the coefficient, the stronger the correlation (Wheelan, 2012, p. 62). These rules of thumb are helpful for understanding magnitude. Correlation coefficients from .0 to .20 (regardless of direction) are weak correlations. Correlation coefficients from .20 to .35 are small relationships, whereas coefficients between .35 and .65 are moderate and often have theoretical or practical value. Coefficients of .65 are considered large and can be used for predictions, and coefficients of .85 demonstrate a strong relationship between variables (Fraenkel et al., 2014, p. 341).

Inferential Statistics

As stated earlier, inferential statistics are a set of mathematical procedures using probabilities and information about a sample to draw conclusions about a population (Gall et al., 2007, p. 137). Samples are used when populations are too big or difficult to gather data from. For example, it may be a challenge to gather data from the 50,000 students at Michigan State University, so a smaller sample of the student population may be gathered. Or it may be difficult to track all students who identify as lesbian or gay. Through the use of inferential statistics, well-chosen samples can provide data that are as useful as collecting from an entire population. A sample has the additional benefit of efficiency because the data-collection process for samples can cost less money and/or take less time. The following sections provide an overview of key concepts that can be useful to those performing student affairs assessment.

Sample Versus Population

The set of statistics called inferential statistics allows for predictions regarding data from a group (population) you want to know more about based on the scores of a subset of that group (sample). Any discussion of inferential statistics must begin with the differentiation of samples and populations. A population is the group of interest, usually denoted as "N." In assessment, a population could be students living in the residence halls, students participating in all student organizations on campus, or students visiting the library during a particular academic year. A sample is a subset of a population from whom data are gathered, usually denoted as "*n*." Samples based on the examples could include students from a couple of residence halls, a few students from each student organization, or students attending the library from 7 p.m. to 10 p.m. every weeknight for a given week. The goal is to have the sample be as representative as possible of the population so as to be confident that inferences made from the sample are also accurate for the population.

Confidence Intervals

There are times when it is helpful to know how similar a sample value is to the same value in the population. A mean can be calculated for the number of organizations in which students choose to participate during a specific year. Perhaps, on average, students participate in .68 organizations. This mean takes into account students who do not participate in any organizations and others who participate in multiple organizations. Unless the campus is small, this mean will be computed to choose a sample from the overall campus population. When this is done it may be informative to know how similar the sample mean is to the population mean.

But how similar? A confidence interval, also called the margin of error, provides a range within which the population mean is likely to occur. Election polls often report percentages along with confidence intervals to describe how many people agree or disagree with a stance. For example, a poll may show a percentage of the population who agree with a particular bill on a given ballot. The percentage may be presented as 75% +/- 4%. The 4% is the confidence interval. This means that 75% of those sampled favored the bill, and the percentage in the population who favored the bill would probably range from 71% to 79% (75% − 4% and 75% + 4%). The confidence level for most confidence intervals is set at 95% or 99%. The confidence level must be decided prior to calculating the confidence interval. The higher the level of the confidence, the more likely it is that the population mean will be within that level. However, as confidence levels are increased, the size of the confidence interval also increases. The decision to have a smaller confidence interval range with less confidence or to have high levels of confidence with a larger range must be made early in the analysis. Details for calculating confidence intervals are included in most statistics texts.

Types of Sampling

There are numerous ways to choose a sample from a population; these methods can be grouped as either random or nonrandom sampling. In random sampling, every member of the population has an equal opportunity to be selected. In nonrandom sampling, every member of the population does not have an equal chance of being selected (Fraenkel et al., 2014). Following are descriptions of the various sampling methods.

Random Sampling

Simple Random Sampling.   As the name connotes, people are randomly selected from the population. This requires that a list of the population be available. With the list in hand, a preset number of names are selected randomly. A table of random numbers is a useful tool for selection. There are also ways to select random samples using Excel and SPSS (an analysis tool for quantitative data).

Stratified Random Sampling.   This process involves a sample where particular subgroups are adequately represented in the sample (Gall et al., 2007, p. 173). For example, if one wanted to measure attitudes regarding climate for diversity on campus and the student population was 54% women and 46% men, then the sample would be selected to be composed of 54% women and 46% men. For a sample to be truly random, it should come out to the same percentages, so stratification should not be needed. But random sampling does not always yield the same proportions of respondents found in the population. In these instances oversampling is needed to achieve a stratified sample. Research may suggest that students of color respond less often to surveys than Whites do. If there are 25% students of color on campus, then of the total number of students receiving the survey, the percentage of students of color would be more than 25%.

Cluster Sampling.   Cluster sampling is used when it is easier to select groups of individuals (a cluster) than individuals from a defined population. Someone may want to understand the study habits of students in the residence halls. Since college students frequently do not check email, it may be easier to pass out surveys by hand rather than send an electronic survey. Rather than randomly selecting any residence hall students, specific residence halls may be selected and all students in those halls would receive the surveys.

Another version of cluster sampling is multistage cluster sampling. Using the previous example and a multistage approach, specific residence hall floors would be randomly selected within each of the selected residence halls. Students on selected floors would receive the survey. This is a way of making large clusters more manageable.

Nonrandom Sampling

Nonrandom sampling simply means that the process to select the sample is not random. These methods are often used when individuals in a population are not included in some type of list from which a random sample can be drawn. Examples of populations that require nonrandom sampling may include all who visit the library in a given week or students who identify as having a disability. For these and similar populations, nonrandom sampling methods must be used.

Systematic Sampling.   One popular method of nonrandom sampling is systematic sampling. This method includes selecting the *n*th person (Fraenkel et al., 2014, p. 98). If there is a list, a random starting point should be selected and then every *n*th person would become part of the sample. If there is no list, every *n*th person would be selected from a group that is accessible. Perhaps a staff member wants to get feedback regarding the new menu in the dining hall. She could select every fifth person leaving the dining hall after lunch or dinner one day until she reached 100 people (or some other predetermined sample number).

Convenience Sampling.   A convenience sample comprises a group of individuals who are available. To understand attitudes regarding a new policy on campus, a staff member might simply talk with students who happen to be sitting in the student union at a particular time during a certain day. The selection of these students is not random or systematic but conveniently accessible. Access and availability influence the use of this method. This type of sampling may be used if the issue being studied is not critical, data must be gathered quickly, or some simple data are needed.

Purposive Sampling.   This is the selection of a sample that is believed to be representative of the population. If it is difficult to collect data from an entire residence hall quickly and easily, a hall director might choose to sample the residence hall government to determine the types of social activities that should be planned for the upcoming semester.

Snowball Sampling.   Snowball sampling is used when it is difficult to identify members of a population from which to sample. For example, there is likely no list of all students on a campus who identify as lesbian, bisexual, or gay. In snowball sampling, once a few individuals are identified who meet the assessment criteria, they are asked to name others who fit the criteria. The second group is also asked to identify people who fit the criteria, and the list gets larger just as a snowball does as it tumbles downhill.

Sample Size and Response Rates
Response rates are an important consideration in assessment as they affect the analyses that can be performed on the data as well as the credibility of the data. The two key issues to address are representativeness and power. Representativeness signifies the similarity of the sample to the population from

which it is drawn. Power is the probability that a particular test of statistical significance will detect an effect when an effect exists.

Representativeness.   Demographics such as gender, race, age, and class are common characteristics that are used to compare the sample and the population to evaluate representativeness. If the sample is similar to the population on the demographic characteristics, there is more confidence that the sample responses are also the same as the population's. However, this is an assumption, and the only way to know for sure is to compare answers from respondents and those who have not responded—not an easy task. Representativeness is another reason why higher response rates are valued. The idea is that the larger the response rate, the more likely that the respondents, and thus their responses, will be representative of the population. This is not always true. Comparing the demographics of the sample and population is one measure for representativeness. It is important to know that the smaller the population, the larger the percentage of the population that must be sampled to be representative. For example, for a 95% confidence interval with a 5% sampling error (or margin of error), a sample of 365 would be needed for a population of 7,500, whereas a population of 10,000 needs a sample of 370. Although there are 2,500 more people in the population, only five more are needed in the sample.

Power.   In addition to representativeness, power is another key concept that may be affected by response rates. Statistical power is the probability that a particular test of statistical significance will lead to rejection of a null hypothesis (Gall et al., 2007, p. 143). As an example, if an academic advisor surveyed her advisees to determine which advising strategies worked best and wanted to compare first-year students with other students, would there be enough students to detect a statistically significant difference between these two groups? The size of the sample is the main factor impacting statistical power. Specific analyses can be done to determine how large a sample would be needed for a specific type of analysis.

Calculating Sample Size.   One of the most frequent questions asked in assessment is "How big should the sample size be?" A simple Internet search will yield a number of web-based sample-size calculators. To use these calculators, the confidence level, usually 95% or 99%, must be decided. In addition, the confidence interval must be identified, which is the size of the range the population statistic should fall within. The population size is also entered. The sample-size calculator then determines what the sample size should be. It is critical to note that this calculated number is the number of responses that are needed, not the number of people who should receive the survey. Assuming a 25% response rate, 400 people would be needed to achieve a sample size of 100. It is important to know that simply getting the "right" sample size does not ensure representativeness. Choose a larger sample if possible.

Statistical Versus Practical Significance

Inferential statistics are used to make inferences regarding a population from a sample of that population. Thus, knowing how similar the sample is to the population is critical. This similarity provides more confidence in the inferences made. Statistical significance represents the probability that findings from a statistical test have not occurred by chance. The results are statistically significant if the probability that they occurred by chance is very small. This probability is called the p value. Typically results are considered statistically significant if the p value is less than .05, which is written as $p < .05$. Although the explanation is a bit more complicated, this p value can be understood to mean that there is less than a 5% probability that the results found will have been due to chance. Most statistics programs include p values as part of the analysis output. However, a statistics text can explain how to compute one by hand and using a table.

Although the results may be statistically significant, this does not mean that they are practically significant. A hall director could survey a sample of residence hall students and find that 86% of women and 83% of men were satisfied or very satisfied living in the residence halls. This difference of 3% might be statistically significant but not practically significant. Would any changes in practice and policy be made because of this small difference? Probably not.

Effect Size

A technique that is helpful in determining practical significance is effect size. It describes the magnitude of results. For comparing differences between two groups, Cohen's d is an easy statistic to calculate and interpret (Cohen's d calculators are available on the Internet). As in the case of a correlation coefficient, a general rule of thumb is that an effect size of .3 is small, .5 is moderate, and .7 is large. The correlation coefficient is also an effect size statistic because it measures the magnitude of the relationship between two variables in addition to the direction of the relationship.

Parametric Tests

In considering which statistics to use to answer various assessment questions, one needs to consider if parametric or nonparametric tests should be used. Parametric techniques make assumptions about the nature of the population (particularly that the population has a normal distribution), whereas nonparametric techniques make few assumptions (Fraenkel et al., 2014, p. 233). Parametric techniques are powerful but can be used only when the assumptions for these methods are met. Consult a statistics text for more detail regarding these assumptions.

t-Tests

A *t*-test is used to compare the means between two groups to see if the difference is statistically significant. The difference is considered statistically significant if the *t* value, which measures the difference, has a *p* value less than .05. If a *t*-test is statistically significant, it is often followed by an effect size analysis, using Cohen's *d*, to determine practical significance.

There are different types of *t*-tests. An independent samples *t*-test is used for two different or independent groups, such as gender or students from different residence halls. Paired samples *t*-tests, also called correlated means *t*-tests, are used to compare the same group over time. This is the technique used for pre/post *t*-tests. Cohen's *d* can be used for independent and paired samples *t*-tests.

t-Test for Proportions

This parametric test for categorical or nominal data analyzes the difference between two proportions. It could be used to determine if responses for a proportion of the 2010 class are different from those of a proportion of the 2014 class. For example, 58% of the 2010 class agree or strongly agree that their critical thinking improved during their college career, compared with 63% of the 2014 class. There are forms for both independent samples and paired samples.

Analysis of Variance

Analysis of variance (ANOVA) is similar to *t*-tests in that it measures differences between means, but with three or more groups. ANOVA would be used to compare means on an item such as race/ethnic groups, majors, and so on. ANOVA produces an *F* value. If the *p* value of the *F* value is less than the *p* value you decide to use (.05 is typical), then there are significant differences between at least two groups in the set. Post-hoc tests, which are *t*-tests between pairs of groups, are then done to determine which groups' means are statistically different.

Nonparametric Tests

Nonparametric tests may be useful when samples are not a random selection, a representation of the population, or a normal distribution.

Mann-Whitney U Test

The Mann-Whitney *U* test is a nonparametric version of the *t*-test and is used to analyze ranked data (Fraenkel et al., 2014, p. 237). The test combines the scores from both of the groups, ranking them in order regardless of group. If the *U* value is statistically significant, the bulk of the scores in one group is higher than the bulk of the scores in the other group (Gall et al., 2007, p. 327).

Chi-Square Test

This nonparametric test analyzes the difference between data in categories. This is done by comparing the observed frequencies and comparing those to the expected frequencies. The chi-square (χ^2) value is statistically significant if its *p* value is below .05, which signifies that the groups are different. A chi-square test would be used to determine if the proportion of students by race/ethnicity were the same for two or more separate student organizations.

Wilcoxon Signed Rank Test

This test is the nonparametric equivalent of paired samples *t*-tests and is used to determine if the distributions of scores of two groups are statistically significant from each other (Gall et al., 2007, p. 327).

Kruskal-Wallis One-Way Analysis of Variance

This test is the nonparametric version of ANOVA. As in the case of the Mann-Whitney *U* test, the scores from all groups are combined into one set and then ranked. The *H* value demonstrates the difference of the ranks between the groups.

Conclusion

Although most student affairs staff did not enter the field to perform statistical analyses, they do have to understand the basic theory behind such analyses and the application of quantitative analysis. They must be good consumers of research and know how they can analyze their own data to make meaning of students' experiences. Statistics are powerful tools in understanding students and their needs and in improving our work. Complicated, complex statistics are fortunately not necessary for student affairs assessment. The goal of assessment is to document student learning and program effectiveness, not to "prove" anything. Information from this chapter will assist in the assessment process. However, a basic understanding of statistics is useful in articulating why a statistical method was used or not used.

Key Points

- It is important to be aware of levels of data because they affect the statistics that can be used.
- Descriptive statistics are statistics that describe a distribution of numbers; inferential statistics are statistics used to draw inferences about a population from a sample of a given group.
- Sampling can be random or nonrandom with different forms of each.
- Parametric tests are statistical tests used when certain assumptions of a distribution are made; nonparametric tests are statistical tests used when assumptions about a data distribution are not made.

Discussion Questions and Activities

- What are examples of each level of data: nominal, ordinal, interval, and ratio?
- When would you choose to use a mean, a median, and a mode?
- What two things does a correlation coefficient identify?
- Why are statistics useful in assessment?
- You are the coordinator of student organizations at a college. The dean of students wants to demonstrate that student involvement is important for student success and asks you if students who are involved in student organizations have higher GPAs and are more likely to be retained than students who are not members. What statistics might you use to answer those questions?
- Your institution participates in the National Survey of Student Engagement in the spring of even-numbered years to track how engaged your students are. You have been asked to determine whether students become more engaged over time and if this engagement is different by reported race/ethnicity. What types of statistical analyses might you use to answer those questions?

IO

QUALITATIVE DESIGN

Qualitative designs offer a different approach to assessment than quantitative designs, one that provides greater depth in the data and can offer a rich description of what is happening. As can be expected, much of qualitative assessment (approach, methods, analysis, and conclusions) is grounded in qualitative research, which is an approach that situates the observer in the world rather than separating the observer (Denzin & Lincoln, 2013) from the activity being observed. The purpose of these designs is to understand how people make sense of their experiences, construct their worlds, and attribute meaning to their experiences (Merriam & Tisdell, 2015). The power of a qualitative approach in assessment or evaluation is that these data tell the program's story by capturing participants' voices (Patton, 2015). As in the case of quantitative designs, there are a number of qualitative designs available to those performing assessment. After the focus of the assessment inquiry is defined, the best choice of design can be made once the similarities, differences, pros, and cons of various approaches are understood.

Characteristics of Qualitative Design

Before we consider the various qualitative approaches to assessment, it is important to understand the characteristics of qualitative research itself. Creswell (2012) as well as Merriam and Tisdell (2015) have identified the characteristics that can be applied to qualitative assessment.

1. The focus is on meaning and understanding.
2. The study is conducted in a natural setting.
3. The researcher is the primary instrument.
4. The study can involve multiple methods such as interviews, observations, and document analysis.

5. Inductive logic is used to build patterns, categories, and themes from the data.
6. The focus is on participants' perspectives, meanings, and multiple subjective views.
7. The study is situated within the context or setting of participants/sites (social/political/historical).
8. It involves an emergent and evolving design rather than tightly a prefigured design.
9. It is reflective and interpretive.
10. It presents a holistic, complex picture with a rich description of the phenomenon.

As discussed earlier, assessment can serve different purposes from those of research. Assessment often focuses on documenting goal achievement and identifying opportunities to improve learning, whereas research typically centers on developing or confirming theory. Thus, the characteristics can be adapted to create characteristics for qualitative assessment:

1. The data are words, stories, and narratives, not numbers.
2. The assessor is the analysis tool.
3. Multiple methods may be utilized.
4. Complex reasoning is used to analyze multiple types of data.
5. The focus is on participants' experiences and the meanings of those experiences.
6. Context is critical to understanding meaning.
7. A holistic picture is presented.

It is vitally important to take these characteristics into account before embarking on a qualitative assessment project, as they help provide the design framing of the overall project and inform the project's goals.

Reasons for Choosing Qualitative Research

Chapter 2, "Epistemology," discussed the different philosophical underpinnings of quantitative and qualitative methodologies. Extending that conversation, Corbin and Strauss (2015) have identified the reasons why someone would choose a qualitative approach over a quantitative one:

- To explore the inner experiences of participants
- To explore how meanings are formed and transformed

- To explore areas not yet thoroughly researched
- To discover relevant variables that later can be tested through quantitative forms of research
- To take a holistic and comprehensive approach to the study of phenomena (p. 5)

Qualitative Designs

Creswell (2012) provided a starting point for understanding qualitative assessment designs by describing five traditions for qualitative research. These approaches are narratives, phenomenology, grounded theory, ethnography, and case studies. The details of each are described next.

Narratives

Narrative approaches rely on stories—written, spoken word, or visual representations of individuals (Lichtman, 2012; Merriam & Tisdell, 2015; Patton, 2015). These stories come in many forms. Some are captured with interviews, with focus groups, or through dialogue between individuals. Other stories are documented through journals, newspaper articles, biographies, or other forms. With the growing use of photos to capture the lived experience (Knoblauch, Baer, Laurier, Petschke, & Schnettler, 2008; Schwartz, 1989; Shulze, 2007), stories can also be presented through visual representations. The underlying similarity between all of these forms is the extent to which authentic narrative reflects a participant's experiences and the meaning he or she makes of those experiences.

Narratives are common designs used in assessment. One example would be interviewing a specific group of students to learn about their experiences after a new policy, practice, or program was implemented—that is, to find out the "story" of their experience of the policy, practice, or program. Another example that may not be readily apparent is through the use of visual collection. In this approach students may be asked to take, find, or create visual representations of some key phenomenon. For instance, student affairs educators may want to understand what community looks like on campus. Thus, they may ask a group of students to take three photographs of what represents community on campus to them and then upload those photos to a common digital repository. Once all of the photos are taken and uploaded, the assessor could then analyze the themes related to the photos that tell the story of community on campus, and students/participants could be enlisted to uncover or confirm a range of interpretations. Themes of community may include athletic events, campus traditions, student organizations, or other esteemed events. In this instance, the narrative is actually a photo wherein the photo tells the story.

Narratives do not have to be long. One-minute papers provide mini-narratives of what students learn from an activity. At the end of a program or an activity, the facilitator passes out index cards and asks students to respond to a prompt in a minute's time. (It does not have to be exactly a minute.) The prompt varies depending on the information the facilitator wants to collect, but it is often something similar to "What are the most important things you learned in this session?" or "How can you use what you have learned today?" These brief statements provide narratives or stories of the participants' experiences in or with the program.

Phenomenology

Phenomenology is an approach that focuses on the lived experiences of individuals (Merriam & Tisdell, 2015; Patton, 2015). Common and unique experiences of a phenomenon are investigated to create an understanding of the universal essence of that experience (Creswell, 2012; Merriam & Tisdell, 2015). In other words, phenomenology seeks to describe "the different ways people conceptualize the world around them" (Gall, Gall, & Borg, 2007, p. 497). Another defining factor of phenomenology is a strong philosophical basis. Phenomenology draws on the works of Husserl, Heidegger, Sartre, and Merleau-Ponty (Creswell, 2012). The bases of this approach are rooted in the following philosophical perspectives (Creswell, 2012):

- A return to the goal of philosophy as a search for wisdom during a time that was focused on exploring the world through empiricism.
- A suspension of all judgments regarding what is real.
- The reality of an object requires one's consciousness of it.
- A refusal of the subject-object dichotomy. An object can be understood only through the meaning one makes of it.

Phenomenology would be a beneficial approach to use for the development of new programs. With the growing number of veteran college students on campus, many colleges are developing programs to address the needs of this population. Using a phenomenological approach, assessors could engage veteran students through interviews and focus groups (and perhaps also talk with faculty and staff) to better understand their experiences. The goal would be to understand the essence of veteran students' experiences and identify the collective needs of the group. Primary themes could form the basis on which to develop educational curricula or support services.

Grounded Theory

The intent of grounded theory is to develop theory that is grounded in, or emerges from, the data (Lichtman, 2012; Merriam & Tisdell, 2015). The inquirer develops an explanation of a process, an action, or an interaction based on views of participants (Creswell, 2012) and by using an inductive process rather than deduction from assumptions at the outset of the study (Patton, 2015). Instead of believing that research must begin with theory, grounded theorists hold that theories should be grounded in data based on actions, interactions, and the social processes of individuals (Creswell, 2012). The goal is to build theory, not test theory (Patton, 2015). Unique to grounded theory, data collection and analysis are interrelated (Corbin & Strauss, 2015). Data are analyzed and, based on the analysis, new data are collected.

Creswell (2012) described the following defining features of grounded theory:

- The focus of the inquiry is a process or action.
- The goal is to develop an explanation or theory of a process or an action.
- Memoing is a step in developing the explanation as the assessor notes ideas that arise during data collection and analysis.
- Interviewing is often the primary form of data collection.
- Data analysis is structured and centers on developing categories from the data and using one of the categories to serve as the focus of the explanation.

Although theory generation is not a typical goal of assessment, the grounded theory approach may be useful in some assessment projects. This design might be used when there is little or no published literature about a particular topic of interest, or it may be helpful in exploring new ideas with few established models. Grounded theory might also be useful to clarify how a process or practice works—for example, how cultures of alcohol abuse are maintained or how student athletes develop leadership skills. This approach would also be useful if an assessor is trying to understand what students learn from living in the residence halls.

Ethnography

The focus of ethnography is to examine the shared patterns of behavior, beliefs, and language of a cultural group (Creswell, 2012; Merriam & Tisdell, 2015; Patton, 2015). Essentially, it is the study of cultures in context (Lichtman, 2012). A variety of data-collection methods can be used with this study approach, including interviews, focus groups, and observations.

Contextualization is a critical aspect of ethnography. Individuals' experiences, behaviors, beliefs, and language all occur within specific contexts. In the case of higher education, "context" can be delineated as the campus environment, but should also include attention to the local or national social, political, and geographic environment. As a result, the assessor wants to get an "emic" or insider's perspective on situations and experiences (Fraenkel, Wallen, & Hyun, 2014). It is easy to make judgments while engaging in ethnography. However, to embed transparency in data collection and analysis, it is essential to interrogate judgments and unpack assumptions (Fraenkel et al., 2014; Lichtman, 2012). Field notes and assessor memos can document decisions and observations and become a part of the data corpus—subject to analysis and interpretation.

There are many opportunities for ethnographic assessment in higher education. For example, in an investigation into the use of alcohol within co-populations on campus, an assessor may want to try to better understand fraternity and sorority culture. She may interview students in fraternities and sororities, students who have attended events, and possibly even observe activities in an attempt to understand the culture around alcohol consumption. Through these interviews and observations, the assessor can begin to understand how community culture might foster behaviors around alcohol use. She can then use those data to develop programs, policies, and services particular to community needs.

Ethnography may also be useful in evaluating the impact of living-learning communities. Although these communities take different forms, a common characteristic is that students who live together also take some courses together. Through interviews, focus groups, field notes, memos, and observations of community activities, an assessor can evaluate the culture of these communities to help clarify what it is about them that aids students' success personally and academically. The findings from this type of evaluation can be used to revise programs and services to better serve targeted groups. The findings may also be transferable to communities with similar profiles and contexts.

Case Studies

The focus of case studies is on a particular case or set of similar cases (Lichtman, 2012) to describe and analyze a bound system (Merriam & Tisdell, 2015) within a defined set of parameters or characteristics. There is an assumption that each case is unique, and attention is given to describing in detail each individual case, with the examination of multiple cases deriving from individual cases (Fraenkel et al., 2014). Gall et al. (2007) identify the following characteristics of case studies: "(a) the in-depth study of (b) one or more instances of a phenomenon (c) in its real-life context that (d) reflects the perspective of the participants in the phenomenon" (p. 447).

A case study approach to assessment might be used to understand exceptional cases. An example in student affairs work may be informative. Many residential life offices perform student evaluations of staff to assess competence and improve performance. If one or two hall directors or resident assistants consistently received extraordinary evaluations, it might be useful to perform a case study to better understand the phenomena under which such extraordinary evaluations occurred. The data collected may include open-ended responses to a survey, interviews or focus groups with residents, observations of the hall director working, or even document analyses of communication with/to students. These data could then be used to inform training and recruitment of future staff.

A similar approach could be used to understand academic success of first-generation college students. A detailed description of the case would require interviews with students as well as their families (if willing and able), friends, faculty, and staff. Analysis might also include review of the students' academic transcripts along with their cocurricular transcripts.

Case study approaches might be used to investigate how higher education structures enable the success of some students but thwart others, with the goal of clarifying how students experience particular conditions. These results could uncover how processes like recruitment and admissions privilege characteristics, behaviors, or skills unrelated to higher education aims.

Data-Collection Issues for Consideration

Data-collection methods including interviews, focus groups, and observations are discussed in depth in other chapters in this volume. Following is a discussion of issues to consider in qualitative data collection.

Access and Rapport

Depending on the goals of the inquiry, another step taken before collecting data is defining the characteristics of the population one would like to assess. Once the group of individuals has been identified, rapport should be established with them so that they will agree to participate in the assessment (Merriam & Tisdell, 2015). Developing a bond with participants is critical for data collection. However, it is important to be neutral in these interactions so the assessor does not lead the participant to certain responses. Neutrality is a stance toward the content whereas rapport is a stance toward the participant (Merriam & Tisdell, 2015). Establishing connection and trust between assessor and participant creates a relationship in which the participant is willing to share abundant, critical, and honest information. Without this relationship building, it will be challenging to collect useful data. Time should be set aside for this type of relationship building. Make the first meeting a "get to know you" meeting. Other strategies for building rapport include fitting the study around the participants' schedules, finding common ground between interviewer and interviewee through self-disclosure, being friendly, and showing interest in the participants and their experiences (Merriam & Tisdell, 2015).

Transparency regarding the reason for the assessment project and explicit description regarding how the results will be used increase the trust participants have in the assessor and the process may enable more honest responses. The assessor's authenticity in his or her role and approach to the topic serves the same purpose. It is good practice to close the loop with participants after the study is done. Although the participants may not be involved with the data analysis or reporting, they are still partners in the assessment process as they share their interpretations of experience. Thus, closing the loop by sharing the results, recommendations, and implemented changes honors that partnership.

Sampling

As described in Chapter 9, "Statistical Overview for Assessment," there are two types of sampling: random sampling and nonrandom sampling. Nonrandom sampling is the acceptable and appropriate sampling method for qualitative assessment as the goal is not generalizability to the larger population.

Purposeful Sampling

Purposeful sampling is a form of nonrandom sampling that is often employed in qualitative research (Creswell, 2012; Gall et al., 2007). Patton (2015) has argued that the benefit of this sampling method lies in selecting information-rich cases. With purposeful sampling, participants or cases are identified and selected with consideration of who has the information or experience necessary to respond to the inquiry (Gall et al., 2007, p. 178). For example, we may not want to engage 60-year-olds in an investigation of first-time voters. Merriam and Tisdell (2015) identify various types of purposeful sampling in which the assessor intentionally selects participants who meet a set of parameters. Typical sampling is used to select an average person, situation, or process. A unique sample is the opposite of typical and centers on unique cases. The goal with maximum variance sampling is to identify the widest range of participants. Convenience sampling relies on a sample that is easy to access. Snowball, chain, or networking sampling involves identifying a small number of participants who then identify potential participants with similar characteristics.

Creswell (2012) offered three considerations for purposeful sampling. The first is to consider the participants. Participants want to be selected because of the experiences they have had or the information they can share, not simply because they are convenient. Convenient samples may not lead to rich data. Although purposeful sampling is the overarching approach, there are still decisions to be made regarding whom to select for the assessment project. This is the second consideration. Sampling can happen at the site level, event level, or individual level. Sampling can focus on obtaining individuals who are similar or who have diverse experiences related to the phenomenon.

Creswell's third consideration is the size of the sample. The recommended size of the sample varies with approach and the kind of data necessary to respond to the inquiry. Patton (2015) phrased it well: "Sample size depends on what you want to know, the purpose of the inquiry, what's at stake, what will be useful, what will have credibility, and what can be done with the available time and resources" (p. 311). Creswell (2012) suggested three to 10 individuals for phenomenology, one culture-sharing group for ethnography with numerous artifacts and other data, and four or five items for case studies; however, others emphasize an approach where size of a focus group is dictated by practicalities of group and conversation management and inquiry focus. For example, it is unrealistic to expect full participation of a group of 25 gathered to discuss a controversial topic. More importantly, focus groups should be repeated until saturation is reached. Saturation is the point when no new concepts are emerging (Corbin & Strauss, 2015). As many as 20 to 60 interviews may be needed to reach saturation (Creswell, 2012), which likely requires more time than a staff member may be able to realistically provide.

Theoretical Sampling
A theoretical sample is chosen in order to help the investigator develop a theory (Creswell, 2012; Patton, 2015). The goal is to collect data that will maximize opportunities to develop concepts and identify relationships (Corbin & Strauss, 2015). This process starts the same as purposeful sampling, but analysis of the data leads the investigator to the next person to interview (Merriam & Tisdell, 2015).

Data Analysis

Depending on the method indicated for the inquiry, data analysis can be undertaken at any point in the data-collection process. As stated earlier, unlike quantitative assessment that often uses statistical tools for collection and analysis, the primary analytical tool in qualitative assessment is the assessor.

The qualitative analysis process is an inductive process in which dimensions emerge from the data without ascertaining what they are in advance (Patton, 2015). For some methods, the analysis process begins with the creation of codes or categories that, according to Creswell (2012), involves aggregating data into categories of information and naming those categories. A code is often a word or short phrase that ascribes meaning to each datum for pattern detection, categorization, theory building, or other analytical purposes (Patton, 2015; Saldaña, 2012). Codes can be predetermined (e.g., they can be based on existing research and/or predetermined hypotheses).

An example may be instructive. An assessor wants to discover what traditional-aged college students learn by living in a residence hall during their first year in college. The following is an excerpt from a fictitious interview with a student. The codes are noted with superscripts in the paragraph and then defined.

> I learned a lot living in the residence halls this year. With a roommate, we figured out how to give and take.[1] We took turns choosing what to watch on TV and set ground rules for guests. I also learned to take care of myself.[2] My dad wasn't going to do my laundry or buy food. One of the most important things I learned was to stand up for myself.[3] Before college I often didn't express my opinion. This year I learned to speak up or else I wouldn't get what I wanted or needed.[3]

[1] Compromise
[2] Independence
[3] Assertiveness

In this example each unit of data received its own code. This is called *open coding* (Merriam & Tisdell, 2015). Each code is then compared with other codes to determine similarities and differences—a process called *comparative analysis* (Corbin & Strauss, 2015). Codes are sorted into patterns or categories. The coding process moves from description to interpretation during this stage. This sorting process is termed *axial coding* or *analytical coding* (Merriam & Tisdell, 2015). Merriam and Tisdell (2015) provide three suggestions for naming categories: from the assessor doing the analysis, from participants' own words, or from literature on the topic. Categories should meet the following criteria:

- Answer the assessment question
- Exhaustive
- Mutually exclusive
- Conceptually congruent (Merriam & Tisdell, 2015)

After codes are grouped into categories, the codes may be reviewed in the context of this newly named category to determine if there is alignment between the codes and corresponding category. This process is similar to zooming in, zooming out, and zooming in again. Within categories, subcategories of smaller but similar patterns of codes may be found (Saldaña, 2012). The process of developing categories may influence continual data collection, which may be done to confirm or disconfirm the emergent patterns. Thus, data collection and analysis often happen simultaneously. Through further comparison of categories and reflection, concepts or themes may emerge.

Although coding and categorizing can be done by hand, software such as NVivo, ATLAS.ti, and MAXQDA is available to assist with the process.

Saldaña (2012) should be consulted for an extensive description of the coding process. Following is a description of a basic coding process that can be used with most assessment projects.

Simple Coding Example

To understand how qualitative analysis works in assessment, a basic example of coding may be informative. An individual has undertaken a study regarding students who have been academically successful; the hope is to learn how the institution has helped them in this regard. After interviewing 15 students, the Word documents containing the notes of each of their interviews are compiled. Since a structured interview approach was used, each student answered the same questions.

It is important to organize the data in a way to make it easier to discern common categories or themes. One approach would be to copy and paste the answers from each participant on question one to a Word document. The focus can now be on the analysis of the answers from the respondent to one question at a time. Thus, there is a page header with the question itself and, underneath, the responses from each participant. As the assessor reads through the questions, he or she looks for common terms and common concepts. Similar words/concepts could be highlighted across participants in one color, electronically, or with a paper copy. A different highlight color represents a distinct category.

Once the assessor has gone through all of the responses to question one, he or she cuts and pastes all of the similarly colored highlighted text and puts it into another document. As this is done, all of the purple (or whatever color) highlighted text is put on one page, all of the yellow highlighted text on another page, and so on until the assessor runs out of highlighted text.

Once the highlighted text is extracted and sorted by color (this is the categorizing phase) the assessor must describe each category with a name or short phrase that defines those codes. After selecting that word/phrase, the assessor reviews all of the codes in each category to determine if the code should still be kept in that category. At this point some codes may be removed from categories and/or transferred to other categories.

Now that the assessor has extracted the highlighted text from the students' answers, he or she should go back to the unhighlighted text to see if there are any new categories in the remaining text that were missed earlier.

The assessor may notice that there are no new categories but that some of the remaining text fits with some of the text that has already been highlighted. For codes that do not seem to fit with current categories, "off topic" categories can be created. The responses are still kept to help provide the holistic picture of these students' experiences although these responses are not part of a theme.

With all codes placed in a category, the assessor should review each code again to ensure it is in the appropriate category and that the category name is still appropriate. Subcategories may also be identified at this time. The assessor then reviews the categories with the goal of identifying a theme or themes that connect the categories. At this stage, identified categories for this example might include "checking in," "providing reassurance," "making referrals," "asking how classes are going," and "motivating and inspiring." The assessor may determine that the theme is "academic and personal support." The categories should be reviewed again to make sure that they align with this newly identified theme. There may be more than one theme that emerges, and all are examined to create an overarching explanation or theory.

In the previously discussed approach, the themes "emerged" from the data. They were not created ahead of time. Another approach would be to create the codes/categories that would represent themes before reviewing the responses. This approach is used when there is already a guide, perhaps from existing theory or research. In this process, the assessor would be looking for statements that align to the categories already identified. As in the case of the emerging themes process, the assessor will want to highlight the statements that align with a category, using a different color for each category. Once all of the responses have been reviewed and highlighted, any remaining text should be reviewed to see if it fits in a current category or if any new categories can be created.

After either of these review processes, the assessor may decide to count the number of statements related to each category. This could help to provide a level of magnitude to each theme or to test the warrants made, but capturing responses quantitatively is not the goal of qualitative approaches. A theme with three statements could have a different magnitude than a theme with 16 statements. It is important to appropriately represent the themes by providing sample statements for each theme to provide the reader with a context for the theme. In the appendix of the report, each theme should be included as well as all corresponding statements for readers who want that level of data.

As with any assessment, qualitative analysis can be basic or complex. Coding can take a great deal of time, which is important to consider in the overall timeline for completing an assessment project. For a more extensive discussion of coding, consult Saldaña (2012).

Managing Bias

An issue arising with any assessment project is the bias of the person performing the assessment. Some constituents may be concerned that the assessment yielded positive results for a program or service only because the assessor wanted to place the activity in the best possible light. Or if the person assessing the program or service created it, it may be assumed that because of this the assessor cannot be objective or accurate. The goal for quantitative approaches is to make the process as structured as possible; thus, quantitative designs should address bias through the designs themselves as well as through data-collection methods and analyses. This ensures that the study will be seen as trustworthy. Qualitative designs, on the other hand, acknowledge, address, and embrace this bias. The perspective of the assessor is critical to the assessment process, as the assessor is the analysis instrument. As such, any assumptions or bias should be made explicit rather than be subjugated to supposed objectivity.

Trustworthiness

Internal validity, external validity, reliability, and *objectivity* are terms used in quantitative assessment to address bias and demonstrate rigor. Under the umbrella of "trustworthiness," the corollary qualitative concepts identified by Lincoln and Guba (1985) are credibility, transferability, dependability, and confirmability (Merriam & Tisdell, 2015). Credibility is the extent to which the findings are credible given the data. In other words, do the findings match reality (Merriam & Tisdell, 2015)? Like generalizability, transferability is the extent to which the findings from one study can be applied to another context or group of people. It is the responsibility of the investigator to provide rich descriptive data so the reader can determine how transferable the findings are. Dependability is the extent to which the results are consistent and make sense. Since the assessor is the instrument in qualitative assessment, the assessor can be more reliable. Confirmability is the extent to which the results can be confirmed or validated. Dependability and confirmability can also be bolstered through the multiple triangulation of data.

Ways to address and make transparent bias in qualitative assessment and ensure rigor, drawn from qualitative research methodology, include audit trails, bracketing, member checks, and triangulation.

Audit Trail

An audit trail documents the process by detailing how data were collected and analyzed (Merriam & Tisdell, 2015). According to Schwandt (1997), the audit trail can serve two purposes. First, an audit trail can serve as a form of record keeping for the assessor; it can also be used by a third party to validate the process. The trail makes the process clear to others for review and critique, and documentation may include "source of and method of recording raw data, data reduction and analysis products, data reconstruction and synthesis products, process notes, and information about the development of instruments" (Gall et al., 2007, p. 474). Another type of audit trail involves assessor memos. Memos can record reflections and perspectives of the assessor at all stages in the assessment process, to include, for example, decisions made, ideas, impressions about relationships, challenges, strengths, and issues to revisit. Memos can be brief, written narratives, created by the assessor to provide context and transparency in the assessment process.

Second, an audit trail is especially useful in assessment as assessment projects are often replicated annually or semiannually. An audit trail can provide the detail to an individual implementing a project in the future. Before embarking on an assessment project, the assessor should consider what to include in the audit trail as it is easier to add to the trail during the process when assessment is actually happening than trying to add documentation after the project has been completed. An audit trail in assessment may include raw data in the form of interview or observation notes, recordings from interviews or focus groups, minutes from meetings discussing the assessment project, drafts of reports, email communications, field notes, and anything else that will help describe the process. A good perspective to begin with may be "If I were to replicate or validate this assessment project, what information would I want or need?"

Bracketing

Another way to address bias is through examining and making assumptions apparent about an assessment project. Bracketing is a way of identifying preconceived beliefs (Lichtman, 2012) by articulating views on the topic and setting them aside (Lichtman, 2012). Bracketing is employed throughout the process (Holstein & Gubrium, 2011), allowing the assessor to reflect upon his or her notions of the assessment and monitor them over time. Bracketing provides a holding tank of sorts for beliefs about the project and its results. Although this device is often associated with phenomenology, it can be applied to any type of qualitative assessment.

In an assessment project, the assessor may take time to make conscious his or her feelings, beliefs, and assumptions regarding what is being assessed. Bracketing makes these beliefs explicit and documents them for both the assessor and readers if bracketing is shared. Hopefully, this process will help the assessor to consider what he or she brings to a project (e.g., prior knowledge, assumptions, prejudice) and how these positions influence study design, administration, and conclusions.

Member Checks

Where the audit trail centers on the process and bracketing focuses on the assessor, member checks, also called respondent validation (Merriam & Tisdell, 2015), revolve around participants. These checks are a way of soliciting feedback on the preliminary findings from participants (Schwandt, 1997). This is a way of checking interpretations of the data (Merriam & Tisdell, 2015), correcting factual errors, and collecting more information to reconcile findings, rewrite a report, or include a contrasting view (Gall et al., 2007). However, member checking may not be appropriate for every inquiry, such as assessment regarding sensitive/controversial topics or point-in-time approaches where it may not be possible to contact members.

There are a couple of ways in which member checks can be used in an assessment project. First, the assessor could share the interview notes or summary of the interviews, focus groups, and so on with each respective participant to ensure that the information collected was accurate. Second, the assessor could share the final draft of the report with the participants for their feedback. In either case, the assessor needs to decide how to handle any feedback. In some cases, such as inaccuracy of information, revisions would be appropriate. However, participants' interpretations may differ and the assessor must decide if they call for any changes. In deciding how to address conflicting feedback, consider the context and purpose of the study and how the data make sense within that context. It is also appropriate to explain to participants at the beginning of the study how their feedback will be handled. This manages any expectations that may arise regarding the solicitation of feedback from members and making revisions.

As another check for consistency, the person who has collected and analyzed the data could have a colleague review the data and findings. The external person is not changing the results, but confirming (or not) that the conclusions drawn from the data are reasonable based on the literature and method.

Triangulation

Triangulation is a process to confirm findings through multiple means of data collection or analysis that converge to support the same inference or conclusion. Denzin (1978) identified four approaches to triangulation: multiple methods, multiple sources of data, multiple investigators, and multiple theories to confirm findings. With multiple methods, focus groups may be used along with interviews. Mixed-methods assessments may be used as a way to triangulate findings by combining interviews and surveys or other forms of data collection. Another approach to triangulation is the use of multiple data sources. If an assessor wants to discover what students learn while living in the residence halls, focus groups may be done with students, resident assistants, and professional hall directors, each of which has a different vantage point on the issue. The use of multiple, independent investigators each analyzing the same data to investigate the same issue is another approach to triangulation. Similar findings by each investigator would confirm those findings, deeming them dependable. Finally, the multiple theories approach is used to explain a phenomenon in multiple ways. This approach would also confirm findings.

In qualitative assessment there would be multiple approaches to managing bias and ensuring the rigor of the process and findings.

Qualitative Assessment Design: An Example

In Chapter 7, an emerging leaders program was used as a basis for designing a hypothetical assessment. In that case, the director of student engagement, who oversees all leadership programming, wanted to know what students were learning from the program. That same topic can be used as a foundation for designing a qualitative assessment to provide an example of how two methodological approaches can be used for the same activity.

As discussed in Chapter 2, on epistemology, one's view of the world affects one's approach to assessment. The director believed that experience is socially constructed through interactions with others and thus chose a qualitative approach. Once the overall approach was determined, a design was selected. Since the goal of the assessment was to describe what students were learning through this program, the director chose the narrative approach. Phenomenology was not the best approach, as the assessment was not examining the lived experience of the students. Grounded theory was not ideal, since the focus was not on the process of leadership development but the outcomes. The culture was not at the center of the assessment, so ethnography was not a good match. Although a case study approach could have been used, the assessor wanted to learn about leadership skills across participants, not just one or two of them. In addition, the focus was not the program overall but individual student outcomes. Thus, a case study was not the best match. After choosing the narrative methodology, the director chose the data-collection method.

Approximately 20 students participated in the most recent program. Given that the number of participants was not large and it was likely that not all students would agree to participate in the assessment, the director decided to employ interviews to learn more about each individual. Focus groups could also have been used and could be a good approach if time were scarce. However, depth would likely be sacrificed with this method. The director could also have selected observation or even journaling as methods of collecting data. But observation would not incorporate the students' perspectives on their own experience. Journaling would be similar to interviews in the ability to gather information-rich data and would also provide an opportunity to see growth over time. Yet, unless the journals were reviewed throughout the semester, follow-up questions could not be asked. Since the assessor believed that probing would be a valuable approach to uncover a deeper understanding of the learning, interviews were selected for data collection.

After securing permission for the assessment from the institutional review board, the director began the process of setting up interviews. First, a room was identified for the interviews and scheduled for blocks of time (both day and night to be aligned with students' schedules) during a two-week period after the end of the program. The director began contacting the students participating in the Emerging Leaders Program, first through the Twitter hashtag the group used to communicate. The director was going to email students but learned that students infrequently check their university email address. The director had the instructor for the Emerging Leaders Program also post to the group's Facebook page asking for participants. Included in the Twitter and Facebook solicitations was a link to a Google doc with a list of available times. After a week, the assessor began calling students who had not responded via social media asking them to participate. Upon completion of these three outreach strategies, 13 of the 20 students set up times to be interviewed. In addition to the student interviews, the director set up interviews with the instructors and the mentors (five upperclass students who were each assigned to a "pod" of four students). Data gathered from these groups enabled triangulation of the findings.

Following the guidance included in Chapter 11, the assessor conducted semistructured interviews with each student. Handwritten notes were taken and the interview was audio recorded on the director's smartphone. Since learning outcomes were already established, the director used those as categories and mapped codes to said learning outcomes. Themes were developed from the categories regarding what the students learned from the Emerging Leaders Program. Since there were codes for each outcome category, there was evidence that the outcome was achieved. Codes that did not align with the learning outcome categories were sorted into additional categories, some of which represented unintended learning outcomes. Rather than mapping codes to categories derived from the learning outcomes, the director could have let the categories emerge from the data and then compared those categories with the learning outcomes to determine whether students reported learning the espoused outcomes. The preliminary findings were shared with the interviewees as a member check to correct misinformation or misinterpretation of data.

Once the findings were confirmed and triangulated through the use of multiple data sources, the director wrote a report outlining the assessment process, findings, and recommendations for improvement. An appendix to the report included the audit trail to detail the assessment process and provide step-by-step instructions if another person wanted to do a similar assessment. In addition to this comprehensive report, an executive summary was created for senior divisional leadership and an infographic was created to share with students. The director also presented the findings at a divisional meeting. Participants were given access to any of the reporting formats if they wished to view them.

When the following program cycle approached, the director worked with the instructors to identify the changes that were made to the program based on assessment. Those revisions were added to the comprehensive report to document the improvements that had been made.

Conclusion

Qualitative approaches provide different kinds of evidence and conclusions as compared with quantitative approaches. In this context- and data-rich environment, student affairs professionals can gain insight by using students' own words and experiences. Although data collection and data analysis can take more time than in a quantitative design, the outcome is much more descriptive and responds better to "how?" and "why?" questions.

Key Points

- Qualitative assessments use data consisting of words, stories, and narratives; their focus on meaning and understanding the assessor is the primary assessment tool.

- Qualitative designs include narrative, phenomenology, grounded theory, ethnography, and case studies.
- Data analysis and data collection are often interrelated in qualitative assessment.
- In qualitative data analysis, codes are ascribed to data and—through a process of constant comparison—those codes are sorted into categories. The resulting categories may be grouped into themes from which theories or explanations emerge.
- Credibility, transferability, dependability, and confirmability are standards of rigor for qualitative assessment that help to manage bias in the assessment process.
- Audit trails, bracketing, member checks, and triangulation are approaches to increase the rigor of a qualitative study.

Discussion Questions and Activities

- Identify five characteristics of qualitative assessment.
- Describe three topics or issues for which a qualitative assessment design is best suited.
- Compare and contrast the following designs: narrative, phenomenology, grounded theory, ethnography, and case study.
- Identify one issue and describe how each qualitative design might be used to assess it.
- Define *credibility, transferability, dependability*, and *confirmability.*
- What are three ways of triangulating data?

11

INTERVIEWS AND FOCUS GROUPS

Although many think that assessment favors quantitative approaches and the collection of data that can be represented numerically, a great deal of assessment utilizes qualitative methods. A key to success in assessment is to choose the data-collection method that will answer the question at hand. The method should not be the driving force in performance assessment. One major goal of assessment is to "tell the story" of the work being done in student affairs. These types of stories are conducive to narratives that emerge from qualitative methods for data collection. As discussed in previous chapters, qualitative approaches focus on capturing stories and experiences and making meanings of those experiences. The emphasis is on depth rather than breadth and, unlike quantitative methods, qualitative approaches allow for and require flexibility and adaptability during most stages of assessment projects. As a result, qualitative methods are distinctly different from quantitative methods. It is important to identify what types of data are needed to answer the assessment question at hand. Some questions require quantitative data and others require qualitative data. This chapter will provide an overview of two frequently used qualitative methods: interviews and focus groups.

Interviews

Interviews are frequently used to collect data. The assessor wants to understand participants' "feelings, intentions, meanings, subcontexts, or thoughts on a topic, situation, or idea" (Lichtman, 2012, p. 190), but interviews are not just casual conversations. They are informed by rigorous methods and research and require forethought and structure (as indicated by the type of interview) and guidelines for implementing them.

Advantages

There are advantages to interviews over other data-collection methods such as surveys. According to Wyse (2014) interviews can enable more accurate screening of participants because the interviewer can talk with the interviewee to gather and clarify demographic information. Interviews allow for capturing verbal and nonverbal cues. Similarly, interviews can capture emotions and behaviors. Video recording is helpful as it can otherwise be challenging to note all nonverbal activity. The interviewer controls the data collection and can keep the process on track.

Limitations

There are a number of disadvantages to interviews. First, interviews are resource-intensive. They take a great deal of time and effort to implement. Staff time translates into a financial cost as well as an opportunity cost for other activities that are not completed as staff perform interviews. Wyse (2014) suggests other limitations. Second, interviews can be the quality of data, as that depends on the skills of the interviewer. If there are multiple interviews, consistency of data across interviews can also be an issue. There may also be data entry error if notes and other data are hand-entered into an electronic format. Finally, the sample size is limited by the time available by staff. As noted in Chapter 10, it may take as many as 20 to 60 people to reach data saturation, but it is unlikely that staff will have enough time to interview 20 or more people.

Types of Interviews

There are essentially three types of interviews: structured, semistructured, and unstructured (Gall, Gall, & Borg, 2007). They are briefly reviewed here. Additional texts provide further detailed exploration (Denzin & Lincoln, 2011; Merriam & Tisdell, 2015; Patton, 2015).

With a structured interview, every participant is asked the same questions in the same order. The benefit of this approach is that the question protocol is standardized and implementation is straightforward (Lichtman, 2012). Responses to interview questions may be analyzed with predetermined codes (aligned with the foci of the inquiry and the questions themselves). In addition, a structured interview ensures consistency across interviewers if a team is used, which increases the trustworthiness of responses.

Semistructured interviews begin with a set of standard questions but utilize probing to search for additional, deeper information (Gall et al., 2007). Although the core questions are the same across participants, the interviewer may vary the additional probes depending on responses.

The final type of interview is the unstructured interview. In this format, there are no focused, standard questions; instead, there are general topics or big-picture questions to guide the interview. This is the most flexible interview format, but it can be challenging to administer as it requires synchronous attention to method and responses to best gather information related to the topic. There may not be a set interview guide for question conformity (Gall et al., 2007), but there may be a protocol of general, open-ended questions (Merriam & Tisdell, 2015). An unstructured interview resembles a conversation and can be free-flowing. These interviews are advantageous when very little is known about a phenomenon and the responses or results will be used to inform future studies and protocols.

There are advantages and disadvantages to each type of interview. As mentioned, a structured interview provides consistency of protocol from one interview to the next. But, depending on the purpose of the inquiry, this rigidity may limit the extent to which an interviewer can solicit clarification or elaboration. With more flexibility in the semistructured and unstructured formats, the interviewer can ask follow-up questions, but those questions can easily deviate from the purpose of the assessment if the interviewer is inexperienced or does not have a well-defined objective for the interview. With a goal of thick, rich description, the probes help and may provide the structure needed for interviewees who are less talkative. The unstructured interview provides the most flexibility, but it also might become a conversation without a purpose if there are no guiding questions or a clear goal. It is also the most challenging to analyze because of the inconsistent questions and answers.

Types of Questions

When preparing to conduct a set of interviews, it is important to consider the types of questions that could be asked. Fraenkel, Wallen, and Hyun (2014) have suggested six types of questions/prompts: background, knowledge, experience/behavior, opinion/values, feelings, and sensory.

Background questions or prompts help to clarify the background characteristics of participants and should be aligned with existing research on the inquiry topic, whereas knowledge questions get to the facts of a situation or phenomenon. Examples of background prompts may include "Please tell me about your educational background" or "Please tell me about the jobs you have held while you were a college student." Background questions can also be asked through a demographic profile sheet that includes pertinent information related to both the interviewee's demographics and other brief background information regarding the assessment.

A knowledge prompt could be "Tell me what you know about the Department of Student Involvement." Experience/behavior questions center on what participants do or have done; examples of these questions might include "Could you walk me through a typical day in your life?" or "Tell me about the responsibilities you have as a student leader on campus."

Opinion/value questions get to what participants think or value. Examples of these types of questions include "What do you think about the climate on campus for LGBT students?" or "What do you think the biggest strength of the Office of Student Involvement is?" followed by "What are the biggest weaknesses of the Office of Student Involvement?"

Feelings questions try to tap into the emotions of participants and include examples such as "Describe how you feel when you walk across campus at night" or "How are you feeling as you begin your job search?"

Sensory questions focus on what participants have seen, heard, tasted, and smelled. Examples of this type of question might be "When you attend a party, what do you see?" or "When you look at the campus population, what types of diversity do you observe?"

Lichtman (2012) has also discussed types of questions, but in a different way. She described question forms that included grand tour, concrete example, compare/contrast, new elements, and closing questions.

The grand tour question is meant to get a person to talk at length about a topic, going into detail regarding the phenomenon. Examples of a grand tour question could be "What is it like to access academic resources on this campus?" or "What concerns do you have as a first-generation college student?"

A concrete prompt allows the participant to provide a concrete example relating to an experience or a topic. Examples of concrete prompts may include these: "Give me an example of a microaggression you witnessed in the last week" or "Describe the conduct hearing you had last week."

A comparison/contrast prompt asks participants to compare and contrast different events or experiences. Examples of a comparison/contrast question could be "Tell me about the differences and similarities of being a leader in organization A compared to being a leader in organization B" or "Tell me how the climate in your residence hall has changed since the new policy was implemented at the beginning of the year."

A new element prompt allows the assessor to move to a new topic if a previous topic has been exhausted or the participant does not want to or is unable to talk about the previous topic. Examples of this type of question include "We have talked about the challenges of being a first-generation college student. Can you now tell me some of the benefits?" or "We have talked about the effectiveness of Career Development Services. Tell me about the effectiveness of Placement Services."

Closing prompts bring the interview to a close and provide an opportunity for participants to add anything else that they may want to say regarding the topic that has not yet been discussed. Examples of closing questions may include: "Is there anything else you would like to tell me regarding the Emerging Leaders Program?" or "Is there anything else you would like to discuss that we have not already covered?"

Pilot testing questions is a good practice with both interviews and focus groups. This helps determine if students understand the terms being used. For example, students may not know what a *microaggression* is. If they do not understand the term, they cannot answer the question. Pilot testing also ensures that the interviewee understands the question as intended. Additionally, by using testing questions, the interviewer also ensures that his or her questions yield unbiased data (Gall et al., 2007) and determines how much time will be needed to obtain the required answers.

Interview Implementation

Following is a general overview of an interview process. Further details may be found in texts on qualitative interviews (Denzin & Lincoln, 2011; Merriam & Tisdell, 2015; Patton, 2015). As with all assessment projects, the purpose of the assessment must be kept at the forefront. Using the purpose of the assessment as a beacon to guide the assessment process increases the chances of obtaining the needed answers to the research/assessment question(s).

Planning and Preparation

Before the interview is conducted, there are a number of tasks to be performed. The interview questions must be developed. This begins by identifying five to eight questions that should be covered to understand the issue being assessed. Using the types of questions just discussed, key questions to ask should be identified. In regard to the question order, easier and noninvasive questions should be put first. Starting with low-risk questions helps build rapport between the interviewer and interviewee. It is useful to develop two to three prompts or follow-up questions for each key question to solicit more information if needed. These questions can be turned into an interview protocol. An interview protocol is a guide to facilitate the interview or focus group. It would include the interview questions and space to write in (or type if using a computer) the participants' answers. The protocol might also incorporate the date, time, and location of the interview as well as the code or name of the person being interviewed (Creswell, 2012). Text that will be read to begin and end the interview would also be part of the protocol. In addition to the key prompts, there may also be possible probes to follow-up prompts. The protocol form may also include areas for the interviewer's reflections. A simple

Internet search will provide various samples of interview protocols. A recorder should be responsible for note taking so that the interviewer can establish rapport with the interviewee. If the interviewer does not have a recorder, it is best to record the interview and then transcribe the data. Transcription services are available to do the transcriptions and thus save time.

Pilot testing is a critical element of interview development because it helps ensure that the questions being asked will be understood as intended. In pilot testing, the interviewer follows the protocol as a practice and asks the practice participants if the prompts made sense and if anything was confusing. The interviewer should select a few participants who are similar to the target population but will not be part of the sample. The interview process is then implemented as planned. After completion of the interview, the interviewer seeks feedback on the process and prompts, identifying questions or places that need clarification. As stated previously, pilot testing also ensures that interview questions yield unbiased data (Gall et al., 2007) and indicates how much time will be needed to obtain the required answers.

In order to implement interviews for an assessment project, guidelines should be followed to ensure quality. The first step is identifying the people to be interviewed. Assessors should identify and select individuals who fit the criteria for the project. If the focus is discovering what students learn while living in the residence halls, talking with students who have never lived in the residence halls will not be useful. Individuals who have access to a group of participants, such as a director of residence life, can help to identify potential participants. The "snowball" method (Gall et al., 2007) can also be used. In this approach current participants are asked to identify other potential participants. It is also worthwhile to select participants who are interested and willing to talk.

One question all individuals new to conducting interviews ask concerns the number of participants. "How many is enough?" This is a difficult question to answer, as the goal of this type of assessment is to understand the phenomenon under study and the context surrounding it. The goal is data saturation. This means that as more people are interviewed, no new information is being generated (Corbin & Strauss, 2015). Usually 12 people is adequate to fully understand the issue being assessed, but there may be times when as few as six participants may be sufficient to clarify an issue (Guest, Bunce, & Johnson, 2006). Keep in mind that the more people interviewed, the more data collected and thus the more time needed for analysis. It is important to know that not all invitees will show up, and twice as many people may have to be invited to make sure that enough people participate.

Selecting an appropriate setting is a critical step in the interview process. Assessors want to make sure that participants feel comfortable enough to speak freely. A mutually agreed on location is often a public place or office space, but it is important to ensure that the space is quiet and that privacy be considered. There are frequently rooms in libraries and student unions that can be used. It is helpful to have a few possible locations in mind to suggest to the participants and ask them where they would feel most comfortable. Assessors should ask the participants if they would like the door left open or closed.

Conducting the Interview

After accessing the interview location, the next step is for the interviewer to make the participant feel comfortable and build trust and rapport. This begins with providing information regarding the purpose of the interview, how the information will be used, and how confidential the responses will be. Participants will be more honest if they believe that their responses will not be shared unless they choose to reveal them. Other strategies for building trust are the use of pseudonyms and allowing the participants to choose their own aliases. The interviewer can also offer to share transcripts with the participants to ensure that no identifying information is included. One effective way for an interviewer to build rapport with the participant is by sharing personal information. The information shared does not need to be sensitive, but making a personal connection increases trust. Even before starting the interview, the interviewer can make small talk about the weather, students' classes, an upcoming campus event, and so on, helping to put the interviewee at ease.

The assessor must decide how the information will be recorded. Recording can include handwritten or typed notes or question responses, audio recording, and video recording. Both video and audio recording allow the interviewer to focus solely on facilitating the interview, as he or she does not also have to keep detailed notes of the conversation. However, video recording may not be appropriate for specific conversations, such as asking members of the LGBT population about the process of coming out on campus or how safe trans-identified students feel on campus. One's visual image is identifiable and participants may be less likely to participate in the assessment. The institution's policies regarding human subjects research may also impact the types of recording that can be used.

Although video recording is the most complete method, as it captures both verbal and nonverbal communication, this type of recording also makes many people feel uncomfortable, which can negatively impact the amount and depth of information participants share. Audio recording may have a similar impact on interviewees. However, the impact is less now, given the ability of smartphones to capture conversations. Given the current prevalence of smartphones, the sight of one on a table may not feel threatening. A laptop computer can also be used for recording. In addition, there are pens that can capture audio recording as well as take notes, allowing the recording and notes to be synchronized. Many times people being interviewed forget that they are being recorded once the interview begins. If this type of documentation is going to be used, the interviewees' permission to record their responses should be obtained. When notes are taken, quotes should be included to exemplify summary findings. Identify key points in notes by highlighting them or marking them another way. The interviewer may also wish to note hunches or thoughts, but these should be noted in an explicit manner so as not to confuse these insights as quotes or comments from participants themselves. Additionally, there are human subjects considerations for some types of data collection. Some review boards may consider video recording more intrusive than audio recording and require specific consent, storage safeguards, and usage protocols.

Fraenkel et al. (2014) offer a number of considerations regarding behavior during the interview. An interviewer may need to ask the same question in different ways to make sure that he or she is being understood. Asking the interviewee to repeat a response also allows the interviewer to confirm the interviewee's understanding of the response. Leading questions can be avoided by asking open-ended questions that do not suggest a specific answer. Closed-ended questions should also be avoided, as they stifle conversation and in-depth answers. An example of a leading question is, "Can you tell me all of the reasons you like your residence hall director?" This question assumes that the interviewee likes the hall director. Questions should be asked one at a time. Finally, assessors should listen actively and be judicious with interruptions. When recordings are confirmed and the interview concludes, thank the interviewee for his or her time and walk him or her to the door. It is also appropriate to provide a small token (such as a free beverage at the dining hall, a discount coupon at the bookstore, or free tickets to an event on campus). This incentive can also be used to invite individuals to participate.

Postinterview Tasks

If an audio or video recording was made, it should be reviewed to make sure that it is understandable. Review any handwritten notes to make sure that they are legible, and take a moment to make sure that all comments are clearly understandable. It is much easier to clarify a comment immediately after an interview than to try to answer the question "What did I mean by that?" later on. The moderator and recorder may also confer to discuss and clarify notes taken during the interview to ensure agreement.

Focus Groups

Whereas interviews center around one interviewee at a time, focus groups are interviews with more than one person at a time, usually six to 12. But this description can be confusing because they are not sequential interviews where each person, in turn, answers the interviewer's questions, nor are they free-flowing, undirected discussions. Rather, the goal is to have the participants interact and build on the responses of others to provide information that could not be obtained in individual interviews. As such, focus groups are indicated when the topic of interest involves a social phenomenon. This approach increases the complexity of the data collected.

Advantages

Stewart, Shamdasani, and Rook (2006) have identified a number of advantages of focus groups. Although ease of collection should not be the guiding consideration when choosing data-collection methods, focus groups may allow data to be gathered more quickly and less expensively than could be done by interviewing participants individually. Unlike other methods, but like interviews, focus groups permit direct interaction between the moderator and participants. The open response format provides a large amount of rich data regarding the issue at hand. Unlike individual interviews, however, focus groups allow the participants to build on the responses of others. The flexibility of this method enables its use for a number of topics and settings, and results are easy to understand and use. In addition, there may be some topics that are especially appropriate for focus groups. The assessment of collective experiences may be one such topic. Focus groups would be better suited than interviews for identifying the pluses and minuses of being part of a student organization, a fraternity or sorority, or an athletic team.

Limitations

The focus of the assessment inquiry should drive the methods selection, and focus groups are not a substitute for individual interviews. For example, focus groups of college students may not be useful if perspectives and experiences considered invasive, risky, or controversial are being assessed. Participants may not divulge their attitudes or behaviors. There are also some disadvantages to the focus groups. Data from focus groups may not be generalizable to a larger population, but generalizability is not a goal of qualitative research. The interaction among the participants and moderator is a challenge, as individual responses can be influenced by other responses and a dominating member of the focus group can skew results. The moderator has to manage and facilitate the discussion. The flow and open-ended nature of the discussion make summarization difficult. The facilitator or moderator and note-taker roles should be explained to the participants at the outset. The moderator may also intentionally as well as unintentionally direct the conversation. This is one reason why staff should not facilitate interviews related to their own office or program. In college settings, securing participation in focus groups is challenging. Even participants who have committed to attend may not show up, so more people than are expected to attend should be invited. Despite these limitations, focus groups do have many advantages.

Focus Group Questions

Krueger (1998) has identified five types of questions/prompts for focus groups: opening, introductory, transition, key, and ending.

Types of Questions

Opening prompts are designed to be responded to quickly and build rapport with other members of the focus group. Examples include "Tell us your name and where you live" or "Tell us your name and a gift that was memorable to you." The purpose of this question is to help participants get connected to one another, not actually to gather such data. Demographic data can be collected on a demographic information sheet prior to the actual focus group. It is helpful to create a seating chart with names and/or pseudonyms of participants. Respondents to each question can be noted on the chart, making identification of participant responses easier.

Introductory questions introduce the topic of the focus group and allow participants to reflect on their experiences. These foster conversations but are not critical to analysis. Examples might include "When you hear the word *diversity*, what comes to mind?" or "What's your impression of residential life here on campus?"

Questions that move the conversation toward the key questions are called transition questions. Often, these questions ask participants to go into more depth about an experience. Examples may include "How have you been involved in service-learning while on campus?" or "Tell us about the activities you have participated in that have improved your problem-solving skills."

Key questions drive the study. There are typically two or three key questions for each study. Examples may include "What resources, including people, have helped you be academically successful on campus?" or "How have you changed in your time as a student at this college?"

Ending questions bring the focus group to closure, allowing participants to reflect on previous responses, add further comments, or sum up their thoughts on a topic. Examples might include "Suppose you were riding an elevator with the college president. What would you say to her about the Greek system on campus?" or "Of all the needs discussed so far, which is the most important?"

Krueger (1998) also suggests a pattern for asking these questions. The outline begins with an opening question, followed by an introductory question, which is then followed by a transition question. Next are three to five key questions followed by an ending question. Here is an example of a question set:

Opening	1. Tell us your name and where you live.
Introductory	2. How stressed would you say you are on a scale of 1 to 10?
Transition	3. What are the things that cause stress in your life?
Key	4. What would help you reduce stress in your life?
Key	5. Suppose that a workshop on stress is held. What would get you to attend?
Key	6. What would be useful to you to include in the destress workshop?
Ending	7. We are going to be putting together programs for residents on how to lower their stress. As we begin this project, what advice do you have for us?

Guidelines for Questions

Krueger (2006) provides a number of suggestions for developing and asking questions. He suggests using open-ended questions, which will elicit more information than closed-ended or dichotomous questions. Rather than asking "Why?," assessors should ask about attributes, characteristics, or influences, as these provide greater depth and clarity. Asking "why?" can sound accusatory; so instead of saying "Why did you decide X?" you can rephrase it to "How did you decide to do X?" or "What was the thought process that led you to decide X?" "Think back" questions help to provide a mental map for participants to reflect on their experiences. It is also helpful to use questions that get participants involved by having them provide examples, make a rating and explain the rating, fill in the blank, role play, or even draw. Focus questions help participants move from general experiences to more specific ones. Questions should serve as mental maps, helping the participants to situate themselves in the topic and move toward the key questions of the study.

An observational focus group is another option. With this type of focus group, the assessor observes individuals performing a task. For example, students in a computer lab might be asked to test residence life's new website. They might be given specific tasks (or no particular task) and could then provide feedback during the hands-on part as well as overall feedback in the course of conversations with their peers.

Focus Group Implementation

Once focus groups have been confirmed as the data-collection method and questions have been identified, participants must be identified. The goal is not necessarily to invite participants who are representative of the population from which they are drawn; rather, the goal is to foster conversation. Participants may be randomly or intentionally selected, depending on the topic. If the topic is the experiences of students of color on a predominantly White campus, there may be a focus group comprising random men and women of color. There may also be one group of students of color who live on campus and another group who live off campus, as their experiences may be different. Another focus group may comprise student athletes of color or students of color in fraternities or sororities, as the experiences of these students may be unique.

Recruitment of participants is challenging. Incentives can be useful for increasing attendance. Feeding participants during the focus group is a popular incentive. The assessor may also consider providing a gift card that could be used for the dining hall or off-campus store as a way to encourage participation. Even when individuals agree to participate, they may not show up. As a general guide, invite twice as many as you need, assuming that one third may not show up (D. Kniess, personal communication). If all show up, the group can be divided in two, in which case two moderators should be on hand.

Though not overly complicated, there are some steps important to implementing a successful focus group. Before actually implementing the discussion, a good location must be identified. The room must be quiet and also private to ensure the confidentiality of responses. The room should also be conducive to a conversation. A lounge setting is more apt to foster a discussion than sitting around a table.

Prior to the focus group discussion, the assessor should set chairs in a circle and set up any recording devices that may be used. If food such as pizza will be served as an incentive to get people to attend, this should also be delivered prior to the beginning of the discussion. Participants can eat while getting to know each other. All of the preparation should be completed 15 to 20 minutes before the start of the focus group so that the moderator can greet participants as they arrive. The moderator may want to give out a cell number in case participants have difficulty finding the location. This is crucial for focus groups held in a location unfamiliar to participants.

If there is a recorder assisting with note taking, the moderator and recorder should clarify roles and responsibilities well before the focus group takes place. Creating a list of responsibilities for each role will make these explicit for each person. The recorder may take notes, check and operate the recording device, and pay attention to time. This person does not engage with the members of the focus group, but having a person assigned to managing those tasks allows the moderator to focus solely on the participants and their responses.

At the beginning of the group, the moderator should explain the purpose of the discussion and how the results will be used. There should also be a discussion regarding confidentiality, including a statement that the data will be held confidential but also encouraging participants to keep the conversation confidential as well.

During the focus group, the moderator should focus on facilitating conversation with the two to three key questions in mind. Probing questions will be needed to draw out more information or to explain what has been said. Facilitating focus groups takes practice to be able to address dominant and nonparticipating members as well as to interpret the nonverbal communications of participants. The moderator may ask some participants to hold back on their input so as to give others the opportunity to speak or to invite quieter participants to speak. Frequently a focus group will go off topic. The moderator should take care not to bias the conversation by leading participants in a specific direction (Stewart et al., 2006).

As the focus group concludes, the moderator should thank the participants, reiterating the purpose of the focus group and how the data will be used. The recorder may also summarize the conversation and the moderator should offer to share results with the participants once they are compiled.

After the participants have left, the recording equipment should be checked to ensure that the discussion was recorded properly. If a recorder was also present, the recorder and moderator may debrief the focus group and review any notes taken. The moderator will also want to take a few moments to reflect on the discussion and any main points raised and to document these to assist the analysis later.

Conclusion

Interviews and focus groups are qualitative methods used to gather assessment data. Both methods can provide in-depth, descriptive data that richly describe a social phenomenon studied. Responses from participants are used to not only identify themes but also provide "texture" for the themes, helping them come to life. Although interviews and focus groups may seem easy to implement, facilitating discussion and selecting questions to yield useful data requires practice and diligence. When an assessor decides that a focus group method is a useful approach to investigate an inquiry, adequate preparation is required to secure skilled facilitation and appropriate data capturing. The quickest or easiest way is frequently not the best way, because often qualitative methods such as interviews and focus groups are the best data-collection methods to answer a question and thus worth the time and effort.

Key Points

- A key to assessment success is selecting a data-collection method that best answers the assessment question.
- There are three types of interviews: structured, semistructured, and unstructured.
- There are six types of interview prompts: background questions, knowledge questions, experience/behavior questions, opinions/values questions, feelings questions, and sensory questions.
- Focus groups have five types of prompts: opening questions, introductory questions, transition questions, key questions, and ending questions.
- Pilot testing is essential for both interviews and focus groups to make sure that participants understand the language and intent of questions.

Discussion Questions and Activities

- What are similarities and differences between interviews and focus groups?
- What are similarities and differences among the focus groups?
- What are the advantages and disadvantages of interviews?
- What are the advantages and disadvantages of focus groups?
- You have been asked to interview student athletes to elucidate their experience on campus. Describe how you would establish rapport with the students. List three key questions to be asked in the interview, including two probes or follow-up questions for each key question.
- Your institution is planning on building a new residence hall and the administration wants student input regarding the type of facilities such as classrooms, labs, and snack shops that should be included. As the assistant director of residence life, you have been tasked with facilitating focus groups to gather the data. Using the focus group seven-question sample question set discussed earlier, develop a question set for these focus groups.

12

ADDITIONAL ASSESSMENT
METHODS

Although surveys and focus groups are the "go to" assessment methods, there are a myriad of other options of which student affairs professionals should be aware. Many of these are more effective and easier to implement than traditional methods and may be more appropriate to the situation—maybe even more fun! They can be formal or informal, qualitative or quantitative, time-consuming or fairly quick. Some methods use indirect evidence of student learning (students' perceptions of their learning), whereas others provide direct evidence (students' demonstration of their learning). Methods can also be formative (during an experience, where changes can be made) or summative (at the end of an experience). Knowing the options and assessment purpose allows customization of the assessment for the individual context.

This chapter provides descriptions of a variety of methods that student affairs staff can use in a variety of settings to measure student learning in the cocurricular area. Rubrics and portfolios will be covered in some depth. In addition, observations, learning contracts, classroom assessment techniques, narratives, reflexive photography, and document review will be highlighted.

Rubrics

Today's college students are probably familiar with rubrics, which measure specific performance, because rubrics are used in the K–12 educational system. Stevens and Levi (2013) define a *rubric* as a "scoring tool that lays out the specific expectations for an assignment" (p. 3) and describes acceptable levels of performance. Thus, rubrics can be both educational, by providing direction for performance, and evaluative. Suskie (2009) has described rubrics as lists or charts that are flexible in design and include criteria used to score student work.

Suskie (2009) explains a variety of rubrics to illustrate the fact that they are flexible assessment methods. The simplest is the checklist, which determines whether or not a specific construct is present. More complex rubrics include a rating scale, which specifies the degree to which the constructs are present (e.g., see p. 186, this volume). The descriptive rubrics have not only a rating scale but also a narrative in each cell that explains the performance level. Holistic scoring guides give the rater a scale with which to rate an entire artifact or demonstration of a skill. Structured scoring guides give raters categories in which to make comments without using a quantitative rating scale.

Uses

Rubrics may be appropriate for advisors working with student organization leaders, supervisors working with student employees, and even student conduct administrators rating reflective papers assigned as sanctions. These not only designate current performance but also describe what better performance looks like. In many cases it is appropriate to show students the rubric so that they will know what level they want to achieve as they move through an experience.

Rubrics can be used as repeated measures to provide direct evidence of student learning. At the beginning of an experience, the student can self-evaluate while the advisor/supervisor also evaluates the student. When they meet, they can discuss areas of agreement and disagreement as well as set goals for improved performance, and the same process can take place once or twice more. The student can keep the rubrics as artifacts of learning.

Advantages

Rubrics have several advantages. Although the nine listed here relate to classroom assignments, they certainly can be adapted to the out-of-class experiences (Suskie, 2009).

1. "Rubrics help clarify vague, fuzzy goals" (p. 139). Staff want students to develop leadership skills but need to define exactly what that entails so that students can know on what areas to focus.
2. "Rubrics help students understand your expectations" (p. 139). Sharing the rubric with students describes performance levels and indicates where they should focus their development.
3. "Rubrics can help students self-improve" (p. 139). Not only can faculty and staff use the rubrics to evaluate students' work, but students can use

them to reflect on their performance. If the student and a supervisor/advisor both rate a student's work, they can compare the similarities and differences and focus on improvements.

4. "Rubrics can inspire better student performance" (p. 139). If students know what exemplary performance looks like, they can strive to meet that level. Not all students are motivated by that; the staff member must also consider the developmental level of each student (a freshman's strong performance and a senior's strong performance may look different).

5. "Rubrics make scoring easier and faster" (p. 139). Once the rubric is created and tested, it facilitates scoring. Although staff are not usually giving grades, they may be reviewing numerous examples of student work in a short period of time.

6. "Rubrics make scoring more accurate, unbiased, and consistent" (p. 139). Having a rubric keeps the important concepts at the forefront.

7. "Rubrics improve feedback to students" (p. 139). Because of the explicit descriptors most rubrics use, students know where they are performing well and where they need to improve.

8. "Rubrics reduce arguments with students" (p. 139). With a standard rating scale, students can see objectively how their performance rates.

9. "Rubrics improve feedback to faculty and staff" (p. 139). If advisors or supervisors see a trend in students not demonstrating a specific skill, they can use that to plan additional training or other interventions to improve performance.

Limitations

Although rubrics have advantages, they also pose some challenges. Like all assessment methods, they take time to develop, especially at the beginning of the process. Novice developers may have to pilot several drafts before implementing a final product. That task is more challenging if the learning outcomes and desired performance have not been determined. Once the rubric has been implemented, it must be reviewed to determine its usefulness and accuracy. If staff and students are not used to rating and being rated by this method, it may seem awkward or too structured for an out-of-class experience. In addition, if more than one person will be rating, the raters must be trained to be consistent in scoring. Rubrics are not always the appropriate method to assess learning experiences, but they can be a valuable direct method to use.

Implementation

Before the rubric is created, the learning outcome or outcomes must be accurately described. This provides the overall goal of learning and performance.

In academic courses, the outcome could be the result of a completed assignment, but in the cocurricular area, that could be a component of leadership skills or one of the institution's learning outcomes.

Next, that outcome can be separated into very specific behaviors or skills that are observable and describable. For example, written communication can be evaluated on not only spelling, grammar, punctuation, and sentence structure but also message and content. Stevens and Levi (2013) called those *dimensions*. The number of dimensions or criteria needs to be manageable yet thorough enough to describe the skill or competency.

The levels of performance (scales) can range from two (yes/no) to five or seven. To keep the rubric manageable, consider the number of scale points that are needed to determine whether participants have mastered a skill. Examples include these:

Beginner/Intermediate/Advanced
Benchmark (1)/Milestone (2)/Milestone (3)/Capstone (4) (Association of
   American Colleges & Universities, 2015a)
Needs attention/adequate/very good/excellent (Suskie, 2009, p. 150)

Each of those behaviors, in turn, can be described in more detail based on the expected levels of performance. Those descriptions qualitatively indicate the behavior for each of the scales unless the rubric is specifically designed as a rating scale rubric.

The Association of American Colleges and Universities (2015b) has created a variety of rubrics called Valid Assessment of Learning in Undergraduate Education, or VALUE for short. The AAC&U states that "VALUE provides needed tools to assess students' own authentic work, produced across their diverse learning pathways and institutions, to determine whether and how well they are progressing toward graduation-level achievement in learning outcomes that both employers and faculty consider essential" (para. 1). The 16 rubrics based on the AAC&U Essential Learning Outcomes are divided into three categories:

1. Intellectual and Practical Skills (inquiry and analysis, critical thinking, creative thinking, written communication, oral communication, reading, quantitative literacy, information literacy, teamwork, and problem solving)
2. Personal and Social Responsibility (civic engagement—local and global, intercultural knowledge and competence, ethical reasoning, foundations and skills for lifelong learning, and global learning)
3. Integrative and Applied Learning (integrative learning)

Each rubric has five to six dimensions to rate performance. For example, the Oral Communication VALUE rubric dimensions include organization, language, delivery, supporting material, and central message based on a Benchmark (1), Milestone (2), Milestone (3), and Capstone (4) scale. Each scale has a description of performance level. The AAC&U has created rubrics using input from faculty and administrators and have also acknowledged that campuses must adapt them to their own contexts. The VALUE rubrics can be accessed from www.aacu.org/value/rubrics.

In creating rubrics, use the resources available, at least as a starting point. For example, the AAC&U VALUE rubrics already exist in the context of higher education and can be adapted. An Internet search can also provide examples for specific topics. Because rubrics are more common in K–12 education and for classroom experiences, student affairs staff may need to do extensive revamping. Campus faculty can also be valuable resources as subject matter experts and may already have developed rubrics for their courses. Also available from an Internet search are online tools that can assist with rubric development.

As rubrics are being developed and implemented, work with others to norm the rubric. As an example, if advisors want to measure critical thinking using a case study rated by a rubric, they will want to agree on the dimensions and ratings of the rubric. What are the components of critical thinking? What do advanced critical thinking skills look like? In addition, before they begin scoring, they will want to practice interrater reliability, also called calibration. This means that there will be agreement about what constitutes a low score versus a high score. After the first round of using rubrics, staff can provide feedback to improve the rubric before using it again.

Portfolios

In some academic programs (e.g., art and architecture), portfolios are a common assessment method to demonstrate student performance. Although portfolios have been used to assess learning in general education and in the major, they are also used to assess learning in cocurricular programs (Banta & Palomba, 2015). Portfolios are qualitative assessment tools with a great deal of potential for student affairs assessment. "Portfolios are collections of student evidence accompanied by rationale for the contents and student reflections on the learning illustrated by the evidence" (Driscoll & Wood, 2007, p. 88). This method supports both formative and summative assessment of student learning.

Huba and Freed (2000) have identified two main goals for the use of portfolios. The first is to evaluate learning. Portfolios provide an opportunity to evaluate learning in a specific program, learning across experiences, or student development over time. The second goal is to promote learning. Since reflection is a key element of portfolios, they are one of the powerful tools that assess and foster learning at the same time.

Suskie (2009) has defined six criteria for portfolios:

1. Portfolios have a clear purpose to help students learn and demonstrate their learning.
2. Students have a choice about what to include in the portfolio (although some criteria might be specified).
3. Portfolios are assessed using a set criterion (e.g., rubric).
4. Portfolios illustrate growth by including early work and later work in a particular area or by providing documentation about the process a student went through in creating the product.
5. Portfolios are dynamic in that students can continually update the content as they develop skills in particular areas.
6. Portfolios include student reflection to synthesize learning and develop metacognition skills.

The focus on reflection is a main distinguishing feature of this assessment method. In order to respond to their own artifacts, students need to develop their own critical and reflective thinking skills.

Implementation

Whereas portfolios have their genesis in the classroom, they can be applied to experiences outside the classroom as well. Portfolios can be used to document learning and development through structured experiences such as leadership development programs, student organization involvement, or student employment such as being a resident assistant (RA), orientation leader, peer educator, or organization leader. This tool would also be useful to demonstrate learning across experiences, including a variety of leadership experiences on campus or participation in a myriad of service-learning opportunities. It could also be used to track growth in general across time and across the entire educational experience—both in and outside of the classroom. The key is to align this tool to established outcomes for a program, a department, a division, or an institution.

Portfolios have some typical content. Suskie (2009) outlined the sections to include a table of contents, examples of student work, evidence of learning and growth, a student overall reflection page, a faculty evaluative summary, an introductory statement, student reflections on each item in the portfolio, and faculty comments on each item. Some institutions have an integrated and online portfolio system that includes out-of-class accomplishments and reflections. Bass (2014) has characterized ePortfolios as a way for students to integrate learning across multiple experiences as well as to combine a record of their learning with the institutional measures of learning. Portfolio options are built into many assessment management systems as well as open-source software made available through Open Source Portfolio (OSP), a nonproprietary organization (Maki, 2010). Free website platforms also provide easy-to-use solutions for portfolios. Students can also upload a variety of artifacts, from written material to websites to audiovisual presentations. If the portfolio integrates both curricular and cocurricular experiences around university outcomes, for example, a student could provide examples of communication proficiency by including a research paper and a video that shows her presiding over a student organization meeting.

Angelo and Cross (1993) have suggested using an annotated portfolio that would represent a sample of student work along with an explanation, written by the student, of how it relates to specific goals. This assessment method may be appropriate for student leaders who will be producing a product, such as a budget, agendas/minutes, marketing materials, planning documents, and so on. With technological advances, it is now easy even to video record a student making a presentation or to provide a link to a student-designed website. The portfolio could be organized by leadership goals or reflective questions.

Advantages

There are a number of benefits to using portfolios in student affairs assessment. As discussed earlier, portfolios are valuable because they both assess and promote complex learning. Given the portability of a portfolio, students can use the artifacts or links to the ePortfolios for job interviews or graduate school applications. These tools engage both students and staff in the learning and assessment process. Staff feedback is crucial for both assessment and promotion of learning through portfolios. Feedback not only assists in documenting outcome achievement and identifying opportunities for program improvement but also helps students see in what areas they are performing well and how to improve. Additionally, these portfolios reward student work as artifacts and can be a source of pride and accomplishment.

Portfolios are advantageous because they provide documentation of student learning in one location that can be enhanced over time. They allow students to demonstrate their strengths and understanding (Sternberg, Penn, & Hawkins, 2011). Students can use their portfolios with potential employers to demonstrate their application of learning, ability to synthesize and analyze, and skill in the reflection and transference of their own learning. If an institution is already using a portfolio system to evaluate curricular work, it may be adapted to include cocurricular experiences. Portfolios provide direct measures of student learning and can motivate students to fully engage in the learning process and develop reflective skills.

In addition to being a useful assessment tool, the portfolio benefits students in many ways. Huba and Freed (2000) have identified the following benefits:

- Develop a view of themselves as learners
- Understand more deeply what they have learned and not learned
- Develop a sense of learning as ongoing through life
- Develop a better understanding of how they learn and what they value
- Gain feedback for improvement from stakeholders who view their portfolios
- Understand how their work is viewed by others
- Develop a better understanding of the faculty's intended learning outcomes
- See relationships among courses
- See relationships among in- and out-of-class learning experiences
- Become more aware of and invested in their own learning
- Become conscious of the role writing plays in learning (p. 263)

Limitations

Portfolios have disadvantages in the out-of-class context. If a portfolio system is not currently in place, significant logistical resources (time, energy, technology, funding, etc.) will be required to create one. As an assessment tool, it requires a process to be in place to determine who will be evaluating which student work at what point in time based on a predetermined set of criteria. This may not be a manageable undertaking for student affairs professionals, who must be realistic about the time and resources needed to evaluate a portfolio (Walvoord, 2010). If portfolios are used only in the out-of-class context, students and staff may not buy into the process because perceived costs (time to collect and reflect on artifacts, development of an evaluation process, not knowing the purpose and audience of the portfolio, etc.) outweigh the perceived benefits (direct evidence of learning, collection of artifacts, etc.).

If staff want to undertake portfolios as an assessment method, they should start with a manageable portfolio size and number of students. Because they can be difficult to score and require expertise (Sternberg et al., 2011), the process must be carefully developed. A team of staff need to develop the content guidelines and other logistics to make the portfolio usable and useful. Staff also need to consider what will motivate students to participate in the process because they will not be receiving a grade as part of a course requirement.

Observations

Whereas interviews and focus groups require talking with participants to gather data, information can be obtained by observation as well. Student affairs educators make observations constantly. However, those observations are rarely systematic in a way that leads to quality inferences and decision making.

Forms of Observation

There are four forms of observation that can be used in assessment. *Participant observation* is where the assessor is actually participating in the situation or setting that is being observed (Fraenkel, Wallen, & Hyun, 2014, p. 444). An example of participant observation would be that of a director of new student orientation who wants to assess the impact of orientation leader training. Since the director is helping to facilitate the training while also observing the impact, both activities are part of the setting and the experience. *Nonparticipant observation* involves observers who are not directly involved in the activity but watch from outside of the situation (Fraenkel et al., 2014). Observing how the executive board of a student organization functions to assess leadership skill of those members would be an example of nonparticipant observation. In *naturalistic observation*, the assessor makes no effort to manipulate variables or control the activities of participants (Fraenkel et al., 2014). An example of this type of observation would be monitoring the location of cigarette butts to assess the impact of a policy that smoking must occur at least 20 feet from the entrance to campus buildings. In *simulation observation*, participants are given certain tasks to perform and are observed doing those tasks (Fraenkel et al., 2014). An example of simulation observation may be residential life professional staff observing RAs engaging in "behind closed doors" training to evaluate their readiness for their jobs. In such training, RAs must address a situation in a residence hall room that is being role-played by other students or staff. Often the RA does not know what awaits until he or she knocks on the door.

Another observation option is using "secret shoppers." Supervisors of student employees who provide customer service on a regular basis might set up fake customers who have scripts to interact with the student employees. The customers may be given a rubric or survey questions to rate the employees' performance. The rating areas might be greeting customers (or answering the phone), answering questions, dressing appropriately, being friendly, and so on. The supervisor can use the evaluations to provide feedback to individuals and determine the effectiveness of training.

Documenting the Observations

As noted earlier, people make observations constantly. However, little of this observation is systematic. One way to systematize the process is to take diligent notes to document what is observed for analysis at a later time. An observation protocol is used for this documentation (Creswell, 2012). Some protocols are quite basic and simply include the location of the observation, start time, and stop time noted at the top with two columns below. The left column includes the detailed observations, and the right column is used for reflective notes (Creswell, 2012). Mapping, photographs, and audio/video recordings are additional ways to document observations.

Errors Related to Observations

There are a number of issues to consider when employing observation. The first set of issues relates to effects of the observer on the observation. In some cases, the fact that a group of individuals is being observed will affect behavior. Observer biases are errors that result from the personal characteristics of the observer (Gall, Gall, & Burg, 2007). Observer contamination can occur when the observer's knowledge of a phenomenon influences the data collected (Gall et al., 2007). For example, in the "behind closed doors" example, if the observer knows who the top-performing RAs are based on their performance evaluations, that knowledge may influence how effective the observer believes the RA is in this activity. In this scenario, the observer may overrate the performance of those RAs who had strong performance evaluations. Another error, observer omission, occurs when the observer does not document a behavior in the protocol (Gall et al., 2007). Observer drift occurs when the observer redefines the variables under study so that the data collected earlier no longer match variable definitions (Gall et al., 2007).

Learning Contracts/Development Plans

Learning contracts, which can also be considered professional development plans, allow students to individually create plans to address an outcome or competency. Students define the goals, objectives, learning methods, and assessment methods. Ideally, the students get feedback in the beginning of the process to improve their plans. During the process, if students have an accountability partner (a peer, an advisor, or a supervisor), they can check in on a regular basis. At the end of the contract term, students demonstrate the accomplishment of their goals. The advantage to this method is that it allows individuals to choose an area in which they want to develop. It can be tied to the curriculum (perhaps the institution's learning outcomes) or to a particular student experience. The disadvantage is that the assessment is not easy to aggregate as evidence of student learning among a group of people.

As an example, students could be given several areas to address in a leadership learning contract in their first month in the position.

> First, describe how this position relates to your curricular or career interests and how you will make an impact. Use the SMARRT method (specific, measurable, ambitious but attainable, results-oriented, relevant, and time-bound) to define your goals for the year. Second, articulate your learning outcomes/objectives, which identify specific knowledge or skills you want to accomplish by the end of the experience. If applicable, connect each outcome to the university's learning outcomes. Third, describe the learning methods you will use to achieve the outcomes (take a course, read books or articles, seek feedback on performance, interview experts, etc.). Fourth, explain how the outcomes will be demonstrated to show proficiency and how they will be evaluated (e.g., monthly presentations will be given in the student organization meetings; peer-used rubrics will be used to rate performance; the score will improve from an average of 2.5 to at least 3.5 by the end of the year).

Once the leadership learning contract has been submitted, the advisor/supervisor provides feedback about the proposal through a rubric or simple feedback. The students then prepare a second draft if needed. Throughout the experience, the advisor, supervisor, or peer accountability partner provides feedback. The peer accountability partner could be a student in the same organization or activity who can give honest, regular feedback to promote completion of a goal. At the end of the experience, the students demonstrate their proficiency or write a reflective paper about their learning process.

The word *contract* does not resonate with some students. If that happens, the learning contract can be called learning agreement, professional development plan, or something else that interests students. In addition, the content of the contract can be adapted to meet the needs of the students and the experience, depending on the developmental level of the student and the length and content of the experience. Contracts can also be used with other assessment techniques.

Classroom Assessment Techniques

Numerous assessment activities used in the classroom can be easily adapted to the out-of-class environment. Wehlburg (2008) enumerated several characteristics of these techniques: They should be learner-centered, teacher-directed, mutually beneficial to the student and teacher, formative in nature, context-specific, ongoing, and rooted in good teaching practices (pp. 33–35). They are used to gather evidence of student learning that an instructor can use to improve specific learning. Students have the opportunity to engage in their own learning and development. In *Classroom Assessment Techniques*, Angelo and Cross (1993) described numerous methods to assess student learning. Many of those techniques can be adapted to out-of-classroom experiences.

One-Minute Paper

One-minute papers can easily be used at the end of a program, a meeting, or an experience to gather feedback. Participants are asked to use one minute to answer a predetermined question or two, usually writing it on an index card or half sheet of paper. The responses can be anonymous or participants can put their name or other identifier on the paper if absolutely necessary. The advantage is that this assessment method takes little time to implement and analyze. The disadvantage is that the amount of time does not allow a depth of response. If the technique is overused, students may tire of the experience and not take it seriously.

The questions need to be designed carefully. Although only one or two questions are provided, they need to be of the highest quality to provide useful results. When the responses are collected, the program coordinator can review the responses for any themes or commonalities. If the participants are an intact group, the responses can be used to spark discussion or clarification at the next meeting. If the group is there just for the one program, the presenter can still take the feedback to improve the experience for the next group.

Examples include the following:

What is the most significant piece of learning you learned from this program?
How will you apply what you learned?
How would you explain this topic to a friend or family member?

Muddiest Point

A similar process can be used to determine the "muddiest point" (Angelo & Cross, 1993, p. 154). Simply put, the assessor asks students to briefly identify what was most confusing about a learning experience on an index card. While this is a fast and easy assessment method, some students may find it difficult at first to articulate what they did not understand. The themes and suggestions of the responses can be analyzed for what information needs to be clarified. If the facilitator meets with the group again, they can clarify confusing points. The themes can be used to make improvements to program delivery.

Misconception/Preconception Check

Another classroom assessment technique that can be adapted for out-of-classroom experiences, especially presentations, is the misconception/preconception check (Angelo & Cross, 1993). As Angelo and Cross describe, "It's much harder for students to unlearn incorrect or incomplete knowledge than to master new knowledge" (p. 132). Asking students to anonymously respond to several brief questions at the beginning of an experience can help students integrate new and correct information into their thinking. This could be particularly beneficial for topics such as alcohol and drug education, sexual health, study abroad, or service-learning—any area in which students may have developed inaccurate information. The presenter identifies the challenging topical areas, creates a short questionnaire, anticipates the answers and how they will be addressed in the learning environment, and explains the purpose and use of the assessment to students. Questions could be short-answer, multiple-choice, or even statements followed by answer choices, such as "I'm absolutely certain this is true, I'm pretty sure it is true, I have no idea whether it's true or false, I'm pretty sure it is false, I'm absolutely certain it is false" (p. 134). This approach could also be used in a pre-post format to measure change.

Focused Autobiographical Sketches

Angelo and Cross (1993) provide several examples of techniques that assess students' self-awareness as learners. Although their examples are course-related, they can be adapted to students' experiences in the cocurriculum. In the focused autobiographical sketch (Angelo & Cross, 1993, p. 281), students write about a single learning experience relevant to a particular program or activity. Students need opportunities to reflect on how experiences influence their learning and development. The person working with the program determines the focus of the assessment to make it manageable for the students—what students will address (experience, time frame, role, etc.). Then he or she determines how the product will be assessed (rubric, for qualitative themes, etc.) and creates clear instructions for students. This method allows students to develop self-awareness about a focused experience and permits the assessor to get feedback about an important aspect of the program. On the other hand, the analysis of the artifacts is not always clear-cut, and finding time to read all of the papers, even if they are relatively short, can be a challenge.

Sample prompts include the following:

(For a service-learning experience) In one to two pages, describe an experience where you served your community for a specific purpose. Focus on what you learned and how this will impact your future contribution to social issues.

(For an intact student organization leadership experience) In one page, describe a conflict you had with another person that was resolved successfully. What were your actions to make it a success? What did you learn that you can transfer to other experiences?

Focused Listing

Focused listing can be used to assess prior knowledge, recall, or understanding. In this method students are asked to recall what they know about a particular topic or concept. Focused listing might be a useful needs assessment in a leadership development class to better understand what knowledge students already have. An example might be the following: "Please identify the characteristics of a successful leader." This method could also be used after a discussion on leadership style or skills to see how much information students retained from the discussion. A focused listing question might be "Identify all of the traits of charismatic leadership."

Empty Outlines

Empty outlines are for educational programming. This technique can serve as an educational guide as well as a test to assess recall of information. Many people who facilitate programs develop a detailed outline regarding content to share during the session. In this technique, selected words are deleted from that outline. This empty outline could then be given to students at the beginning of the program to keep them engaged as they pay attention for the words to fill in the blanks. For assessment, the empty outlines could be given at the end of the session and students would be asked to fill in the blanks. The number of correct, incorrect, and empty blanks could be tallied to demonstrate acquired knowledge, and the incorrects and blanks could be analyzed to determine how the program could be changed to increase the number of correct items.

One-Sentence Summary

A one-sentence summary helps foster and assess synthesis and critical thinking. This method asks students to summarize an activity or a set of information but do so in only one sentence. This method gives students practice in taking a large amount of information and condensing it into smaller, integrated pieces (Angelo & Cross, 1993). It also enables educators to find out how concisely, completely, and creatively students can summarize a large amount of information. This would be a useful technique for student activities staff who meet with students to discuss event registration processes. At the end of the meeting, the staff member could ask the student to summarize the process in one sentence.

Directed Paraphrasing

Like the one-sentence summary format, directed paraphrasing assesses application and performance. Directed paraphrasing is an assessment technique designed to assess and help develop the ability to translate highly specialized information into language that clients or customers understand (Angelo & Cross, 1993). Students are directed to paraphrase part of a policy or practice for a specific audience and purpose. This method provides feedback on students' ability to summarize and restate important information or concepts in their own words. Describing the alcohol policy to students at a first-floor meeting in a residence hall is often a scary event for many new RAs. The RAs do not want to be seen as policy enforcers in their very first formal interaction with residents, but their supervisors are also expecting them to be accurate in their description of policy. Directed paraphrasing is a useful educational and assessment tool. During a staff meeting or one-on-one meeting, a hall director could ask each RA to paraphrase the alcohol policy in the way they would tell their floor. This provides an opportunity for the RA to practice this along with providing the hall director an opportunity to review the paraphrase for accuracy and offer suggestions and revisions.

Documented Problem Solutions

The bane of many high school students' existences was the requirement to show all work in math problems to get full points on a problem. Documented problem solutions is similar. This technique, centering on problem solving, prompts students to keep track of the steps they take in solving a problem—to "show and tell" how they worked it out (Angelo & Cross, 1993). By analyzing these detailed protocols, in which each solution step is briefly explained in writing, educators can gain valuable information on their students' problem-solving skills. Documenting problem solutions has the following aims: (a) to assess how students solve problems and (b) to assess how well students understand and can describe their problem-solving methods. This might be a helpful tool for RA or orientation leader training. Students could be given scenarios or case studies that they could expect to encounter and then asked to articulate their solution to the dilemma and describe their decision-making process.

Application Cards

Application cards are useful to foster and evaluate application and integrative learning. After students have heard or read about an important principle, generalization, theory, or procedure they receive an index card and are asked to write down at least one possible real-world application for what they have just learned (Angelo & Cross, 1993). Students who serve on student organization executive boards could be asked how what they are learning in this setting could be used in their classes. After a program regarding effective oral communication, students may be asked to give three examples in which they could apply the information they learned. In addition to helping educators understand if students grasp certain topics, this method helps students connect learning to different parts of their lives.

Narratives

Also a form of qualitative design, narratives are a powerful assessment tool because, in addition to providing useful assessment information, they foster learning through reflection about an experience that employs metacognition and synthesis (Suskie, 2009, p. 185). Journaling can take many forms, from Twitter posts that are 140 characters or less to multiple-page reflection papers. The goal is for students to describe experiences as a means to articulate what they are learning.

Students document their experience over time in either a handwritten or electronic journal. Journals can simply be descriptive, but from an assessment perspective it is more helpful to also include reflection on experiences. The inclusion of thoughtful prompts daily or weekly can help evoke this type of reflection.

Similar to journals are blogs, which can be public, private, or semiprivate depending on the purpose of the blog. The benefit of blogs is that they can easily be archived for later analysis. Blogs have become a popular way for individuals to share their lives, thoughts, and feelings with the public. As such, they may be more readily accepted by college students than journals.

The documentation of experience and reflection in blogs can be enhanced by the inclusion of photos or videos. Free websites such as Wix, Weebly, and WordPress can be used for blogs. There are also tools such as edublogs; these are specifically set up for student blogs and provide settings for how the blogs can be shared.

Microblogging in the form of Twitter is a growing trend in higher education. Students, faculty, and colleges alike are using the tool to share their thoughts and connect with each other. It is also being used in the classroom to foster engagement (Junco, Heiberger, & Loken, 2011). Microblogging could be used to foster discussion regarding a topic or reflections regarding an experience. The Twitter feed could then be archived and analyzed for themes.

Reflection papers are another form of narrative that is often used in student affairs. In this form of narrative, students write two papers, each about five pages in length, regarding their experience. This is a common educational sanction in student conduct cases. Given the length of these papers, it is typically difficult to have students write them voluntarily. When used, reflection papers offer a depth of reflection and experience that can be mined to elucidate the shared experience of a group of people.

The key to successful use of narrative assessment is the prompt. Without a clear, concise, and thought-provoking prompt, participants may provide brief statements that do not include rich data. Students may be good at writing the what (e.g., what the service-learning trip entailed), but they are not always as good about the why or the how (e.g., how the service-learning trip affected their opinion of a social issue or their likelihood to get involved in a community organization). Suskie (2009) makes four suggestions regarding how to get useful information. First, ask both pros and cons of an issue that forces participants to see at least two sides of the issue. Second, questions that are uncomfortable should be avoided as people will not provide honest responses. Third, questions should be phrased in a way that will elicit insightful replies. Finally, people should be allowed to admit they do not know or do not have a response. In some situations, that is appropriate.

For students who need structure in their narratives, one option is to use a version of "What? So what? Now what?" They can describe a significant experience they had, what they learned, where they learned it, and how they learned it. Then, they can describe why that was important and to whom. It provides more context. Finally, they can explore how they will apply what they have learned in future contexts or what they will do differently based on their learning.

Reflexive Photography

Reflexive photography, also called photovoice, allows for meaning to be created by a person taking a picture and reflecting on it, although it could also be that participants are reflecting on a picture taken by someone else. Harrington and Schibik (2003, p. 24) have described it as a "phenomenologically-oriented, individual-environment interaction" technique. The pictures initiate reflections and conversations, particularly about social change issues (Cook & Buck, 2010). Interpretation of the photograph may elicit associations or ideas that may not be obvious at first glance (Harper, 1988). This method provides an opportunity for students to reflect on experiences or questions using pictures as a prompt for their text or oral presentation. Most people today can take pictures with their phones; students frequently post pictures and comments on social media that could be analyzed for deeper meaning. As technological advances continue, more people also have access to video as a means of data collection and interpretation.

Reflection and photography could be used during student experiences that encourage students to think critically and deeply about a particular topic. For example, students who attend a week-long "alternative spring break" service trip may be assigned to photograph the experience and to journal about specific pictures. They could be asked to keep a video diary that records their reflections. The questions could address not only the topic of their service but also the root causes of the need, the impact of the service on the community, what they learned from the people they worked with, and how this changed their involvement in their community for the future. This method could also be used for study abroad experiences, in student leadership or organizational experiences, or in first-year experiences, for example. Additionally, a sample of students could be recruited to take pictures that answer a particular question of interest. For example, if the topic of the assessment is inclusive spaces on campus, students could be asked to take pictures of places where they personally feel included and excluded. Alternatively, students could be asked to reflect on or react to pictures that someone else has taken.

Assessment of the reflection could be done by using a rubric, rating presentations that students make, or documenting conversations that students have as a group. The rubric could rate students on their ability to analyze an issue, synthesize their learning, or describe their learning. As a programmatic assessment, the reflections could be qualitatively analyzed to understand what students have gleaned from an experience. The assessment is not about the quality of the photograph itself, so students should know they will not be evaluated in that respect.

The University of Minnesota's Orientation & First-Year Programs (2014) coordinates its First Year Photo Project to document students' personal transitions. Students are given seven assignments that span the academic year. Topics include defining themselves and what they want from their college experience, their first days on campus, events before classes begin, their confidence and anxiety levels, and their plans for the future and advice for others. At the end of the experience, students present an exhibit in the campus art gallery.

Sample questions include the following:

How does this photograph represent the values of our organization?
What areas on campus do you consider inclusive/exclusive and why?
What has made your transition to college easier/harder and why?
What has had a positive impact on your college career?

Simon (2015) suggested several considerations before choosing this method. The topic has to be carefully chosen to be narrow enough, but it must also elicit multiple perspectives. Not all topics are appropriate for photography. If the topic, and resulting pictures, may be considered lewd or inappropriate, the assessor should use a private collection method (e.g., email rather than Facebook).

In terms of process, Simon (2015) proposes several logistical considerations. The data-collection time frame and platform must be decided. Depending on how the assessment is to be implemented, you may need to develop a marketing plan to get students to participate. Determine whether you need to get any releases/permissions to use the photos and whether they will be anonymous. If the photos are to be shared beyond your department or might include sensitive topics, consult your institutional review board. Once the pictures have been collected, decide how long they must be kept and where they will be stored.

Document Review

Sometimes a formal assessment of already created documents can reveal important information about a program or student learning. Student affairs and academic affairs professionals have access to documents and records that can also be used for assessment purposes. Examples include the minutes of student organizational meetings or planning documents; training manuals and schedules; health records; appointment or interview schedules; requests for presentations; scholarship essays; published letters to the student newspaper; housing demographics; high-failure-rate courses; and membership, employment, or leadership position applications. Of course, depending on the document, identifiers such as names or student IDs should be redacted. Specific assessment questions may be defined before the document review (e.g., "What are the busiest times for appointments at the career center?" or "What topics do students address in their scholarship application essays?"). Student organization advisors new to their positions could find valuable information about the health of the organization and their needs by reviewing the organizational documents (minutes, transition documents, etc.) for the past few years. The student health services department could review the number of flu shots given compared with the incidence of flu, or they could review medical records to determine how often physicians asked patients about symptoms of depression. Document review and ongoing audits could also reveal a deficit in documentation; an assessment of planning documents for an annual student conference could reveal lack of receipts, contracts, and risk-management planning.

Cooper (2009) identified several advantages of document reviews: Access is based on the researcher's schedule and convenience, data are already transcribed or documented, and data collection is unobtrusive. The disadvantages include potential difficulty in accessing private or personal data, data may need insider knowledge or context to be understandable, and documents may be inaccurate (Cooper, 2009).

Conclusion

Student affairs staff have more assessment resources than surveys, focus groups, and interviews. Other options may be appropriate for use depending on the situation and the purpose of the assessment. Some methods are best suited for onetime interactions, whereas others require a longer-term commitment for data collection. Many of the highlighted methods in this chapter actively engage students in the process of data collection, which may make them popular among their peers.

Key Points

- Student affairs staff need to develop program or learning outcomes and the overarching assessment question before choosing the data-collection method.
- Each method has advantages and disadvantages, which must be weighed before a method is chosen.
- Although some methods are relatively quick and easy, staff need to devote time and energy to developing a quality instrument.

Discussion Questions and Activities

- What assessment methods are appealing to you in your environment? Why?
- What are the challenges of choosing methods that might not be generally accepted?
- How can you engage stakeholders in these methods to achieve buy-in?
- You are asked to assess your institution's orientation program. Which of the assessment methods discussed in this chapter would you use and why?

13

SHARING ASSESSMENT
RESULTS

In this era of increased accountability and transparency, student affairs administrators are focused on sharing information. Many divisions and departments talk about "telling our story" without knowing exactly what that means or how to do it. Assessment data can assist with the effort if done well. Banta, Jones, and Black (2009) have encouraged assessment sharing to ensure that it is a continual process and that it documents program improvement. Specifically they said, "Those charged with compiling assessment results at the campus level must find ways to share information about findings that can help to improve teaching and program processes with those teaching and/or designing and carrying out programs at the unit level" (p. 19). Sharing results can reflect positively on a department, garner resources, and build a solid reputation.

The Process of Sharing Results

Unfortunately, many staff think that once they have the results of an assessment, they are done with the project. The goal of assessment should not be to put a report on the shelf to gather dust. Rather, from the beginning of the assessment cycle, staff should be considering how they will share the information, with whom, when, and for what purpose as a step toward closing the loop. As Suskie (2009) posited, sharing results is inherently a teaching process and must be considered as seriously as the assessment itself.

In the student affairs context, results should be shared in aggregate to protect the respondents' identities (Suskie, 2009). As covered in Chapter 15, assessors should be following ethical standards about the confidentiality parameters. If individuals can be identified when the data are disaggregated, the analysis should not be reported to that level of granularity. Much of the time data about programs and services are most useful in the aggregate.

Suskie (2009) also encouraged staff to provide results in a complete and objective manner. That includes stating the actual wording of the question, a description of the sample, the response rate, and the precision of the results. The reported results should be unambiguous and clear to the audience. Conclusions and recommendations should connect to the results that are reported. Individual biases should be recognized and mitigated.

There are numerous factors to consider in sharing information. Initially, consider who would be interested in the information and what actions, if any, they could take based on that information. Each audience may require a different method of communication, a different level of complexity, and a different timeline. For example, good practice suggests sharing results with the participants who provided the data. If students responded to a survey in late spring, it might be appropriate to wait until the fall to send an email, create posters, or report the assessment in the student newspaper with a few key results and how the unit has implemented changes. If participants know how information is valued, they may be more loyal to the program and assessment.

Staff should provide information to their up-line supervisors, department heads, and other staff in the division. There are also times where it is appropriate to share with faculty, community members, and other external stakeholders. For some projects, the institution might be interested in sharing information with the general public, accreditors, boards, and donors. Faculty may pay more attention to the methodological details, accreditors may be more interested in how the results were used to make improvements, and donors may want to know the impact of their contributions on individual student learning without caring about the in-depth statistical analyses.

Although multiple stakeholders may be interested in the information, all constituents do not receive the same information. Just as it is important to identify the "who," the assessor has to determine the "what." Options range from very brief snippets of information to more lengthy reports. Student affairs staff may have the intimidating misperception that all assessment reports must be written as published refereed journal articles that are more research-focused. Not all recipients will be interested in or knowledgeable about methodology or complex data analysis. There are options for the appropriate format or formats for the audience, ranging from very detailed to a focus on recommendations (Schuh & Associates, 2009). Knowing one's audience directs how to share information. Some people want to hear about individual stories or impacts whereas others value the numbers and the bottom line.

Timing

Understanding the importance of timing in sharing information and making recommendations is crucial for success. As mentioned, waiting until students return to campus to share results may have a positive impact. Current campus events should also be considered. Depending on what is happening on campus, results will be welcomed, ignored, or criticized. For example, if the campus conversation revolves around assessing learning outcomes, student affairs may benefit from learning that students who live on campus, who are employed by student affairs departments, or who participate in leadership programs score better than students who do not. In addition, the campus may be struggling with issues of alcohol abuse, sexual assault, or guns on campus; assessment results may or may not support the administration, which is making policies and responding to media inquiries.

In making recommendations, assessors also have to consider their timeliness. Those made too late become irrelevant because they cannot be implemented (Schuh & Associates, 2009). Think about when funding decisions are made, when policy changes are made, and when the information can have the most impact on the campus community. Since assessment promotes positive change, these issues are critical to implementing improvement.

Addressing Shortcomings

Though using the same methods as research projects, many assessment projects have more limitations. The sample may be smaller (and more convenient), the response rate may be less than hoped, the instrument may not have been tested for validity and reliability, and the results may not be generalizable. Based on realistic time and other resource constraints, assessors may need to accept more error in the results. No assessment results will be perfect, but they can be useful and should be used with a variety of other information and professional judgment. Schuh and Associates (2009) recommend acknowledging those issues up front rather than being challenged by others who may criticize the results based on methodological flaws. Be open about limitations while also emphasizing that the results provide more information or another perspective on an issue.

To avoid having results ignored or dismissed, it is important to know the story to be told, to whom, and why. What are the key points? Is this for general information or a call to action? What will the readers relate to? The United Nations Economic Commission for Europe (2009a) has provided several tips to help make assessment results comprehensible and more likely to be accepted while still addressing limitations. The suggestions include using language that the audience understands, writing short sentences and paragraphs, using appropriate subheadings, using the active voice, and including bulleted lists. In addition, it suggests things to avoid: elevator statistics (i.e., this went up, this went down), jargon, acronyms, all capital letters and all italics, and table reading (i.e., describing every piece of data in a table). The audience should be the focus in deciding how to share data—their knowledge, time, need, and interests shape how, when, and why the story is told. If the audience does not easily understand the message or the limitations, it cannot support the results and/or make accurate decisions.

Methods of Sharing

There are a myriad of choices when it comes to sharing information, from very simple, brief, and targeted, to fairly complex and comprehensive. Planning how the results will be shared from the very beginning of the assessment process will make it easier to implement and more timely. Even without actual data, templates and outlines can be prepared throughout the process; when analysis is completed, the data can be inserted into the framework.

On the brief side, an executive summary is a one- to two-page report that highlights the project's methods, important results, and conclusions or recommendations. It is meant to be easily digestible and to focus on the big picture. This method may be preferred by upper-level administrators who do not have time to read extensive and detailed reports. If you have a large survey, it may be helpful to divide it into smaller sections. For example, you could create a one-page summary for each area of analysis. Each page could have a consistent look and format and could indicate where more information can be found.

A brief written report or several short reports can be tailored to a variety of audiences. Each report may not include all of the results but rather focus on a particular area of data. These reports could be four to five pages. For example, a campus climate assessment that addresses gender, religion, race/ethnicity, and disability could be in the form of four different reports in addition to one overall report. On the other hand, in order to create appropriate educational material for their audience, staff who work in orientation may be interested in how freshmen or transfer students responded to the survey.

Either a long or a summary report could be written to cover all of the questions in the assessment. Realistically these reports take time to compile, but they are also a good source of documentation and provide a complete picture of the assessment results. Depending on the audience members' interests, they may or may not take the time to read the report. Because of this, including an executive summary at the beginning of the longer report may be helpful. Long reports could also include literature, theories, or models related to the issue at hand as well as a section on the background and purpose of the assessment project.

Some units, departments, and divisions compose annual reports as a way of sharing their strategic plans, accomplishments, and future plans. These are also places to share assessment results to support their accomplishments and provide transparency. The annual reports are typically published on websites and as high-quality booklets that can be shared with alumni, donors, and administrators.

Technology promotes a variety of alternatives to share information. Results can be posted to a website (think of sharing quotes from past participants in an event or a percentage that indicates success). Brief statements or pictures can be uploaded to Facebook, Twitter, Instagram, Pinterest, or other social media that attract several audiences. Because those are typically brief statements, the message has to be carefully crafted. For example, 140 characters in Twitter do not allow the assessor to provide detail about the methodology or supporting theory. Alternatively, if there are many followers to that Twitter account, a positive message will reach many people. In recent years, infographics have become a popular way to use graphics to represent data. They use graphics, color, and visuals to represent data in an engaging manner. They are typically used on posters or websites. As with all visuals, you need to have a clear message to communicate easily rather than relying on the style to represent your meaning.

Assessment results can also be shared on websites, particularly if the information can be updated frequently. This is another way to be transparent about program quality. The results can also be used as marketing for the program (i.e., using quotes from past attendees or positive ratings). To understand the reach of the website, you can determine the number of website hits and even how long people stay on the web page. Technology has progressed to where you can have interactive data so your audience can do their own analysis for areas that interest them. How technology can assist with sharing results will be addressed in Chapter 18.

Email can be used to share results. This is a convenient way to share results with a specific audience. If a known sample of students was used to collect data, send the respondents an email thanking them for their participation and sharing key results. Similarly, share results over an electronic mailing list if the members would be interested in the results. The email can include a few results and refer people to a website for more information.

Some units already have regularly published newsletters that can be used to communicate with stakeholders. Another publication option could be a magazine that goes to potential students, alumni, or other groups. Rutgers University created *Assessment in Action*, a quarterly magazine, to share results and educate about assessment (Rutgers University Division of Student Affairs, 2015). Assessment results can also be added to brochures or other publications that the public receives.

On a smaller scale, posters, table tents, or flyers highlight results. The University of North Carolina Wilmington (n.d.), uses its "We've Heard Your Voice" campaign to share not only results with students but also actions that have been taken because of them. Students feel valued because their opinions have been taken into consideration, and student affairs staff are accountable for using assessment results for improvement. The flyers are posted around campus with a consistent format to promote campaign recognition and branding.

The campus newspaper is another method to share information. Results could be shared through advertising space or could be through an article. If students were your audience, this is a good way to get the information back to them. Sending the newspaper an interesting press release could motivate the student reporters to follow up.

Student affairs staff frequently present to their own staff, to the division, and at conferences. This is a prime opportunity to explain assessment results. Unlike the print formats, presentations are more interactive, but you still need to keep in mind the background, knowledge, and interest of the audience. They may or may not understand or care about the purpose of the assessment or the methodology, results, or recommendations. Presenters need to understand their audiences to design an appropriate presentation. A discussion of multilinear regression may not be comprehended by some audiences, but basic descriptive statistics might be too elementary for others.

Presenters have to consider detailed logistics. The amount of presentation time impacts the presentation. Be sure to allocate enough time for a question-and-answer period (probably about 15 to 20 minutes for an hour-long presentation). Many presentations use PowerPoint or Prezi to support the verbal presentation. As with other presentations, be sure that the font is large enough for the audience to read, the graphics are clear, and the language relates to your audience. The slides are not the focus of the presentation; the presenter is. Slides should have minimal text, and the final slide should include contact information. Charts and tables are better visual representations of the data. Handouts with summary information can be useful supplements to a presentation. Practice the presentation to understand the timing for each slide (about two minutes per slide). Think about the room for the presentation. In a large room, everyone needs to see the screen clearly and hear the presenter. Dark font on a light-colored background typically provides the best visual results in most rooms. Graphics and other visuals should be accessible to those with visual impairments. Using alt-text (alternative text for images) to describe graphics allows the same information to be portrayed for text-only readers. Prior to the actual presentation, the presenter should ensure that the technology works and is compatible with the file format.

Portraying Results Visually

Once you have determined the best way to illustrate the data, you will be able to guide the reporting process. Some say that a picture is worth a thousand words, but if the picture is not relevant, the message will not be helpful. Suskie (2009) provides these tips for using tables and graphs to represent information:

- Give each table and graph a meaningful, self-explanatory title.
- Label every part of a table or graph clearly.
- Make each table and graph self-explanatory.
- If there are many possible results, group them.
- Make it easy for readers to see differences and trends.
- Avoid putting too much information into a table or graph.
- Present your results in an order that makes sense to readers and helps convey your point.
- Draw attention to the point you want your table or graph to make.
- Don't assume that a software-generated table or graph is readable.
- Date each table and graph and note its source. (p. 287)

Many student affairs professionals and stakeholders are not familiar with interpreting assessment results, so it is imperative for the person writing the report to be as clear as possible. Tables, graphs, and figures should be clearly labeled and explained in the text. In addition, they should be as close to the text explanations as possible. By highlighting key findings in the text, you can help the reader to interpret the significance of the visual or numerical representations. Always have other people read reports for errors and comprehension before releasing the final version. Reports with typographical errors or incorrect grammar will not have the desired impact.

By paying attention to the small details, you will also help the reader to understand and remember the key points. Rounding percentages to the nearest whole percent (Suskie, 2009) makes it easier for the reader to see the big picture and/or put the information in context. Decimals should be used only with technical audiences who will want that level of precision. Tables and graphs should not be cluttered with too many columns, too much information, or irrelevant information (Suskie, 2009). Also make sure that all graphs and figures are appropriate. Novice assessors often create a two-bar chart that takes up a great deal of space when a simple table or even reporting the data in the text would be clearer and more efficient. Graphs and figures should not be created just because they can be. According to the United Nations Economic Commission for Europe (2009b), tables and graphs presented in a concise way can support accompanying text, but they should also be clear and include a descriptive title and source.

Tables should be arranged in a logical order—descending mean, chronological, alphabetical, and so on. Descending mean or frequency order highlights differences in the responses and illustrates what is most positive and perhaps those items that were not rated as highly. Tables and graphs can use shading and color to be more descriptive, but remember that some readers may print the report in black and white, which may negate any visual cues. For more formal documents student affairs staff may find it useful to consult the *Publication Manual of the American Psychological Association* (American Psychological Association, 2010) or refereed journals for specific guidance in creating tables and charts.

Tables and graphs should be thoughtfully designed. The title should be descriptive and answer the "what," "where," and "when." The column headers should provide relevant data, such as units of measure. Each row should be clearly labeled. Footnotes that follow the table are used to provide any additional data (United Nations Economic Commission for Europe, 2009b). The table should also be labeled with a number and a name (e.g., "Table 1" with the table name) and be referred to in the text (e.g., "As seen in Table 1"). Each data cell should contain information, even if it says "Not Applicable" (which should be explained), and it should be sized to be readable.

Graphs, if they are clear and concise, to illustrate results can be an effective means for telling a story. Tips include using solid lines rather than patterns, starting the Y axis at zero, only illustrating points that add value, using one unit of measurement per graph, and making the text easy to understand (write labels from left to right, and avoid legends unless on maps) (United Nations Economic Commission for Europe, 2009a). Graphics take a fair amount of space on the page, so they should be used mainly to make important points. When colors are used in graphics, they should be created with the knowledge that some of the audience may be color-blind or have difficulty distinguishing similar colors or patterns.

Charts are another convenient way to represent data, especially when you want to illustrate comparisons, change over time, frequency distribution, correlation, and relative share of a whole (United Nations Economic Commission for Europe, 2009b). There are different types of charts: pie, bar, area, donut, bubble, line, and so on. You may have to experiment with various types for clarity, space, and story. As with all of the ways to represent data, the chart must show the relevant information without being confusing to the reader. Data should still be presented in a logical order that tells an accurate story. Be sure to pick the appropriate chart for data. For example, a pie chart, which is typically used for data that sums to 100%, should not be used for "all that apply" questions whose total will be more than 100%.

Sharing Negative Results

Sometimes staff are reluctant to share "negative" results for fear of looking bad. One of the consequences of not sharing is being accused of lack of transparency. Stakeholders may also be skeptical of results if all are positive. When negative results are shared, it is very important to choose the right language that does not place blame or insult (Schuh & Associates, 2009). The report may also highlight the positive results and focus on possible recommendations. Suskie (2009) endorses using a phrase such as "suggestions for further improvement" (p. 279) so as to be sensitive to your audience. Before problematic results are released to the public, the assessor can share the information with the affected department or unit ahead of time. That personal discussion can provide more context that could be included in the report, but it also gives people an opportunity to prepare a response and a plan. Ideally, the assessor and the client or other stakeholders will have had a conversation at the beginning of the project about the potential for disappointing results, so no results should come as a complete surprise. At no time should assessment results be used in personnel evaluations. Assessment can be a job function and engagement in assessment can be evaluated, but using results in an evaluation can make staff fearful of doing assessment.

Rather than hide less-than-positive results, a different tactic would be to share the results but spend more time explaining which possible actions would lead to improvement. In this way the writer maintains control of the message. The important part of that decision is to commit to making the change and then follow up by assessing the change. If no action is taken, constituents may lose their trust in the unit and the assessment process, thereby reducing the likelihood of their future participation in assessment and programs and services.

Cautions

The language used in any report or presentation should be carefully constructed for inclusion and clarity. Incorrect word usage can interfere with the message and findings or be misleading. In particular, language used to refer to particular groups should be carefully chosen (Schuh & Associates, 2009). Writers need to know the terms used on their own campuses as well as what is appropriate in larger contexts, which may change over time. The *Publication Manual of the American Psychological Association* (American Psychological Association, 2010) provides specific guidance on inclusive language and word choice.

An important knowledge area in student affairs assessment comprises the legal and ethical context. In the United States, public institutions are subject to the Freedom of Information Act or open records requests. Although states vary in their implementation and specific laws, it is important for student affairs professionals to know what is expected of them. Public institutions usually have legal and administrative staff to coordinate the requests. They are the ones who decide what information must be released to the requestor, not the person who maintains the information.

Another consideration includes the confidentiality or anonymity promised to your participants. Sometimes sharing results includes providing quotes from the data collected, whether from an online survey, in-person focus group, or some other qualitative method. Be careful to avoid providing too much description of demographics, as this might reveal the identity of the respondent. For example, if a quote names a particular student organization or class and then provides multiple demographics such as gender, ethnicity, academic classification, and academic college, it might be easy for the reader to identify the specific respondent. Asking respondents for their permission to use their identities also builds trust between the assessor and the respondents.

Conclusion

Sharing assessment results is one of the most important steps in the student affairs assessment cycle. It not only increases the knowledge base about a particular program, service, or issue, but also shows a commitment to transparency and accountability. In addition, it provides a foundation for making data-informed decisions to improve student experiences on campus.

Key Points

- The sharing of results takes planning and coordination.
- Information should be individualized based on audience, desired action, and timing.
- Graphical displays of data, used appropriately, can enhance the message.

Discussion Questions and Activities

- What are the barriers to sharing assessment results effectively?
- What resources do you have and need to be able to share results effectively?
- How can sharing information impact programs and services positively?
- How can "negative" results be used to create positive actions?

14

USING ASSESSMENT RESULTS

Closing the Loop

In thinking about the use of assessment results, the old adage of a tree falling in the woods comes to mind. The philosophical question goes like this: "If a tree falls in the forest and no one is around to hear it, does it make a sound?" The question challenges assumptions and understandings of reality. Perhaps a sound is a sound once it is heard. Similarly, if assessment results are not used, is assessment really being done? That is an interesting question to ponder. At the root of this question is the definition of *assessment* and the current understanding of the assessment process. Although this chapter comes late in the book, the topic is actually important to consider and address from the very beginning of any assessment project.

Suskie (2009) concisely outlines the assessment process for student learning. The first step in the process is the establishment of learning goals, which leads to the second step of determining strategies to accomplish the learning goals. The third step is what many people consider assessment to be. Data are gathered to determine if students are learning, they are then analyzed, and finally the results are used to improve learning. This step closes the assessment loop. For Suskie, closing the loop by using results is a critical step in the assessment process. With this model in mind, assessment does not happen if the results are not used. It is important to note that although Suskie focuses on the assessment of student learning, her model can be adapted to any type of goal or outcome.

Closing the loop may be easier said than done. Many departments do an outstanding job of collecting data but may not make use of them. The collection of data is already an integral part of their process, and thanks to the growing use of assessment technology (e.g., Campus Labs, OrgSync, LiveText), many can produce piles of data regarding a number of activities. Institutions may be data-rich but evidence-poor (Kuh et al., 2015). These piles of

215

data can lead to "data paralysis," where data sit in binders, on computer hard drives, or on servers, never to be put into use to document goal achievement or improve programs and services. This chapter outlines concrete ways in which data can be used.

Linking to Institutional Assessment

In addition to using results, it is important to link them to structures, processes, and cultures of the division or institution (Baker, Jankowski, Provezis, & Kinzie, 2012; Bresciani, 2010). Assessment results aligned with department or divisional priorities can demonstrate association between the goals of a program, department, and division.

Whereas assessment may be decentralized across a division or an institution, it is crucial to connect all assessment processes. Thus, it is important to have program or departmental assessment results inform divisional assessment, which will then inform institutional assessment. Many student affairs divisions have a centralized or standardized structure to prepare annual reports. These often include departmental annual reports that are culled and aggregated into a divisional annual report. Since it is critical for these divisional annual reports to focus on impact rather than to report only the number of programs implemented or students served, departments must also focus on results-oriented evidence demonstrating goal achievement in their assessments so that they can be included in the departmental report.

Departmental assessment results can inform strategic planning (Baker et al., 2012). The evidence can be used to set strategic goals, identify strategies to achieve those goals, or establish targets or related milestones at both the departmental and divisional levels. Student affairs units can provide evidence of their contribution to important divisional goals priorities.

Finally, assessment results should be built into accreditation processes (Baker et al., 2012). Accreditation is not an episodic process that happens every 5 or 10 years when a progress report or self-study report is required but rather an ongoing process of gathering data to demonstrate goal achievement and identify opportunities for improvement. More importantly, the data collected should be used to make improvements. Thus, departmental and divisional assessment results should support institutional accreditation. Many regional accrediting processes have shifted focus to demonstration of how assessment data are used to make improvements. This is a shift away from an emphasis of demonstrating goal achievement. Few student affairs professionals are involved in the actual institutional accreditation processes, but they should be knowledgeable about campus progress and how they can provide evidence for the report. Accreditation can be a wonderful opportunity for departments within a division of student affairs to demonstrate their impact on student learning and success.

Purposes of Assessment Results

Whereas results should be linked to institutional processes, there are a number of specific ways in which assessment evidence can be used. Despite the fact that the most frequent use of assessment data is for regional accreditation (Kuh et al., 2015), this evidence can also be used to make decisions, inform resource allocation, inform planning processes, refine goals and outcomes, and improve assessment processes. Upon reviewing a number of institutions that use assessment results well, we found that one defining factor was that a goal for use of the results was set at the beginning of the assessment process (Baker et al., 2012). Just as with assessment, use of the results should be goal-directed. In addition, it may be helpful to consider the end use of the results as assessment in addition to the goal being served (Kuh et al., 2015). There are various ways of using results.

Using Evidence for Decision Making

Assessment data can be used to make a variety of decisions, including if a program should be continued, how it should be revised to be more effective, what strategies would be most effective for reaching a particular goal, and how staff time would be best utilized on a project. The basic point is that decisions should not be made without some type of evidence. Schuh and Associates (2009) appropriately summed up the importance of using data to inform decisions that are made:

> Without a systematic approach to gathering information and using that information to determine effectiveness of student affairs units, initiatives, programs, and procedures, unit leaders will have difficulty determining whether organizational goals are being met, thus making their organizations vulnerable to reorganization, outsourcing, or even elimination. (p. 9)

While data should be used to inform decision making, it is also important to note that other information besides data affects decisions. Decisions may be based on values, resources, politics, stakeholder opinion, benchmarking, "best" practices, and other influences. Thus, *data-informed* decision making may be more accurate than *data-driven* decision making.

Decisions center around the two main purposes of assessment: goal and mission achievement and opportunities for continuous improvement

(Doyle & Meents-DeCaigny, 2015). Underneath this dual umbrella are decisions related to resource allocation and student issues. Resource allocation decisions are often connected to the assets needed to achieve goals or make improvements so that goals are met. In regard to student issues, there are a variety of decisions related to this constituent group. Critical student needs must be identified along with strategies to address those needs. In addition, the extent to which students are successful and how to ensure success must be measured. The chief senior student affairs officer advocates for student issues and student success, and to do this effectively, this person needs to efficiently identify these key areas (Doyle & Meents-DeCaigny, 2015).

In addition to having the data to make decisions, the process regarding how evidence is used in decision making must be understood. Walvoord (2010) suggests that mapping the flow of data from all areas of the division to decision makers is a useful exercise to document this process. Once data are visible, it will be possible to determine how effective the data flow is in regard to informing decision making. There may be important data that never reach decision makers because there is no process to distribute them to that constituency.

Using Evidence for Resource Allocation

Another primary use of data is decision making regarding resource allocation (Bresciani, 2010). With constrained resources, assessment is a crucial process to ensure these limited resources are used as effectively and efficiently as possible. There are five types of resources to consider: fiscal (money), physical (facilities), human (people), technological, and intellectual (skills and knowledge of staff). In 2001, Schuh and Upcraft wrote, "Student affairs [was] under considerable pressure to demonstrate its importance and worth. In an era of declining resources and increased competition for what precious few resources there are, student affairs has come under the institutional financial microscope" (p. 9). Today, resources are still declining at many institutions, and student affairs divisions must effectively steward the funds they are allocated as well as advocate for additional resources (Doyle & Meents-DeCaigny, 2015). Culp (2012) echoed this sentiment: "Cultures of evidence provide a degree of financial protection for student affairs professionals, as they document with hard data the significant contributions student affairs makes towards the institution's mission and goals" (p. 1).

Measuring Impact or Return on Investment (ROI)
With increasing demands on student affairs divisional budgets, the impact of programs and services must be assessed to understand which are effective in supporting divisional goals or priorities and which are not. Programs

deemed ineffective should be retooled or eliminated to better support divisional directives. Assessment data in this case can be used to tell us the extent to which a program achieves goals that are desirable for the institutional community and if the cost of having the program is worthwhile. There are many issues to consider as one examines the use of assessment data in a cost-versus benefits analysis.

Costs are more than just how much money was involved in administering the program. The effectiveness of a program can be even more challenging to determine because it can include value judgments in addition to quantitative evidence. In evaluating a program or service, one should consider participation rates, the number of activities comprised by the program, satisfaction rates, and outcome achievement (Doyle & Meents-DeCaigny, 2015). Suskie (2009) has reiterated the importance of considering student learning evidence in this type of analysis. This does not mean that all programs must be evaluated all of the time or that every program must have the same depth of learning outcomes and assessment.

The overall impact of a program or service must be considered together as components of overall outcomes. Participation rates must be interpreted in the context of the outcomes achieved. A program with 100 attendees is not necessarily a success if the participants do not achieve the intended outcomes. On the other hand, there could be a program with five participants whose lives were transformed as a result of the activity. Although those five participants may have exceeded the outcomes by far, the resulting student outcomes may not be worth the resources expended on the program. However, the participation rate can help to determine the impact of a program. If two programs have similar outcome achievements and one program has 10 participants and another has 30, assuming the same costs for each program, the latter program would have a larger cost/benefit ratio.

These lessons can be applied to using assessment data as part of a cost/benefit analysis to some widely applied student affairs programs. "Welcome week" activities occur on many campuses. They (hopefully) attract a large number of students to a variety of events. Those events may or may not include learning activities, but they are probably geared toward helping students meet other people, get acquainted with campus resources, and build their affinity with the institution. Depending on the length and complexity of activities, the cost of staff and materials may be fairly low or fairly high. Another example is institutions that have intensive programs geared toward students with alcohol or drug problems who have been through the conduct process. In order to stay enrolled, these students might need to see a substance abuse counselor weekly, meet with conduct staff on a regular basis, get alcohol/drug tested frequently, and have an assigned staff mentor. In this case, the number of students involved is low, the staff cost is high, and the impact on individual student learning and development as well as retention is probably tremendous. In such cases, assessment data may be used to make decisions about which programs should continue and which ones should be cut. The process of using assessment data to inform decisions may not be as easy as just determining the reach and breadth of a program. Deciding which program is more valuable is not straightforward.

Satisfaction rates must be contextualized in a similar manner. Often high satisfaction rates are used as a proxy for learning. The idea proposes that if participants are satisfied, they are engaged, and thus they learn. This may be true, but it depends on the content. Students who are being challenged on their behavior in individual meetings or in student conduct proceedings may be very dissatisfied but may be learning a great deal. This is because cognitive dissonance fosters learning. In this case, assessment might focus on the process (fair, timely) and the student interaction with staff (Did the student feel respected and listened to? Did the staff member explain the process and potential consequence so the student understood?). Like participation rates, satisfaction rates must be interpreted in the context of outcome achievement. Without the outcome data, it is difficult to know if higher satisfaction rates are associated with outcome achievement.

Impact must also be understood in relation to divisional goals and priorities. A program can have a cost/benefit ratio for the outcomes of that program, but the program may not be aligned with the divisional goals. It is essential to make sure that outcomes for programs are aligned with divisional goals at both the program development stage and the program assessment stage. As one uses data to make decisions, it is extremely important to look back to the intended outcomes of the program and the overall goals of the division and institution.

Using External and Internal Evidence

In making resource allocations, external evidence as well as internal evidence should be considered (Suskie, 2009). External evidence may afford additional leverage for resource allocation because it provides external validation. There are two types of external evidence to contemplate. The first is benchmarking to standards. The Council for the Advancement of Standards in Higher Education (2015) provides standards for 44 functional areas in higher education. In addition to the standards, CAS provides self-assessment guides (SAGs) that steer the evaluation process. Other professional associations also provide specific standards for professional practice. Using standards such as these can validate an assessment process and add credibility to its results. The results of these self-study guides can provide direction for changes and improvement.

The second type of external evidence to consider is benchmarking against peers, competitor programs, aspirational programs, or itself over time. Peer or competitor benchmarking compares institutional data with those of similar institutions. *Similarity* can be defined by many things: geographic region, institution type, athletic conference, or Carnegie classification, for example. In benchmarking against aspirational groups, the institution or organization is comparing itself against a group that is slightly "ahead" in order to strive for change. This process offers the opportunity to set a target to strive for and make decisions regarding resource allocation accordingly. These types of comparisons provide contextual data that can not only help to pinpoint areas of strengths and challenges compared with peers but also be used as a basis for judgment regarding resource allocation.

Internal evidence is also useful in making resource allocations. Comparing performance over time is another form of benchmarking. To understand its performance in addressing alcohol abuse, a student affairs division may review specific metrics over time, such as the reported binge rate of students, medical transports for alcohol abuse, or alcohol-related policy violations. Tracking these metrics over time can provide some understanding of effectiveness. Resource allocations can be based on past performance and future intended performance.

Using Evidence for Planning

In addition to using assessment evidence for resource allocation, it is a critical tool for ongoing planning. This planning can be informal or formal and may take many forms, including priority setting, strategic planning, program revision, or action planning around a specific program or initiative.

Baker et al. (2012) have described how assessment evidence can be used for setting institutional priorities. The same concept applies to divisional priorities. The evidence can help determine what is working well and what needs improvement at the departmental and divisional levels. Areas of improvement can be identified as departmental or divisional priorities for the coming year. With priorities such as "decrease the alcohol binge rate," "increase residence hall retention," or "increase learning related to microaggressions," attention can be focused on addressing these issues.

Bresciani (2010) has identified nine steps to follow when using data for strategic planning in student affairs:

1. *Establish a strategic plan.* A plan is needed to get the process started.
2. *Gather forecast and trend data.* Much data needed for the strategic planning process already exists on campus. These data may include results

from national surveys, data from the College Board, or data from the Integrated Post-Secondary Data Systems.

3. *Conduct a capacity review.* This type of review determines if the division has the resources to implement its strategic plan. Limitations can be identified at the beginning of the process.

4. *Articulate indicators of success.* It is important to identify how one would know whether goals in a plan are achieved. These indicators should be quantifiable and possible to measure.

5. *Prioritize action plans to meet the strategic goals.* Prioritizing parts of the strategic plan provides direction regarding what goals to start with and which resources should be expended.

6. *Align divisional resources with institutional priorities.* Following on step 5, this step ensures that the use of resources is aligned with institutional goals as well as divisional goals. This alignment ensures vertical connection between goals within the organization.

7. *Implement outcomes-based assessment program review.* Once the priorities are set and indicators are established, a process must be implemented to determine the extent to which the goals are achieved.

8. *Allocate and reallocate resources to help realize the goals.* Findings from the outcomes-based assessment review are used to make allocation decisions moving forward.

9. *Make it all systematic.* After this process has been followed once, it is important to ensure that it continues in an ongoing rather than a sporadic way. The process should be institutionalized in the practices of the division.

Bresciani (2010) identifies steps in the process, and Suskie (2009) discusses additional ways in which data can be used for planning. As in setting priorities, assessment evidence can be used to refine goals and targets (Suskie, 2014). Suskie (2009) provides three suggestions for using assessment data to refine goals and targets. The first is in regard to the number of goals. It is difficult to achieve a large number of goals. Thus, assessment data can be used to identify the most important goals to focus on. Four to five goals are generally achievable. Second, consider the appropriateness of the goals. Some goals may be too ambitious given a specific time frame. A goal of decreasing the alcohol binge rate on campus by 15% in one year may be too high. More time may be needed to achieve aspirational goals. Third, there should be consideration for how goals should be refined. Departmental goals may be more achievable or better aligned with divisional goals if revised.

Strategic planning is a more complex form of goal setting. After a process to identify strengths and opportunities for improvement, strategic priorities are developed. This typically happens at the divisional level, but may be used by larger departments. Assessment evidence is integral to successful strategic planning. Bryson (2011) defines *strategic planning* as "a deliberative, disciplined approach to producing fundamental decisions and actions that shape and guide what an organization is, what it does, and why" (pp. 7–8). In other words, strategic planning provides a map of action for an organization. Most plans are for a three- to five-year period and do not include everything an organization does. Rather, strategic plans include only the most important goals or strategies. These plans often include the priority, strategies to achieve the priority, resources required for the strategies, shepherds for the strategies, and targets for priority achievement as well as milestones to monitor progress toward targets. Assessment data can help to identify the priorities or goals for strategic planning as well as the specific components of the plan. Assessment is then used to describe progress of the plan and achievement of goals.

To use evidence for strategic planning is important to identify assessment data needs for planning and implementation of the strategic plan (Doyle & Meents-DeCaigny, 2015). These data may include evidence to establish priorities as well as evidence to identify strengths and weaknesses (Doyle & Meents-DeCaigny, 2015). A SWOC (strengths, weaknesses, opportunities, and challenges) analysis is a popular technique for strategic planning (Bryson, 2011). Assessment data are useful in this analysis as they help to set a baseline that can be used to establish targets and milestones whereby to monitor progress and success (Doyle & Meents-DeCaigny, 2015).

There is a current movement toward a different type of strategic planning called SOAR, which stands for strengths, opportunities, aspirations, and results. This systems-based, action-oriented approach to strategic planning focuses on strengths rather than weaknesses or what needs to be improved (Capela & Brooks-Saunders, 2012).

In addition to setting priorities and developing and implementing a strategic plan, assessment evidence can be used for action planning around a specific program. After a program or service has been assessed and its impact determined, planning can take place to make improvements. Revisions may be made to increase the impact and achievement of outcomes or perhaps scale up the program or service to influence more students. Improvements may also focus on making more efficient use of resources, be they financial, human, physical, technological, or intellectual. Regardless of the change, staff should document the decisions and rationale for decisions and actions. When a new staff member takes over a program, he or she needs to know why certain decisions were made.

Using Assessment Evidence for Improvement

Although assessment data are integral to planning and resource allocation, the most important use for this evidence is improvement of programs and services. This may be the most authentic use of assessment and where it has the biggest impact. According to Baker et al. (2012), one central feature of institutions that use data well is that they focus on increasing the use of evidence to impact processes and practices that improve student learning.

Assessment of effectiveness should be built into every program or service to clarify what is working and what is not. All of the assessment methods discussed in earlier chapters play a critical role in program improvement. Residence life staff will want to assess the room-selection process to determine improvements to be made for the next year. Student conduct staff will want to determine how fair the conduct process feels to students and to address the feedback appropriately. Student involvement staff will want to gather data about the effectiveness of advisors in order to provide additional training to these individuals. These are all examples of activity-level assessment. However, a department will also want to perform larger-scale assessments. Health services staff typically perform a student health evaluation periodically to determine how effectively each area within the department is functioning and to seek feedback regarding how to improve. Career services may perform a self-study to determine the effectiveness of the various programs and services they offer and how these are viewed by the students they serve. Although one goal is effectiveness, the other main purpose is to identify ways to improve (Ewell, 2009). A true culture of assessment is established when staff, programs, and departments consistently seek ways to gather evidence to inform improvement.

Program Reviews

Many colleges and universities have academic program reviews as part of their assessment cycle. Every five to seven years an academic department goes through a self-study process to identify what is working well and what can be improved upon. The main goal of these processes, which can range from basic to quite involved, is program improvement. This practice is becoming popular in student affairs divisions as well.

Student affairs divisions that have these program-review processes provide step-by-step instructions for performing the program review. At many institutions, these program reviews begin in the fall; they come to a close in the spring or early summer with a summary report and action steps. Once a review has been approved, the department begins implementing the recommendations.

Functional area standards developed by the Council for the Advancement of Standards in Higher Education (CAS) (2015) often provide the framework for this self-study process. CAS has extensive worksheets called SAGs, which identify questions to be addressed within a set of functional area standards. CAS (n.d.) also provides guidance on facilitating a program review that will result in evidence for improvement. The steps are as follows:

1. Assemble the team.
2. Educate the team.
3. Conduct ratings.
4. Complete the action plan.
5. Prepare the report.
6. Close the loop.

The program-review process may just be internal or it may also have external review steps. Some institutions bring in an external review team from outside the institution to review the self-study and provide feedback and recommendations. Some institutions ask staff or faculty outside the department or division but still from within the institution to provide feedback. The choice to have an external review step in the overall program-review process depends on overall goals for the process and resources available. Although serving as an external reviewer is often considered service to the field, there may be travel costs to cover and it is customary to provide a small honorarium for the reviewer's time.

Program-review processes have multiple benefits. They are often part of a larger institutional assessment process; therefore, they have institutional value and are resourced. The use of models such as the CAS standards for program review brings external credibility to the activity. Because these are often formalized processes, the results and action plans are often implemented, resulting in change. In addition, they provide time for reflection in an otherwise busy schedule to see the big picture and gain a fresh perspective.

Types of Improvements

A variety of improvements can be made based on assessment data. First, the delivery or content of a program or service could be revised. An assessment of new student orientation might reveal that students are not fully aware of the academic resources on campus. Rather than just having a panel of directors discuss what a particular office does, students could compete in a scavenger hunt to find pieces of information about each office. An evaluation of resident assistant (RA) training may suggest that RAs are not prepared to be first responders to a sexual assault. Sexual assault training could then be added.

Second, consider developing a new program or service to address an identified need. To ensure safety on an urban campus, an assessment may be done to determine how many students are walking alone at night. Noting that there are many students doing this, the college may choose to implement a "safe ride" program, which provides free transportation across campus between 9 p.m. and 4 a.m. Or a university may be increasing its recruitment of international students. After an evaluation of international students' experience on campus, the findings may suggest that staff do know how to interact with students from countries outside the United States. The division of student affairs may then choose to develop an "international intercultural" training program for all staff.

Third, expand a current program. The assessment of a pilot summer bridge program for underprepared students may suggest that these students form stronger bonds with faculty and staff than students who did not attend and that they also were more academically successful after their first three quarters. Given these positive results, the campus may choose to expand the program, doubling the number of students who can participate. A student/ staff engagement program meant to connect first-year students with a staff member on campus during the first six weeks of a semester may be assessed to determine if the program was effective in helping students become socially integrated at the college. Results may suggest that students' confidence increased and they reported more connections than students in a control group. As a result, more students could be recruited to participate.

Expansion of a current program or service is related to the fourth type of improvement—increasing resources. Resources may include staff, money, or other material resources. For the previous example regarding student/staff engagement, additional resources may be required in order to increase student participation. Staff may be given free meal passes to take students to lunch or coffee. To enable more students to participate, more meal passes may have to be purchased. A university may be comparing two alcohol education programs—one that is homegrown and a research-based program developed by an outside company. Results may suggest that the outside program is more effective in decreasing alcohol consumption. The division of student affairs may then spend more money to make this program available to all incoming students.

There may be other types of improvements resulting from assessment, but these are four changes that are frequently made.

Using Results Fairly, Ethically, and Responsibly

Although there are many ways of using results, there is a certain manner in which they should be employed. Suskie (2009) was emphatic that assessment results be used fairly, ethically, and responsibly and outlined 11 ways in which this can be accomplished (Suskie, 2009).

The first way to be responsible with results is to make assessments planned and purposeful (Suskie, 2009). By being intentional, the results can be used in a thoughtful manner with a focus. Unintentional or random assessments may do more damage than good and are not a useful allocation of resources. These types of assessments may be reactionary or self-serving rather than centered on accountability or improvement. Realistically, if results are not going to be used, do not do the project.

The second way Suskie (2009) suggests is focusing assessment on the overall goal of helping students learn. This suggestion also applies to operational and programmatic goals as well as setting metrics and targets of a division. The purpose of this recommendation is to intentionally align assessment with established goals. If not done so already, student affairs divisions and departments need to move in the direction of writing, assessing, and documenting learning outcomes to demonstrate the impact they have on student learning, which can help the division gain more credibility in the academy.

The third way of using the assessment results in a responsible manner is to assess teaching and learning processes as well as outcomes (Suskie, 2009). This suggestion can be broadened to student affairs divisions by ensuring that the assessment includes evaluations of learning strategies in addition to outcomes. Therefore, units are focused on accountability of outcome achievement and improvement of processes. For example, think about residence life assigning students to residence hall rooms, or the union facilities staff processing room reservations, or the recreational sports department coordinating intramural sports teams.

For the fourth way, Suskie (2009) recommends involving stakeholders in decisions stemming from results. This ensures that the results are used fairly as the voices of important individuals are included in decisions and creates an inclusive decision-making process. This practice also establishes checks and balances on evidence usage. It is important to identify stakeholders early and keep them informed along the way. In particular, keeping a supervisor informed can prevent unpleasant surprises.

Fifth, it is also responsible and ethical to communicate assessment findings widely and transparently (Suskie, 2009). This action serves multiple purposes. First, it demonstrates that assessment is being done, and this validates the process. Second, the sharing of results shows that administrators are not trying to hide anything from constituents. However, it does call for distributing negative as well as positive assessment data. Third, and perhaps most importantly, the reporting of assessment information helps tell the story of an organization—a key role of assessment. By transparently sharing results, the organization can tell the story it wants to tell instead of allowing others to interpret the data. The sharing of results focuses on improvements to be made, and different audiences may want different information.

One of the biggest challenges with the ethical use of assessment data is how others use it once it has been distributed. In her sixth recommendation, Suskie (2009) states that it is important to discourage others from making inappropriate interpretations of the results. This is difficult, as it does take some understanding of data and context to know how to interpret them accurately. To uphold this suggestion, the assessor must know the knowledge level of those with whom the data are being shared and must frame any results for the users appropriately. This is a reason why raw data or even raw results should not be shared widely. Any data that are shared should be contextualized regardless of the form in which they are disseminated. Appropriate framing requires forethought and diligence. Response rates to surveys are important because they provide guidance regarding the generalizability of the responses. If a sample is chosen appropriately, a survey with a high response will likely be more representative than one with a low response. However, response rates are not part of the raw data. Thus, by providing a report that discusses the response rate and the implications, you can help to contextualize the survey responses.

Not all assessment data are positive. When results are less than positive, staff should not be penalized (Suskie, 2009); this is the seventh suggestion. Rather, they should be commended for performing assessment and provided the opportunity to make improvements. If staff are penalized for poor results, they may become apprehensive about assessment and avoid it or choose to assess only things that will have positive results. Or worse yet, they may fabricate results. Penalizing staff for negative results hinders the improvement process. The focus should be on engaging in the assessment process and using results to improve effectiveness and efficiency. It is important to set expectations for doing assessments and using assessments from the outset.

Since one assessment measure provides only part of the whole picture, multiple assessment methods should be encouraged (Suskie, 2009), which is the eighth suggestion. This could mean that different measures such as a one-minute paper and "muddiest point" are used or that information is gathered from different groups of individuals. The goal is to gather data using multiple methods that support a central conclusion. This provides a stronger argument for resources as well as evidence of student affairs' alignment with institutional priorities.

Although assessment evidence is critical to decision making, it is just one piece of information to be used in making decisions (Suskie, 2009);

this is the ninth suggestion. In addition to assessment data, other sources of information—including experiences, values, and missions—should be considered in making decisions. This is Suskie's tenth suggestion. Context, environment, and politics affect decision making.

Eleventh, while closing the loop by putting the results into action is the final step, it is not enough. That closure must be communicated. Suskie (2009) recommends informing all constituents regarding how findings support decisions. This transparency demonstrates to students, faculty, and staff how assessment data are used to make decisions. Communication could be as simple as an email to stakeholders with a few highlights of results and actions. Constituents are more likely to continue to engage in assessment processes if they know the data are being used for improvement. They are also more likely to support changes based on the evaluation of evidence.

These 11 strategies ensure that assessment data will be used in a fair, ethical, and responsible manner. One of the challenges addressed is using results that are less favorable. Even if the findings are disappointing, there is still an ethical obligation not only to address the findings but also to share them with stakeholders

Addressing Negative Results

Unfortunately, not all results are positive; however, this is a good thing, as negative results lead to change and improvement. As stated in the previous section, negative results should not lead to punitive action (Suskie, 2009). This leads to distrust of the assessment process and limits participation in future assessments. It is also important not to hide negative results (Suskie, 2009). When constituents read only positive results, they become skeptical because they expect a balance of positive with negative. Rather than hiding the results, an assessor should share the negative results as often as he or she shares positive results. Even fairly negative results can indicate improvement. After the strategies have been implemented, another assessment should then be performed to see if the strategies were more effective and/or efficient. It is also important to determine if the assessment itself has impacted results. In other words, assessment should be assessed. Assessments may not be accurate in measuring what they are supposed to measure; they may not be asking the right questions of the right people at the right time to provide usable results. The use of multiple sources of assessment data can address this issue and ensure confidence in the results.

In addition, the best way to tackle negative results is to identify strategies for improvement prior to sharing findings and including those in communicating the results. Having an action plan for acknowledging weaknesses and a commitment to improving those results is critical. It is extremely important to then follow through with the changes. When assessment results suggest a change that cannot be made (Who does not want free tuition, a personal parking spot in front of the residence hall, and gourmet meals delivered to his or her room?), it is just as important to explain the rationale for not making changes. That typically centers on legal or policy issues, funding challenges, safety concerns, and institutional priorities.

Making Sure That Results Are Used

If results are not used, assessment really is not done, since assessment is contingent upon closing the loop, not simply collecting the data. In other words, assessment data must be turned into action. Evidence does not automatically foster change (Kuh et al., 2015). Middaugh (2010) framed this issue well when he stated,

> All too often the products of assessment activity fail to undergo an important transformation. . . . The data are not, in and of themselves, equivalent to information. Data have to [be] massaged, manipulated and interpreted to render them into a form of information that is readily digestible and [can be] used for planning, decision making and the allocation of resources. (p. 173)

Perhaps a new standard for assessment should be considered. Assessment should be evaluated on its use to facilitate change (Kuh et al., 2015). Rather than focusing on reliability or validity, this concept, consequentiality, should be the barometer used to measure the value of any assessment.

Kuh and colleagues (2015) note three challenges to using assessment evidence. First, the evidence is not available to those who could use it. This is why stakeholders must be considered at the outside of an assessment. Second, those who have evidence and can make change do not act on those data. Third, data are used, but this does not lead to change. How can those challenges be overcome?

The following are suggestions to help ensure that action is taken. It is important to develop a culture of improvement. The American Association for Higher Education (1992) suggests that "assessment is most likely to lead to change when it's part of a larger set of conditions that promote change" (p. 3). Thus, it is critical to develop a culture that embraces change as the norm and values improvement. Change should not happen just for change's sake, but people should challenge themselves to reject the idea that "we've always done it that way."

Henning (2009) has identified 10 steps for turning assessment into action. Step one: Do not assess if there is no interest (Henning, 2009). If people are not interested in the assessment itself, they will not be supportive of the results, so it is best not to engage in the assessment at all and thus avoid wasting valuable resources.

For step two, assessment should not be done if it will not be addressed (Henning, 2009). There are some issues that administrators do not want to know the answer to. As a result, they avoid addressing the results of an assessment related to such an issue. Another reason that assessment results are not addressed is lack of sufficient resources to make improvements. The implications of results being addressed should be considered before embarking upon an assessment. The political and practical ramifications may indicate that an assessment does not have to be implemented in the prevailing time and environment.

In step three Henning (2009) also recommends that the assessor should be a change agent rather than an objective researcher. An objective researcher merely gathers the data and reports the findings. He or she may or may not interpret the findings depending on the charge. The assessor's role does not include implementation of the recommendations. In contrast, at the beginning of the assessment process, an effective change agent considers how the results will be used. The change agent perspective assists in developing a plan that includes use of the results. As student affairs structures change, there might be a position whose responsibility is to collect, analyze, and disseminate data and results. But the student affairs practitioner has the responsibility to actually make changes.

In step four, Henning (2009) states that the nimble bird gets the worm. Although administrators may not be interested in an assessment project now, they may be interested in the future. As such, one should ponder how an assessment on a particular topic might be implemented. When the need arises, the assessor will have a plan that will likely be accepted. A good student affairs practitioner will always be thinking about the future and what information is needed to meet the needs of students.

In step five, Henning (2009) recommends producing a worthy product. Without a quality product, constituents are not likely to value the results of an assessment. Thus, the method itself must be appropriate and visualization of the results must be clear and compelling.

Collins (2011), in his book *Good to Great*, discussed that a key element to making great companies different from good companies is that they get the right people on the bus and in the right seats. Step six is identifying the stakeholders and the scope of their involvement in the assessment process is critical. Some should be involved from the beginning, helping to drive or navigate the project. Other stakeholders must be updated along the way. Then there are others who may simply need to be informed at the beginning of the project and notified of the results at the end.

"Be one with the audience" is step seven (Henning, 2009), taking a lead from the *Star Wars* saga, where Luke Skywalker is told by Obi-Wan Kenobi to be "one with the Force." This step focuses on the need to know what the audience wants or needs in order to support the findings. Some people want quantitative data with attractive graphs and charts or the bottom line. Others want compelling stories of individuals. Yet other individuals want a bit of both. There may also be specific questions that audience members need answered. The wants and needs of the audience must be understood from the beginning of the project.

Step eight relates to connecting results with funding priorities as a way to ensure that results are used (Henning, 2009). Citing the work of Suskie (2009), Henning reiterates the importance of aligning assessment projects with priorities that are already funded and also aligning projects with persistent issues that the division or institution has been trying to address. This strategy ensures that results will be used as the project is connected to an issue that is already deemed important. As an example, the student health center, student counseling center, and recreational sports department may collaborate on the health and wellness issue of depression and suicide. If campus funding is not available, they may be able to apply for grants to help them implement innovative programs for students to be able to identify signs of depression, resources available, and healthy strategies to cope with stress.

Step nine is concerned with culpability. To ensure that results are implemented, someone needs to serve as the champion overseeing the implementation process. Like a sports mascot who keeps the fans engaged and excited, a champion needs to ensure that staff are engaged and changes are moving forward. This person is also the one held accountable if the results are not realized. Depending on the division or department structure, the person who collected the data may or may not be the person who takes action.

Step 10 focuses on inclusion. While there needs to be a champion overseeing the implementation process, there are often a number of folks who are involved in the implementation of results from an assessment. Implementation may impact multiple processes over multiple offices over time. To ensure collaboration and support across processes and offices, all people involved in the implementation should understand their roles and importance of them performing their functions.

Kuh and colleagues (2015) have identified "Seven Principles for Fostering Greater Use of Assessment Results." Although their focus was assessment of student learning, particularly at the institutional level, their suggestions regarding institutional assessment data can be adapted for student affairs assessment as well.

1. Gauge the value of assessment work by the extent to which the results are used.
2. Identify a target use of the evidence when designing assessment work and sharing results.
3. Begin with the end use in mind.
4. Leverage the accountability processes for meaningful action toward improvement.
5. Connect assessment work to related current divisional and institutional initiatives and projects.
6. Link assessment activity to campus functions that require evidence of student learning as the program review-process.
7. Work purposefully toward the final stage of assessment—assessing impact, closing the assessment loop—and remember that assessment is a continuous process.

Applying the suggestions from Henning (2009) and Kuh et al. (2015) can help ensure assessment data are used.

Challenges of Closing the Loop

Although it is the most important step in the assessment cycle, closing the loop can also be the most challenging to implement. Part of this challenge stems from the fact that closing the loop can be seen as a product, such as a report, an executive summary, or an infographic that depicts the data and results. But, these products do not close the loop. Even the recommendations listed in the report do not close the loop. Changes need to be made; that is when the loop is closed. Making changes is a process, not a product.

This process requires reflection and discussion with staff and stakeholders, first to make sense of the results. Kuh and colleagues (2015) remind us that "evidence does not speak for itself. Instead, it requires interpretation, integration, and reflection in search for holistic understanding and implications for action" (p. 3). St. Olaf College spent an entire year reflecting on assessment results (Baker et al., 2012). Putting them in context is essential. For example, there may have been a virus outbreak on campus right before the health services evaluation was disseminated; therefore, the outbreak negatively impacted the image of health services. This reflection takes time, time that few staff have in their already busy days. However, assessment should be seen as an investment in quality. Taking time to reflect on how to improve programs and services will likely save time later on as that program and service will be more effective in achieving its explicit goals.

Once the data are contextualized, staff must carefully consider what changes would address identified shortcomings. Given resource constraints, remedies need to be creative. This part of the process may take a great deal of time as it may include consultation with colleagues at other campuses, attending workshops on the topic, or talking with experts as ways to explore all possible options before settling on the best solutions for a particular campus.

The next step is implementing the change. Anyone who has gone through change on a college campus knows how difficult it can be. The change can be as simple as keeping the library open later for late-night studiers or it may include reorganization of a division to provide a more integrated student services model. The more complex the suggestion solution, the bigger impact on the status quo and the more challenging the change. Implementing and managing change is a complicated process in itself.

If a person begins the assessment process seeing himself or herself as a change agent and understanding that the ultimate result is change, the process of closing the loop will be easier because, from the beginning, assessment will be seen as a process, not a product or destination.

Although it seems that process ends with implementation, it does not; the assessment process must continue.

Continuing the Loop

Use of results is the fourth step in Suskie's (2009) assessment cycle, and it is also called "closing the loop." But the term *closing the loop* may not accurately describe this step or the end of the process. Assessment should not end with implementing evidence-based recommendations. Although this action is critical, assessment should be an ongoing process. Thus, once results are put into action to make improvements, another assessment should be performed at an appropriate time to determine if the implemented changes had a positive impact. If the results do not have a positive impact, other strategies may need to be implemented to realize improvement. The key is to think about the assessment cycle as an ongoing process rather than a finite process with a distinct end point.

Conclusion

Using assessment results is a challenge for student affairs professionals. Change is difficult, especially in an ever-changing environment. Finding the time to reflect on the results and process how to make improvements is tough for people with already demanding schedules. But if student affairs staff do not take steps to improve the student experience, students lose out.

Before undertaking any assessment project, assessors should be sure that they are assessing something important, something over which they have control, and something that stakeholders support. Keeping this in mind will ensure the success of the project.

Key Points

- Purposes for using assessment results include decision making, resource allocation, planning, and improvement.
- Results should be used fairly, ethically, and responsibly.
- It is critical to close the loop by putting results into action, but this process must also continue, making assessment an ongoing endeavor.

Discussion Questions and Activities

- What are the different types of improvements that may be made using assessment results?
- Identify five ways in which assessment results can be used fairly, ethically, and responsibly.
- Identify five steps to ensuring that results are used.
- You have been asked to assess the needs of trans-identified students on all campuses of your university. What steps might you take to make sure that the needs identified in the assessment are addressed?
- As part of a semiannual health survey conducted on campus, you notice that alcohol abuse and related negative consequences are on the rise and should be addressed. Your institution has traditionally avoided public discussion of alcohol use on campus for fear of tarnishing the university's image and impacting recruitment efforts. What actions can you take to make sure that the results of this assessment are used and the issues are addressed?

ETHICS

S tudent affairs professionals make ethical decisions on an almost daily basis and have a responsibility to follow ethical standards, which is no less critical when performing assessment. There may also be legal regulations to adhere to, but not every ethical situation has legal repercussions. Thus, understanding the ethical implications of this work and adhering to expectations of moral behavior is vital for those performing assessment. This chapter explores those implications and expectations.

Foundations for Ethics in Assessment

Two complementary ethical frameworks serve as the foundation for ethical practice in student affairs assessment: research ethics and general ethics for student affairs practitioners. Much of our understanding of ethics in assessment comes from ethical issues in research. Before beginning a discussion of ethics in assessment, let's define our terms. *Ethics* is a branch of philosophy regarding how people should behave toward others, as well as judgments regarding actions that are used to develop rules to guide choices (Kitchener, 2000). According to Lichtman (2012), "Ethical behavior represents a set of moral principles, rules, or standards governing a person or profession" (p. 51).

Three major documents form the foundation of ethical principles in human subjects research and thus also assessment. The first document is the Nuremberg Code. This document, written in 1947, was an ethical response to the human experimentation done by Nazi physicians and investigators during World War II and identified the fundamental rights of research participants and responsibilities of researchers (Ravindra, 2011). The second foundational document regarding ethical behavior in research is the Declaration of Helsinki. This 1964 document outlined ethical principles and practices for those performing medical research involving human subjects or identifiable human material or data (World Health Organization, 2001). The third document governing ethical research involving human subjects came from the U.S. Department of Health, Education, and Welfare, now the U.S. Department of Health and Human Services. *The Belmont Report* was written in 1974 and outlined the basic ethical principles that should underlie practice of biomedical and behavioral research involving human subjects (U.S. Department of Health, Education, and Welfare, 1974). In addition to these foundational documents, the U.S. Department of Health and Human Services has outlined federal regulations for research involving human subjects that is funded directly or indirectly using federal monies (U.S. Department of Health and Human Services, 2009). These regulations govern the establishment of the institutional review boards (IRBs) that will be discussed later in the chapter. Current ethical practices for research have evolved from these documents and also inform ethical practice of assessment in higher education.

Conceptual Framework for Ethical Practice

Although there are historical and regulatory documents to inform ethical behavior in assessment, the employment of a conceptual framework provides a set of overarching guiding principles. Schuh and Associates (2008) has suggested using Kitchener's ethical principles for student affairs. Kitchener (1985) outlines the following ethical principles that should guide student affairs practice:

- Respecting autonomy
- Doing no harm
- Benefiting others
- Being just
- Being faithful

In performing student affairs assessments, the autonomy of individuals should be protected, including their free agency to decide their desired actions and their freedom of choice (Kitchener, 1985) to participate in the assessment project. Doing no harm is another basic element of ethical practice. In regard to assessment practice, this means that any assessment performed should not risk harming others. This tenet is the foundation for providing privacy to individuals participating in assessment. Assessment should also provide benefits for others. Often the benefit of assessment is reaped by the organization performing it or by others participating in a program or service that has been improved because of a previous assessment. But when possible, benefits should be provided to those who actually participate in assessment, and those benefits should outweigh the costs of participating.

For Kitchener (1985), being just translates into being fair and includes the standards of impartiality, equality, and reciprocity. In assessment, this could mean that all participants are made aware of results and have equal access to any programs or services or other resources that are being assessed. For example, if two programs are being assessed with participants randomly assigned to either program A or program B and results demonstrate that B is much more effective than A, participants in A should be given access to B if they choose. In this way all participants have access to effective programming. Being faithful means being honest with assessment participants. Participants should be fully informed regarding assessment activities and should not be deceived. Using Kitchener's (1985) framework as a springboard, the more specific issues regarding ethical assessment practice will be discussed next.

Respecting Autonomy

Christians (2011, p. 65) has provided a philosophical and sociological foundation for respecting autonomy in the research process by stating that proper respect for human freedom must include voluntary participation. Respecting autonomy, in connection to assessment, can be understood as "recruiting people without any form of coercion or pressure to participate in assessment projects and respecting their perspectives as they contribute data" (Schuh & Associates, 2009, p. 192).

Although understanding and witnessing explicit coercion is easy, anticipating and recognizing implicit coercion is challenging, and student affairs practitioners performing assessment should be cognizant of the latter. Implicit coercion may happen when the assessor has a relationship with potential participants where there is a power differential. This occurs in the supervisor/supervisee, hall director/resident, or advisor/student organization leader and similar relationships. In these cases, although there is no explicit coercion on the part of the staff member, the potential participant may feel that there will be a penalty of some kind for nonparticipation. For example, assume that a residence hall director (RHD) wants to assess interpersonal communication between resident assistants (RAs) and students who isolate themselves from the floor community. The RHD knows that getting students connected to the community positively influences success. Identifying strategies that connect students could be used by others on campus and help many students. To gather these data, the RHD would like to observe two interactions between the RAs and the isolated students and then briefly interview the students about their connections in the building. The RHD, Ayana, asks the RAs which students seem disconnected and isolated. Once those students are identified, Ayana asks the RAs if they can be observed along with the isolated students. This assessment is to take place during the spring semester. Omar is an RA who just began his position this semester because the previous RA is studying abroad. Omar is still a little nervous about the position and wants to do well so that he can be rehired after his contract ends. When asked to be observed, he feels that the only possible answer is to say "yes." Although there is no explicit coercion here, there is implicit coercion, since he wants to do well in Ayana's eyes, receive a good evaluation, and hopefully be rehired. Omar fears that saying "no" would undermine his chances of being rehired or could lead to repercussions, as Ayana is the supervisor. One solution would be for Ayana to have someone else, perhaps even another student, perform the observation. This would address the power dynamic in the assessment. Ayana could also provide a statement in writing for RAs that participation is voluntary and choosing not to participate will not result in any negative repercussions. Informed consent forms (discussed later in this chapter) would be used for the RAs participating, and nonparticipation forms could be used for those RAs who do not want to be part of the assessment. Both the RA and the RHD would sign the forms.

With voluntary participation, participants also have the right to withdraw from the assessment project whenever they choose. Although this is an unfortunate circumstance for the assessor, the request should be granted and all previous data from that participant should be deleted from the study. These deleted data should include any pretest or other longitudinal data. If students stop taking a survey midway, the assessor must determine whether to keep the partial data or delete all of them. An example may be helpful. Some assessment projects are longitudinal, in which case participants complete surveys or participate in focus groups or interviews over a period of time. This could occur during a specific intervention or could go on throughout their entire college careers. At any point, the student has the ethical right to withdraw from the assessment project. Although data may already have been collected, all data related to the student should be deleted from the project data unless the student gives permission to keep them. Participants may also agree at the beginning of the study that all data can be used unless they request removal of data upon withdrawal from the study.

As noted earlier, voluntary participation in assessment is based on ethical principles in social science research. Assessment is not the same as social science research. There may be instances where mandatory assessment would be appropriate: for example, grading of assignments in a course. Grading is a form of assessment of learning performed by instructors. Students usually do not have a choice to participate in these types of assessments. There may be parallel circumstances in student affairs. One example may be assessment of a new method of providing alcohol education to students who have violated college alcohol policies. With the goal of determining the value of this new alcohol education program, participants may be required to take part in a learning outcome assessment as part of the program. Another example involves student employees. Student employees at a university student center might be required to respond to reflective prompts asking them to connect their work experiences with academic learning and describe how they have applied practical, leadership, and multicultural skills as part of their daily work. These reflections are then analyzed for performance on key learning outcomes, students are given individual feedback, and the program is revised based on results on a regular basis. This kind of assessment is perhaps better thought of as an integral part of the teaching/learning process rather than as external research. However, if the data were presented at a conference, some IRBs would say that these data now constitute research. Staff performing assessments should carefully consider the pros and cons of mandating assessment participation.

Doing No Harm

A critical responsibility for those performing assessment is reducing any risk to participants. Although this is a greater issue in medical research than in social science research, there may be opportunities for harm to participants in assessment. Often risk of harm is associated with responses to questions that are sensitive or critical or that cast a negative light on a program, service, or department. For example, participants could be asked to reveal illegal or embarrassing behavior. A respondent's status could be jeopardized if individual responses are revealed. Maintaining respondents' privacy to minimize this risk is a critical ethical issue in assessment.

In regard to privacy in assessment, there should be a focus on two forms: anonymity and confidentiality. Although these are similar, there are distinct differences between the two notions. *Anonymity* means that no one, including the researcher, knows the identity of any respondents. Quantitative assessments typically provide the opportunity to offer anonymity. However, when data are collected electronically, there could be instances in which data are not anonymous: With most online survey tools, the IP address or some other identifying information is collected. Although it may be difficult for the person doing the assessment to gain access to this identifying information and even more difficult to connect this information to the individual, it is still possible, and anonymity cannot be ensured. Some online survey tools do allow the collection of IP addresses to be turned off.

With *confidentiality*, the person doing the assessment is able to connect responses to specific individuals but vows not to share those connections publicly. An effective way to ensure confidentiality is to remove all identifying information—such as real names, student IDs, email addresses, and so on—from the data (Lichtman, 2012). The only exception would be if an identifier was needed to connect assessment data with institutional student records or subsequent longitudinal assessment data such as a posttest assessment or an assessment completed later in students' college careers. When possible, students should create identifiers of their own that cannot be traced back to them. Using the last four digits of their Social Security numbers or student ID numbers is a useful suggestion as there is little chance of there being duplicates, the numbers are too few to allow the Social Security number to be deciphered, and such numbers are easy for respondents to remember if they need to include them on pre- and posttests. It is also possible for demographic data to be preloaded into survey responses based on a unique identifier created by the survey software. It is the responsibility of the assessor to keep this information secure. In the case of qualitative data arising from focus groups or interviews, assigning participants pseudonyms or numbers can be used to name individuals without identifying them (Creswell, 2012).

Even when an assessor wants to ensure confidentiality, there are circumstances when privacy may ethically be violated. These situations include when participants report intent to harm themselves or others, admit to committing a crime, or discuss sexual or physical abuse (in the case of children). It is incumbent upon staff to know state and federal laws as well as institutional policies regarding what circumstances must be reported. One way to be proactive in this situation is to describe the types of information that are required to be reported. Participants can be more attentive to what they choose to share after instructions are read. For very sensitive research topics, the National Institutes of Health issues certificates of confidentiality to protect participants' identity even from legal demands.

Whereas sharing names along with responses is an obvious violation of the privacy mandate, other situations are not as explicit. Lichtman (2012) urges caution in using verbatim quotes, as they may be traced back to the respondent and this may cause harm. Considering how participants are characterized in published results is also critical. In describing participants, particularly in a qualitative assessment, descriptions should not be so precise as to make the respondent evident by providing a number of personal characteristics. A similar circumstance happens in quantitative assessment when there is a small response rate for a question. Disaggregating responses by ethnicity, gender, and other variables and sharing this information publicly may lead to identification of individual respondents.

Benefiting Others

Like research, assessment should benefit others. Beneficiaries often include the department, office, or individual performing the assessment (Schuh & Associates 2009). The individual or office benefits from the assessment since they learn what is working and what is not and are able to make improvements based on that. Beyond benefits to those performing the assessment, future participants also benefit, as they reap the rewards of improved programming or service delivery. Benefits for the actual assessment participants may not be as obvious. For many, helping improve programs and services is a benefit. For others, knowing that their input made a difference is a benefit. Thus, it is essential not only to share assessment results with participants but also to describe how those results lead to positive change. Tangible benefits also include free food, gift certificates, extra credit, or other incentives for people to participate. As with any study, those overseeing the assessment should weigh the advantages of providing incentives and also how the presence of incentives could influence participant responses.

Being Just

As Kitchener (1985) pointed out, being just means being fair and includes three standards: impartiality, equality, and reciprocity. *Reciprocity* relates to the Golden Rule: Treat others the way you would want to be treated. This is a valuable overarching principle in assessment. *Equality* and *impartiality* suggest that there should be equal treatment. This issue has an impact on access to an intervention. One type of assessment is a quasi-experiment. Group A may experience an intervention, perhaps a new model for academic advising, while Group B does not get the intervention. If the intervention proves beneficial, being just would require that Group B also get access to the intervention after the assessment is over. Thus, both groups would get access to the beneficial intervention.

Being Faithful

As noted earlier, Kitchener (1985) associated being faithful with being honest. The use of deception in the assessment process is not consistent with being faithful. *Deception* can be defined as "the act of creating a false impression in the minds of research participants through procedures such as withholding information, establishing false intimacy, telling lies, or using accomplices" (Gall, Gall, & Borg, 2007, p. 71). Only in rare instances would deception be appropriate. In those cases, the assessor would debrief the participants explaining the deception and the rationale for it. While intentional deceit in the form of lying is infrequent, deceit may occur in the form of an unintentional omission of information. The assessor may not fully explain how the responses will be used or may not tell participants that data will be connected to institutional data for each respondent, such as GPA, race/ethnicity, or major. Participants should be given as much information as possible before participating in voluntary assessment. Participants should have the appropriate information, especially regarding how their responses will be used, to make an informed choice regarding their participation. Participants can then provide informed consent acknowledging this. Informed consent will be covered later in the chapter.

Another element of being faithful is being cognizant that assessment regarding sensitive topics may cause discomfort or reintroduce past trauma for some participants. In working with delicate issues such as sexual assault and discrimination, assessors should provide access to counseling and educational resources. Web links or contact information for these resources could be included in the introduction to a data-collection tool or as a handout for in-person assessments.

Timm and Lloyd (2013) have described another aspect of faithfulness: sharing the data and utilizing the results. Abiding by this concept requires the sharing of negative in addition to positive results. After the assessment findings are shared, they should be used to improve the programs or services being assessed. For more details, see Chapter 14.

Additional Considerations

Ethical frameworks for research can be useful when applied to assessment because of the similarity in practice. However, additional guidance provided by Zeni (2006) is informative. Zeni (2006) discusses the shortcomings of traditional approaches to ethical considerations to research done in schools by teachers. The goal in most of this type of research is to improve practice, similar to a major purpose of assessment. But, since the teacher is part of the context of the researcher and has an ongoing relationship with the students who are participants, there are different, and additional, issues to contemplate. Zeni (2006) posited a series of questions to answer prior to engaging in this type of research. These questions revolve around the project, methods and settings, subjects and subjectivity, risks and benefits, ethical questions specific to "insider" research, and the Golden Rule. Space limitations prohibit providing identification questions in each of these sections. The concepts expressed center around the role of the students in the research. Since they are part of the teaching and learning experience, they are cocreating that experience with the teacher. They are not anonymous subjects objectively distanced from the researcher. As such, it may be beneficial to have students be active participants in the research. This issue applies to student affairs assessment as well. There are times when the students are cocreating the learning and thus the assessment. Zeni's (2006) ethical questions should be considered before engaging in qualitative assessment.

Timm and Lloyd (2013) have identified additional issues with ethical implications. The first relates to hidden agendas in assessment. Although many assessment projects are used to evaluate the effectiveness of programs, some assessors may be looking for or expecting positive outcomes. Intentionally or unintentionally, the data collection, analysis, and reporting processes are then designed to highlight those anticipated outcomes. It is the responsibility of the assessor to report all findings honestly, including negative results. Another situation may be when an assessor wants to see a particular change to a program, perhaps decreasing welcome activities by a day. To support this claim, the assessor designs an assessment that will produce data to back the intended goal. A useful solution to these two issues is to have multiple people work on assessment projects, specifically people from outside the department doing the assessment. The additional benefit of this approach is adding a new and fresh perspective.

Another issue identified by Timm and Lloyd (2013) is use of the appropriate methodology. A methodology and corresponding method should be selected depending on the assessment question. However, assessors may choose a particular methodology or method because they are comfortable with one over another. Providing professional development around assessment helps staff add tools to their toolbox, thus alleviating these types of ethical situations.

Ethics in Professional Standards

Whereas the previous discussion has provided an overview of ethical issues related to ethics in student affairs assessment, there are also professional standards that should be consulted.

The Council for the Advancement of Standards in Higher Education

The Council for the Advancement of Standards in Higher Education, known as CAS, is a consortium of over 40 higher education associations that develops and promulgates standards for professional practice. In addition to these standards, CAS has developed a Statement of Shared Ethical Principles (Council for the Advancement of Standards in Higher Education, 2012c). This statement is modeled on Kitchener's (1985) ethical principles of respecting autonomy, nonmalfeasance (doing no harm), beneficence, justice, and fidelity (being faithful). In addition to these principles, the CAS document includes veracity and affiliation. Veracity is the ability to be honest and "convey the truth in words and actions" (Council for the Advancement of Standards in Higher Education, 2012a, p. 22). Affiliation is the promotion of connected relationships and fostering of community. Given that CAS's goal is self-assessment and that these standards are approved by the 42 associations in the consortium, a review of these ethical standards is useful.

In addition to the Statement of Shared Ethical Principles, ethics is a part of the general standards that are included in all functional area standards. Of particular significance to the topic of this text are the ethics standards and guidelines included in the Assessment Services Standards. A few of these ethical principles are worth highlighting. Assessment offices

- Must seek approval from an IRB if the findings will be published outside beyond internal review of the institution
- Should seek IRB approval for all assessment studies when an institution considers assessment generalizable research
- Must ensure privacy or anonymity of study participants
- Must regularly purge identifiable information collected to protect the privacy of participants
- Should maintain raw data for a period of time after the results are published to respond to any questions about the study or results
- Must acknowledge methodological limitations of assessment studies (Council for the Advancement of Standards in Higher Education, 2012a, p. 75)

ACPA—College Student Educators International

ACPA has developed a set of ethical principles for members, some of which apply to assessment practice. This set of standards has four sections: professional responsibility and competence, student learning and development, responsibility to the institution, and responsibility to society. Principles related to assessment practice include the following:

- Informing students of the purpose of assessment as well as discussing how results will be used.
- Complying with institutional policies regarding transmission of electronic data.
- Providing appropriate contextual information prior to participation in evaluation processes.
- Evaluating programs and services regularly to ensure conformity to published standards and guidelines. Evaluation should be performed using rigorous methods.
- Acknowledging contributions of others to evaluation reports. (ACPA—College Student Educators International, n.d., pp. 3–5)

NASPA–Student Affairs Administrators in Higher Education

NASPA specifically supports the CAS Statement of Shared Ethical Principles and has Standards of Professional Practice that provide direction for ethical behavior in assessment. According to these standards, NASPA members should perform assessment regularly to determine whether goals and published standards are met. Assessment results should also be made available to appropriate constituencies so that programs and services can be improved (NASPA–Student Affairs Administrators in Higher Education, n.d.).

In addition to professional association ethical principles, the topic of ethics is also addressed in competencies related to assessment. The *ASK Standards* were published in 2006 by ACPA. Those standards identified the following ethical principles related to assessment practice:

- Understanding the role of IRBs
- Ensuring privacy of participants
- Interpreting Family Educational Rights and Privacy Act (FERPA) guidelines for assessment projects (ACPA—College Student Educators International, 2006, pp. 8–9)

The joint ACPA/NASPA *Professional Competency Areas for Student Affairs Practitioners*, (ACPA—College Student Educators International & NASPA–Student Affairs Administrators in Higher Education, 2015) have a competency area for assessment, evaluation, and research. Specific ethical principles are denoted within the competency area. These principles focus on the following:

- Understanding regarding ethical assessment including IRB approval and informed consent
- Ensuring confidentiality of results
- Using culture appropriate terminology and methods to conduct assessment
- Ensuring compliance with professional standards concerning ethical assessment activities (ACPA—College Student Educators International & NASPA–Student Affairs Administrators in Higher Education, 2010, pp. 8–9)

Institutional Review Boards

IRBs are governing bodies developed to review and monitor research involving human subjects. The overarching purpose of these boards is to ensure that the rights of human subjects are protected. Boards want to be sure research participation is voluntary, benefits are optimized, and risks are minimized. These boards are mandated for any research that involves human subjects and that is funded by federal government monies. However, institutions may choose to use IRBs for research that is not government funded to provide the same safeguards for participants. The IRBs resulted from *The Belmont Report* (U.S. Department of Health, Education, and Welfare, 1974), discussed at the beginning of the chapter, and their authority was enhanced in 1989 when the U.S. Congress passed the National Institutes of Health Revitalization Act and formed the Commission on Research Integrity (Christians, 2011). Currently, IRBs are governed by regulations found in section 45, part 46 of the Code of Federal Regulations (U.S. Department of Health and Human Services, 2009), which can be reviewed for further details.

It is crucial to clarify what is considered "research" according to the federal guidelines, as it may impact IRB review of assessment projects. IRBs are required to review any research that is "generalizable" in nature. This means "empirical findings that are reported in a formal manner and the investigator claims to be contribution to research knowledge" (Gall et al., 2007, p. 79). Like many other federal regulations, IRB scope is subject to interpretation. Some institutions may consider assessment projects "quality improvement" that are internal to the institution and thus not generalizable research. These IRBs may provide blanket exemption from review or may still want to review individual projects. Other IRBs may consider any data that are collected and shared publicly in the form of a report, data on a website, or a conference presentation as "generalizable research" and subject to review. Anyone performing assessment should consult his or her campus IRB to understand the parameters for review at their institution. Some smaller institutions that do not engage in federally funded research may not have IRBs. In this case it is useful to seek approval from an institutional leader before performing assessment.

There are three levels of review: exempt, expedited, and full review. The exempt level is for research that poses minimal risk such as observation or occurs in commonly accepted educational settings involving normal educational practices (University of New Hampshire, 2013). The next level is expedited. This is for research with minimal risk, but more risk than exempt research. Finally, full review is for research that does not qualify as exempt or expedited (University of New Hampshire, 2013). In student affairs, that may include projects with sensitive questions. Most assessment projects, including those using existing data, will likely fall within the exempt category. It is important to note that the IRB must make this classification upon review, not the person doing the assessment. It should also be noted that several IRBs may not allow retroactive approval, although some institutions do have "existing data" categories that can be used when data may be of use for assessment after they have been collected. As such, it is critical to consult with the IRB before doing any assessment project, as obtaining IRB approval after a study is rare.

Informed Consent

There are a host of issues to consider when adhering to Kitchener's principles. One of these is informed consent. Christians (2011) states that all participation in research studies should be based on full and open information. This statement is consistent for participation in assessment projects as well. Lichtman (2012) suggests that it is an investigator's responsibility to inform participants as much as possible about the study. Informed consent respects autonomy as the participants can choose to participate or not in the assessment based on information regarding it. Doing no harm and benefiting others is maintained as informed consent outlines both the known possible risks and the benefits of the assessment. The informed consent itself is also a form of faithfulness as the person doing the assessment is trying to provide as much information as possible to the participants. The focus should be on transparency of the purpose of the assessment including how data will be used and the benefits.

In more formal assessments such as institutional surveys, participants may sign consent forms that are kept on file to document that consent was given or acknowledge their consent in other ways that can be documented. With online data collection, after text that describes the study, there may be a question that participants answer to acknowledge that they consent to participate. If they select "yes," they are given the first question of the questionnaire. If they say "no," they exit the assessment. Since many focus groups or interviews are audio recorded, as discussed in Chapter 11, informed consent can be recorded as well. On the recording, the participants can state their names and acknowledge that they have read and agree with the informed consent statement. Participants should always receive a copy of the signed consent form.

There are other ways to obtain informed consent aside from signing a form. For surveys, a description of the study could be included in the introduction of the survey and the first question asks the participant to respond yes or no to agreeing to participate in the study. Other surveys may say that completing the survey signifies that the respondent has read and understood the explanation of the study and their rights and agrees to participate.

Consent can be given only by individuals 18 years or older. In working with individuals under 18 years of age, a parent or guardian must consent and the person under 18 must assent, or agree, to participate. Without consent, an individual should not be allowed to participate in an assessment even if a parent or guardian provided consent.

Informed consent forms or descriptions have specific information included. Most IRBs provide examples of informed consent, making it easier to know what details to include. A simple Internet search would also provide examples. The following are descriptions of the main components of informed consent.

Reason for Contact

Participants should know why they were contacted. The contact could be a result of random selection, participation in an activity being assessed, or the possession of characteristics that are being studied.

Study Description

The study is described in sufficient detail for a participant to understand what the assessment is and how the data will be used.

Time Commitment

For participants to make an informed decision whether or not to participate, they need to know what the time commitment is. A simple survey may take only a couple of minutes, but a longitudinal panel assessment may take many hours over multiple years.

Benefits

Informed consent information should also include a description of the benefits. It is important to be honest and not manufacture benefits. If there are benefits to an organization or future participants in a program or service but no benefits to those sharing information, that should be stated.

Risks

Potential risks should be described. Like side effects listed for a medication, even remote risks should be included in the informed consent information. The more details potential participants have regarding all possible risks, no matter how small, the better able they will be to make the most informed decision regarding participation.

Use of Data

Potential participants must know how the data will be used. Providing this information serves a couple of purposes. First, this may be an incentive for people to participate as they believe the results will be used to make improvements in a program or service. Second, it allows potential participants to be aware of the purpose of the data collection, allowing them to make an informed choice regarding their own participation.

Privacy

A critical element of any informed consent document is the section regarding how participant responses will be kept private. There should be a discussion regarding how any assigned identifiers such as numbers or pseudonyms may be used; how data will be securely stored; and if, and when, raw data will be destroyed.

Contact Information

The email address and phone number of the individual performing the assessment should always be included if any questions arise. For in-person studies, assessors should provide a copy of this information to the participant to take with them when they leave. Having the contact information on the consent form that the participant signs and returns is not helpful to them later on. For online surveys, this contact information should be in the email invitation as it adds legitimacy to the request.

Resources

Finally, assessors should include any resources that may be useful for participants if the topic of the assessment is a sensitive issue, such as sexual assault or discrimination. Resources may include contact information for the campus counseling center or online information. Again, this information should be provided in a format that participants can take with them.

Data Interpretation

In addition to data collection, ethical behavior must be adhered to regarding the analysis and interpretation of assessment data. Care should be taken to avoid incorrect statements, misinterpretations, and inaccurate analyses (Lichtman, 2012). In qualitative assessment, sharing findings with participants when their specific statements are included in the results will ensure that they have been depicted accurately. Relevant literature and/or experts on the topic should be consulted as another means of verifying findings. Sufficient contextual information should be provided when results are shared so that others can evaluate the interpretations of the data. In addition to ensuring accurate data interpretation, these steps ensure rigor of the assessment, as described in Chapter 10, on qualitative methods. In addition, Creswell (2012) warns against siding with participants and disclosing only positive results.

Power Dynamics

As in educational research, power dynamics can exist in assessment. Care should be taken to level power differentials between participants and those conducting the assessment. As discussed earlier, power dynamics may lead to intentional or unintentional coercion to participate in an assessment project if the assessor supervises, advises, leads, or manages potential participants. Participants may feel compelled to participate or respond in a favorable way to please their supervisor or because they fear retaliation or penalties. The best solution is to have someone other than the supervisor perform the assessment.

Assessors should be cognizant of sensitive issues related to special populations such as children or incarcerated individuals. Although these individuals are not likely to be college students, there may be programs such as service-learning activities that interact with these populations; therefore, collecting data from them may be helpful. Vulnerable populations such as these may experience similar coercion to those being supervised. Therefore, procedures should be in place to protect the autonomy of vulnerable populations. For IRB requests, these procedures need to be detailed.

With the growing diversity of individuals in college communities, people doing assessment must be culturally competent in order to respect the norms of different cultures. There may be varying expectations when approaching or communicating with individuals from different cultures. Perform due diligence regarding accepted cultural behavior to be appropriate and respectful.

Conclusion

There are a number of ethical principles to be adhered to in performing assessment activities. These are influenced by research standards as well as professional and functional area standards. This chapter provided an overview of those principles as well as commentary from professional associations regarding ethical assessment practice. Kitchener's (1985) five principles—respecting autonomy, doing no harm, benefiting others, being just, and being faithful—provide solid guidance in acting ethically.

Key Points

- Kitchener (1985) provides a useful framework for being ethical in assessment. It includes five tenets: respect autonomy, do no harm, benefit others, be just, and be faithful.

- Power dynamics, hidden agendas, and methodological decisions can all have ethical implications.
- Assessment activities at colleges and universities may need to be approved by IRBs, which are tasked with making sure that the rights of participants are maintained.

Discussion Questions and Activities

- In your own words define each of the following in the context of assessment: respect autonomy, do no harm, benefit others, be just, be faithful.
- Identify five different assessment situations that could have ethical implications. For each of these, describe what can be done to avoid the situation or to address it.
- Imagine that you are an assistant director of residence life and want to evaluate RHDs in the middle of the academic year on their effectiveness; you therefore plan to interview all RAs across campus. You are cognizant of the power dynamics of being in a position of power and asking the RAs to report on their own supervisors, with whom they must continue to work. How would you resolve this ethical dilemma?
- Imagine that you have done a campus climate assessment to determine how safe and comfortable students feel on campus. The results suggest that over 60% of students of color and 30% of LGBT students do not feel safe. To address the climate issue, you recommend sharing these results in the student paper and convening a group to identify solutions. Your supervisor wants you to shelve the report and share it with no one out of fear that the results would reflect poorly on the institution, which is struggling with admissions. What would you do?

16

POLITICS

On the surface, assessment may appear simply as a process to identify what is working well and how that work can be improved. However, Upcraft and Schuh (2002) have stated that assessment "virtually always occurs in a political context that the investigators must take into account in designing the assessment" (p. 19). There are multiple constituencies within a college or university with different interests and goals; these may constitute this political context. These groups try to utilize their power to gain control of various resources to achieve their goals. As such, assessment is inherently a political activity, as it involves the allocation of resources, decision making, and power. When assessment is used to measure effectiveness, the underlying issue is whether a program or service achieved its goals or intended outcomes. In other words, were the resources efficiently and effectively used? A corollary question relates to efficiency. Were the resources devoted to implementing a program or service used as effectively as possible? Both of these are critical issues to explore, given the tightening of budgets. When an assessment is performed to determine opportunities for improvement, the subsequent issue relates to how resources should be reallocated to ensure effectiveness and efficiency.

Although financial resources may be the most evident type of resource to allocate, there are four other types of resources. First, physical resources can be considered more valuable than money on many campuses. There are many stories of students, faculty, and staff fighting for offices or parking spaces. The second type of resource is technology. Although expensive, technology can increase effectiveness and efficiency, resulting in long-term financial savings. Human resources are the third type. Given the number of additional responsibilities assigned to student affairs professionals, human resources become critical in fulfilling those duties. Related to human resources are intellectual resources, the fourth type of resource. Human resources are the people themselves, whereas intellectual resources are the skills and knowledge of the staff. Despite sufficient staff, programs and services cannot be effective or efficient if those staff members do not have the ability to implement them.

In order to truly define the term *politics*, further discussion is critical. Easton has provided the most commonly used definition of *politics* (Lesperance, personal communication). In his 1965 text *A Framework for Political Analysis*, Easton describes politics as the authoritative allocation of values for a society (p. 50). These allocated values influence how resources are distributed. Lasswell, in a much earlier text, provides a much more concise definition in the title of his 1936 book: *Politics: Who Gets What, When, How*. As can be seen by these descriptions, politics can be reduced to resources and who has the power to allocate those resources to support specific values and goals.

To further the conversation of *politics*, this topic must be understood in the context of higher education. Although Lasswell's definition is concise and to the point, it may be too simplistic to be applied to complex organizations such as colleges and universities.

The Contextual Lens of Politics

Higher education is a unique context, and politics must be examined specifically within this context to fully understand its implications. Bolman and Deal (2013) have provided assumptions regarding politics in higher education. One assumption is that organizations are coalitions of different individuals and interest groups. These coalitions have differing values, beliefs, and interests that impact decisions regarding the allocation of resources and who has the power to make those decisions. Colleges and universities are organizations with these same characteristics. For example, alcohol abuse is an issue on virtually all college campuses. This problem can be addressed in multiple ways by multiple groups of people on campus; some of these are individuals and others are coalitions of individuals. Faculty may say that alcohol policies should be more lenient so that students can learn to drink responsibly rather than abusively. Health care professionals may approach alcohol abuse as a public health issue and want to address it through education. Residential life staff may view alcohol abuse as a community issue, given the negative impact on residence hall communities, while campus safety may view this as a policy issue. The community outside of campus may be concerned with the negative behavior happening in town, which needs to be addressed. These last three groups may believe that addressing the issue requires vigilant enforcement. Each of these groups approaches the same issue with different values, beliefs, and interests, all of which influence how resources can be allocated to address the issue.

Roberts and Osters (2006) have built on this discussion of politics in higher education and bridged the concept with assessment. They note that politics is challenging in higher education and specifically in assessment because it affects resource allocation. Lis Dean (2013) continued by stating that conflicts occur when individuals or groups compete for resources. Assessment can cause conflicts because it may facilitate competition for resources. If a program has been assessed and it is determined that its goals and outcomes are not achieved, reallocation of resources is discussed. Questions arise including the following: Should the program be revised? Should the program be eliminated and resources used for a different initiative to achieve the same goal? Should the resources be allocated somewhere else in the division? Answers to these questions reduce the issue to who makes the decision to reallocate resources. That is why it is critical for student affairs professionals performing assessment to understand who makes decisions, who controls resources, and who has positional power (Roberts, 2015). This information will help to decide when and whether an assessment is to be conducted; the type of assessment to be done; the type of data to be collected; the analyses to be performed; and how, when, and with whom the results are to be shared.

Some decision makers focus on outcomes whereas others may focus on resource expenditure, satisfaction, or student needs. Some decision makers prefer quantitative data, some prefer qualitative data, and others prefer to see a balance of both types. In regard to how results are shared, some decision makers want to have access to an entire assessment report including recommendations, some want only a brief overview, and yet others would like the assessor to explain the results in person. All of these preferences are useful to know before engaging in assessment. Power is the central element of politics.

Power

Power is the control of the decision-making process for resource allocation and is at the heart of politics. According to Pfeffer (1992), "Power is the potential ability to influence behavior, to change the course of events, to overcome resistance, and to get people to do things they would otherwise not do" (p. 30).

Sources of Power

Where does power come from? What are the bases of power? More than 50 years ago French and Raven (1959) identified bases of power that are still discussed today: legitimate, reward, coercive, referent, and expert. Information power was added six years later (Raven, 1965).

Legitimate power may be the most recognized form of power. This type of power is centered on the position a person holds. People in positional power have control over resources, policies, and decision making based on their level in the hierarchical structure (Roberts, 2015). Merely by being a director of a department, someone holds power. The individual responsible for the work of a department is given power through this role. Legitimate power is tied to the position, not the individual. When a person leaves a position he or she also loses the power derived from it. The higher the position in the organizational hierarchy, the more perceived and authoritative the power held in that position. A department head has power; the vice president supervising his or her department holds more power. As Lis Dean (2013) stated, identifying who is at the top of the chain of command is fairly obvious, but there are also other forms of power.

Reward power is derived from one person's ability to provide a reward so as to secure the compliance of another person. Rewards may include money, gifts, departmental resources, recognition, or prestigious roles. They may be formal or informal. These rewards may emanate from a specific role held or from an individual. A supervisor may provide a financial reward in the form of a raise that he or she has the power to bestow. However, an individual may provide reward in the form of praise or positive feedback, which may not depend on the positional role held. Nevertheless, the role of the individual providing the praise may amplify the importance of this type of reward. Some divisions of student affairs have annual awards to recognize assessment efforts. Different people require different rewards to ensure compliance. One type of reward may be effective for one person but not for another. People who often confer authentic compliments on others are building reward power even if they do not intend to.

Punishment is the basis of coercive power. Some may even view assessment as a form of punishment. Individuals comply because they fear repercussions if they do not obey a request. Coercion can mean loss of job, diminished valued responsibilities, or reprimands. Like rewards, different forms of coercion will ensure compliance by different people. Shaming, embarrassment, or neglect can be coercive. Punishments do not necessarily have to come from a supervisor, since coercive power may or may not depend on the position held.

When people are viewed as attractive, worthy, or respected by others, they hold referent power. This form of power is directly tied to the person as an individual and not the position that he or she holds. Charismatic people and informal leaders hold referent power. They may not have positional power, but people listen to them and comply with their requests and demands. Such people develop relationships with others.

Expert power, as the name suggests, is derived from expertise. The particular proficiency can be a unique skill or special knowledge—some competence not commonly held. People with assessment skill and knowledge may hold expert power. For experts, the power is situational in the sense that others will defer or comply on issues related to the expertise but they may not do so on other issues. As such, expert power is tied to an individual, not necessarily a position, although people may be placed in certain positions because of their expertise.

Information power is based on the amount and type of information someone has. Often people with information power are gatekeepers. Data constitute information and thus can be a basis for power. In this postindustrial information age, many people have acquired power rooted in the amount and type of information to which they have access. However, given the evolution of the Internet and easy access to large amounts of information, this type of power may not be as useful as it once was. On college campuses, such information could be about campus decisions, people, policies, assessment results, and so on.

In addition to the five bases of power identified by French and Raven (1959) and the additional base suggested by Raven (1965), Bolman and Deal (2013) include reputation power. Reputation builds on expertise and is rooted in accomplishments and records of achievement that an individual builds up from prior performance. This type of power may linger even when the individual is no longer an expert.

There are many forms of power that can influence resource allocation. Some of these sources are dependent upon a role or position, others are not, and there may be intersections of different bases of power. Recognizing these various sources of power and identifying people in the organization and the power they hold is essential when one is maneuvering within a political environment. This is especially important in the assessment process. Power can be enhanced through the length of tenure in a position or at an institution, authentic relationships with others, hard work, involvement in professional associations, and knowledge.

Politics in Assessment

Those performing assessment must be aware of the political context to successfully implement assessment results. As Schuh and Upcraft (2000) have noted, "Perhaps the most compelling reason that assessment findings often end up gathering dust on some policymaker's shelf is that the investigators fail to take into account the institutional *political* context" (p. 15). There are three aspects of assessment that become political. The first reason is the allocation of resources. Assessment is used to determine if resources are employed effectively and efficiently. The second reason is because "assessment exists within organizational political context with the purpose to influence policy and practice" (Lis Dean, 2013, p. 67). There could be multiple perspectives regarding how a policy should be crafted or a practice should be implemented. The decision ultimately resides with the individual(s) who have power. The third reason that assessment is political relates to the first two. In a data-informed culture, decision making regarding resource allocation, policy development, and practice implementation is driven by information. That information may or may not align with various beliefs, values, and interests related to those decisions. Information may differentially influence decision making depending on the decision maker.

Lis Dean (2013) has described how politics can influence the assessment cycle. These steps include creating appropriate outcomes, choosing what to assess, allocating resources to implement strategies for assessment, reporting results, and closing the loop. Decisions regarding each of these steps are ultimately being made by the individual or individuals with legitimate power. This is because most of these decisions impact resource allocation either directly or indirectly. Often the legitimate authority is the department or division head. Understanding who has the power to make decisions regarding assessment is vital. The people in power may not want potentially "bad" results collected or shared, so communication with those stakeholders needs to happen early and often.

Assessment is based on data—data that are collected, interpreted, shared, and used in decision making. The information process is a political one because the information can impact how resources are allocated even if allocation decisions are made by a person not directly involved in the assessment process. The individual collecting and disseminating this information has a great deal of power because of the data he or she has access to and how those data are understood. Much power is afforded to the individual performing the assessment. This reinforces the idea for staff to assess their own programs and services so that they maintain as much power as possible over the process and decisions made. If someone else does the assessment, this power is transferred to that individual.

Tips for Success

It is clear that assessment is a political process. How can one successfully navigate this political system? Roberts and Osters (2006) identify eight tips to consider:

1. Consider legal and ethical implications.
2. Know your stakeholders.
3. Collaborate with interested parties on instrument design, background information/literature review, and data dissemination.
4. Tie assessment to the mission and goals of the institution, the division, and the department if at all possible.
5. Prepare with the end in mind.
6. Think about the accountability factor in assessment before creating the assessment.
7. Plan for dissemination of information.
8. Be aware of (and use advantageously) the economic realities on campus.

As is true of many issues in higher education, it is important to know stakeholders. Henning (2009) has identified three groups. The first, and most readily recognized stakeholders, are internal stakeholders. These are the individuals who are directly connected to the assessment process. Internal stakeholders for the assessment of a residential curriculum would include the students who are engaging in the programming, the staff implementing the programming, and the residential life central office staff who are allocating resources for the implementation of this curriculum. Second, external stakeholders are those outside of the institution who may have an interest in the issue at hand. In the current example, external stakeholders could be parents of students living in the residence halls, prospective students, and parents of prospective students. External stakeholders may also include state legislators, especially if the residential curriculum affects persistence and retention. The final group of stakeholders are "mixternal." These are individuals inside the institution but not directly linked to the assessment. In regard to a residential curriculum, mixternal stakeholders would include the vice president of student affairs (or a comparable individual), admissions staff (as this programming could be an initiative to highlight), and deans, whose faculty provide programming in the curriculum. It will be useful to identify the stakeholders for each assessment project so as to understand any political issues that may arise.

Collaboration is a key strategy in a political environment and should be considered along each step of the assessment process, including literature review, instrument design, data collection, and data dissemination. Collaboration serves two purposes. First, it involves key stakeholders early in the process, which allows buy-in to occur. Second, collaboration often leads to coalition building, which increases the power of all stakeholders in the coalition, allowing the coalition to be more effective.

Another way to navigate politics is to connect assessment to the missions and goals of the institution, division, or department. These higher-level missions and goals have already been accepted and validated by legitimate power holders and provide the approved direction of the organization. Connecting assessment to one of these missions or sets of goals helps to legitimately validate the assessment project. Alignment with important priorities helps gain support.

The fifth tip is to prepare with the end in mind. Henning (2009) suggests that assessment is a change process. As such, the person doing the assessment needs to view himself or herself as a change agent, not an objective detached researcher. When such an individual considers the end in mind, he or she must think in terms of what will need to happen to foster change. If the legitimate decision maker is compelled by student stories, not faceless numbers, the collected data should include student stories. It is important to note this at the beginning of the process rather than at the end.

It is critical to consider the accountability element in the terms of assessment as a change process. In other words, it is important to contemplate what needs to be done to ensure that the data are used to make improvements. Kotter (2007) suggests several steps to ensure that change is adopted throughout an organization. His eight-stage process is as follows:

1. Increase a sense of urgency.
2. Create a guiding team.
3. Create a compelling vision.
4. Communicate the vision.
5. Empower action from others.
6. Create and reorganize short-term wins.
7. Don't let up: reinvigorate.
8. Make it stick—institutionalize.

Following a structured process helps ensure that change can be adopted throughout the organization. The change that happens is actually a form of accountability as it demonstrates that the assessment is having an impact. Assessment for improvement contributes to assessment for accountability.

The assessor must understand this at the very beginning of the assessment process. As Henning (2009) has stated, assessment should not be done if there are no resources available to support changes. It may be useful to have a discussion with the leaders who allocate resources to determine what could be available to implement change before the assessment is undertaken. It is frustrating for all involved if assessment indicates a particular change that is not feasible or supported. It is also helpful to identify a point person whose responsibility it will be to manage the change.

It is critical to plan for the dissemination of information. A dissemination plan should be developed that includes a variety of modalities to meet the diverse ways in which people digest information. Dissemination formats could include full reports, executive summaries, oral presentation, newspaper articles, data visualization, and infographics. This plan should also include time frames for dissemination. It would be detrimental to share assessment data that could impact a beloved program during the summer, when students and faculty are not accessible. Intentional dissemination can moderate political challenges or create them if not considered carefully.

As stated earlier in this chapter, assessment is political because it is reduced to resource allocation and decision making. Thus, understanding and leveraging the economic realities on campus is critical. On many campuses retention and persistence are issues. First, high graduation rates imply a successful college or university. Second, there are economic impacts of students leaving an institution, including lost revenue for the time that students were expected to be enrolled and additional expenses stemming from the recruitment of students to fill the empty seats. As such it may be useful to focus assessment on initiatives that are positively correlated with retention and persistence.

The final tip is to consider legal and ethical implications. The last thing one wants to have happen as the result of an assessment is a legal case against the institution or a negative headline plastered on the front page of the *New York Times* or *The Chronicle of Higher Education*—above the fold! Study the laws and policies regarding data collection and protection of those data. In some cases the data can be accessed through open-records laws. This public display of assessment data has political ramifications. Also consider the information being sought and the potential implications. Some information, such as admitted sexual assault of a minor, if known, must be reported to law enforcement officials. Even if there is no legal requirement to report sensitive information, there may be an ethical duty to do so. There are ethical implications in all assessments. Chapter 15 provides a useful overview.

Conclusion

Assessment can become a complex process given the political ramifications of the data or decisions made from the data. A review of the different types of power described helps to provide a conceptual understanding of the political issues. Suggestions and lessons learned from others implementing assessment, such as those included here, can help one anticipate issues that may arise. Talking with colleagues and brainstorming possible implications of data collection, data dissemination, or data-informed decision making can uncover otherwise unanticipated issues. Given the political nature of assessment, it is a process that should not be rushed into. Thoughtful and careful planning is a must to prevent political missteps.

Key Points

- Assessment impacts resource allocation, which is a political process.
- Politics can impact each step in the assessment cycle.
- To effectively engage in assessment, one must be able to navigate politics in higher education.
- Seven types of power are: legitimate, reward, coercive, referent, expert, information, and reputation.

Discussion Questions and Activities

- In what ways do the various sources of power affect the assessment process?
  - What are the positive impacts?
  - What are the negative impacts?
- As someone implementing an assessment project, what types of power do you possess?
- How can you use the power that others possess to assist you in implementing an assessment project?

17

A CULTURE OF ASSESSMENT

S tudent affairs professionals in a division of student affairs have numerous roles and responsibilities that each person must juggle. But one of the most important tasks is cultivating a culture of assessment. Regardless of position, before cultivation can be discussed, a *culture of assessment* must be defined. *Culture* is defined as an organization's shared values, symbols, behaviors, and assumptions (Goffee & Jones, 1998). In other words, it is "the way we do things here" (Martin, 2006). In relation to assessment, a culture is related to people, behavior, and data. Culp (2012) defined a *culture of evidence* as "a commitment among student affairs professionals to use hard data to show how the programs they offer, the processes they implement, and the services they provide are effective and contribute significantly to an institution's ability to reach its stated goals and fulfill its mission" (p. 5).

Another definition of *culture of assessment* is that it is a set of pervasive actions and behaviors by staff across an organization (e.g., unit, division) focusing on the use of data in decision making regarding the accountability and improvement of programs and services. But the use of data to demonstrate impact of programs and services is not sufficient. Data must also be used to identify ways in which the programs and services can be continuously improved.

Characteristics

After defining a *culture of assessment*, it is helpful to define the characteristics of such a culture. What does a culture of assessment look like? For divisions with cultures of assessment, assessment is not performed just for program

A version of this chapter was previously published as Henning, G. W. (2015). Tenet two: Cultivating a culture of assessment. In K. Yousey-Elsener, E. M. Bentrim, & G. W. Henning (Eds.), *Coordinating student affairs divisional assessment: A practical guide* (pp. 11–34). Stylus Publishing, Sterling, VA. Copyright 2015 by ACPA-College Student Educators International & NASPA-Student Affairs Administrators in Higher Education.

review or during the regional reaccreditation self-study process but rather on an ongoing basis with participation from multiple stakeholders throughout the division. In other words, assessment is engrained in the everyday practice throughout the division. Assessment is not simply an activity. Rather, it is a state of mind and being practiced unconsciously as part of the daily routine (Henning, 2013a). Because of this pervasiveness, assessment functions do not fall on a small number of people. Although there may be a coordinator and/or an assessment committee that lead and support the efforts for the division, assessment is the responsibility of all staff members seeking to improve their own programs and services.

When assessment is distributed throughout a division and is part of the daily routine, it follows that data collection also involves a variety of techniques and is not isolated to surveys, focus groups, and interviews. Strong cultures of assessment also evolve to incorporate multiple methods of data collection to provide the most complete possible picture of the program or service. Having a culture of assessment also means that once the data are collected and analyzed, they are used to "tell the story" of the unit. Information is packaged in a format for distribution to stakeholders and typically differs depending on the stakeholders, as each group is compelled by different reporting formats and has needs for different types of data. Finally and most importantly, data are used to "close the loop" by enacting improvement. This implies that data are being used to effect change and are more than a list of recommendations at the end of an assessment report. Once the loop is closed, the process begins anew.

Strategies

Cultivating a culture of assessment across a division of student affairs is easier said than done. Often, student affairs staff members don't believe that they have the skills or knowledge to perform assessment. Others feel that they have limited time for assessment activities. Additionally, Bresciani (2006) has suggested that professionals do not understand the value of assessment, other staff may fear the process, and assessment activities are not appropriately allocated.

Now that a *culture of assessment* has been defined and characterized, how exactly do student affairs staff cultivate a culture of assessment? Suskie (2009) outlined four keys to fostering a culture of assessment:

1. Value campus, culture, and history.
2. Respect and empower people, especially faculty.
3. Value innovation and risk taking, especially in improving teaching.

4. Value assessment efforts, especially by supporting them with appropriate resources and infrastructure and using the results to inform important decisions on important goals. (p. 70)

Schuh (2013) has outlined 10 characteristics of institutions with cultures of assessment:

1. Recognition that assessment is a commitment not only of accountability to stakeholders but also to continuous improvement.
2. Commitment to student affairs practice that is called positive restlessness and a commitment to improvement.
3. Institutions with a culture of assessment are self-critical.
4. Use of an approach called data-driven decision making.
5. Assessments need to be conducted across the institution.
6. Use of multiple forms of assessment contribute to a culture of assessment.
7. Learning outcomes are identified and measured.
8. While someone needs to be in charge, all student affairs staff members should pitch in when it comes to assessment.
9. Results are communicated and acted upon.
10. Discretionary resources are used to seed assessment projects.

The 3 x 5 Plan for Cultivating a Culture of Assessment

Built on the work of previous assessment scholars, the 3 x 5 model for cultivating a culture of assessment incorporates some of those strategies in addition to others in a three-pronged model. The prongs focus on three main domains of building a culture of assessment: foundation, implementation, and support. Each domain has five components. A division that has a foundation for assessment is mission-centered, goal-grounded, outcome-directed, culture-specific, and literature-based. Regarding implementation, assessment is focused on the several purposes and characteristics of assessment: accountability and improvement, embedded in daily practice, collaborative, transparent and ongoing and never ending. Support for cultures of assessment includes a vocal and unyielding leader, a champion, infrastructure, continuous skill and knowledge development, and robust resources. Each domain and component is described in detail next.

Foundation for Assessment

Regardless of what is being built, be it a house or skyscraper, the foundation must come first, as it supports all that is above. The same is true for a culture of assessment. Without a strong foundation the culture cannot be appropriately developed or sustained over time.

Centered on Mission

The mission should be the base for all work within a division of student affairs. Bryson (2011) has stated that a "mission . . . clarifies an organization's purpose, or why it should be doing what it does" (p. 127). He went on to explain that the mission should answer six questions if it is going to be a declaration of organizational purpose. Those questions can be stated as follows:

1. Who are we?
2. What needs do we exist to address?
3. What do we do to respond to these needs?
4. How should we respond to our stakeholders?
5. What are our philosophy, values, and culture?
6. What makes us unique? (pp. 138–142)

The mission derived from the answers to these questions provides the foundation for the organization's work.

Just as the divisional mission should guide the overall work of the division, it should also provide direction for assessment activities. Assessment helps to support the mission by providing evidence documenting the extent to which the mission is being addressed and how mission-related work can better support the strategic direction of the division. Although there may be times for non-mission-related assessment activities, it is prudent to allocate assessment resources for programs and services that directly support the mission. As the staff develop the short- and long-term items on the assessment agenda, the divisional mission should be at the forefront of that decision-making process.

Grounded on Goals

A culture of assessment cannot be cultivated simply by centering work on the mission. Missions undergird the work of an office, a department, or an entire division. But as such, missions are somewhat broad. The mission must be honed into goals that provide further illumination of how work must be done. Goals provide guideposts or beacons giving direction and illuminating the end result (Henning, 2009). Goals provide the "destination postcard" for what that end result looks like.

It is often helpful to embed the goals in a strategic plan, as this provides a structure for intentional goal achievement. However, strategic plans do not include all goals an office, a department, or a division will strive to achieve. Regardless of the fact that goals may or may not be part of a strategic plan, the goals should provide an additional layer in the foundation for a culture of assessment. Without these beacons, staff are not clear about what is to be achieved.

Directed Toward Outcome

Types.   Outcomes are more specific, measurable elements of goals. There are often multiple outcomes for each goal. Henning (2013b) has defined three types of outcomes: *operational, learning,* and *program.*

Purposes.   There are many ways in which outcomes can be advantageous:

1. They help provide direction at the beginning of the activity. A specific product or result is conceptualized and agreed upon.
2. Outcomes keep all staff consistent so that each person is collaborating for the same conclusion.
3. The specificity of the outcomes provides clarity for what exactly to assess.
4. Once the end result is known, the process for identifying strategies to achieve the effect is easier.
5. Knowing the end result and identifying strategies for achieving that result, a unit can then determine the resources needed to implement those strategies.
6. For learning outcomes, the statements themselves assist students in articulating to others what they have learned (or at least should have learned).
7. Since outcomes provide a clear end point, the process for fostering outcomes is focused. The outcomes can be revisited to ensure strategies are on track allowing for midstream readjustment.
8. Explicitly stating outcomes provides critical information to constituent groups regarding an office's intent, role, and purposes. During times when many stakeholders are unaware of the value of student affairs units, this transparency is essential.

Specific to the Culture

Although similarities abound, no two organizational cultures are identical. Organizational structure influences and is influenced by organizational culture. Sandeen, Winston, Creamer, and Miller (2001) identified the following factors that influence student affairs organizations: institutional mission and culture, professional background of the student affairs staff, student characteristics, presidents and senior academic officers, academic organizations, financial resources, technology, and legislation and court decisions. In addition to these institutional characteristics, additional attributes that influence culture include size and prestige. The culture for a division of student affairs is influenced by institutional characteristics as well as the division's approach to student affairs. These approaches are student services, student development, and student learning (Manning, Kinzie, & Schuh, 2006). A culture of assessment must be situated in the larger organizational culture and alignment between these cultures must occur in order to successfully cultivate a culture of assessment.

When cultivating a culture of assessment there are a few components of organizational culture to be cognizant of: the value of assessment, direction of authority, centralization, transparency, and integration with academic affairs. The first component to consider is the value placed on assessment in the division. Cultures that place high value on assessment have an already established infrastructure, assessment is a part of multiple conversations on various levels, and resources are allocated toward these efforts.

The second component to consider is the direction of authority. For staff who have worked in different divisions or for different vice presidents or deans, the culture can vary, from being hierarchical to flat or somewhere in between. This approach to authority has implications for how the culture of assessment is developed. In a hierarchical structure, the chief student affairs officer may want to be involved in all (or most) decision making regarding assessment. As such, the culture will be imbued with the values of that individual. In a more egalitarian structure, the culture has the ability to take on the values of the entire division because the coordinator can involve many individuals in the cultivation of the culture.

Centralization is the third component of culture to consider. This is similar to the direction of authority in that a centralized culture is characterized by the power in one individual, whereas a decentralized culture has power radiating from multiple individuals. Centralized cultures have assessment functions overseen or led by one person or office and processes occur in a more controlled fashion. Decentralized cultures, on the other hand, have assessment happening in multiple offices across the division but not necessarily in a coordinated fashion. It is important to note that not all divisions with an assessment coordinator or office operate in a centralized culture, as there are many decentralized institutions with a full-time assessment coordinator. As a result, many processes created by these coordinators will either look highly centralized (e.g., divisional planning and reporting templates) or highly individualized by department or unit.

Transparency, the fourth component, will be discussed later but should be touched upon briefly here. Some organizational cultures are more transparent than others. This is dependent, to an extent, on the control of the institution, as public institutions are required by state and federal law to share more data than private institutions are required to do. Transparency of an organization, be it a department, a division, or an institution, is also impacted by leadership's philosophy. The level of transparency will have implications for how assessment is implemented and the extent to which the data are shared internally and externally.

The fifth component to consider is the level of integration with academic affairs. Some divisions of student affairs are separate from academic affairs. This integration could result when both divisions report to the provost or vice president for academic affairs. At some institutions, the integration is related only to assessment functions, as there may be one assessment director for the entire institution. The culture of assessment must be cultivated in a way that corresponds to this integration with academic affairs. In some cases the assessment directives may come from academic affairs, whereas in other institutions they come from student affairs administrators. It is essential to understand the institutional and divisional cultures as one cultivates a culture of assessment in student affairs.

Based on the Literature

Student affairs as a field is becoming more professionalized, and a key factor in that professionalization is a growing literature base. All of this literature provides building blocks for a foundation of practice. Student affairs educators can no longer develop programs and services based on anecdotes and personal experience. Although those provide some useful information, student affairs work must be based on the systematized collection, analysis, and synthesis of data and the development of theory. The use of theory and data for program development is even more important in an era of limited and declining resources. It is critical that we integrate current literature into our assessment practice to inform program development, data collection, and analysis.

Just as we need to build programs and services on theory and research, assessment must also have the same foundation. Theory must be integrated with assessment practice. In cultivating a culture of assessment, the student affairs staff should perform a literature review (even a small one) before embarking on an assessment project. Research can help staff hone outcomes, provide direction for strategies to achieve those outcomes, and help contextualize assessment results so that the loop can be properly closed and resources can be used most effectively and efficiently. There may be instances where research does not exist for a particular issue or problem. In these situations, it is important to take the time to develop a conceptual framework that can provide an intentionally considered context for the project.

Consider a new program developed to help students increase their moral development as they proceed through a student conduct process. For this program, it would be essential to understand the various theories of college student moral development. All theories may not be used as the foundation of the program as they have distinctions, but they all should be considered and one should be chosen. The theory can be used to help establish appropriate outcomes for students, identify probable strategies for achieving those outcomes, and assist interpretation of the assessment data.

Implementation of Assessment

Once the foundation is set for assessment, the focus should turn to how assessment should be implemented across the division. The following components outline considerations for implementation.

Accountability Combined With Improvement

Accountability and improvement are the two overarching purposes of assessment. Accountability is demonstrating with evidence "that we do what we say we do" and also demonstrating the "extent to which we do that." In other words, accountability is the demonstration of goals and outcomes achievement. Of course, this assumes that there are goals and outcomes to start with. Accountability was catapulted to the top of the national higher education agenda with the 2006 *A Test of Leadership: Charting the Future of U.S. Higher Education* report (Spellings Commission, 2006) launched by then U.S. Secretary of Education Margaret Spellings. This report decried higher education and was a rallying cry for holding colleges and universities, individually and collectively, responsible for student learning. Since then initiatives such as the Voluntary System of Accountability (www.voluntarysystem.org), Voluntary Framework of Accountability for Community Colleges (www.vfa.aacc.nche .edu), University and College Accountability Network (www.ucan-network .org), and College Scorecard (www.whitehouse.gov/issues/education/higher-education/college-score-card) initiated by President Obama in his 2013 State of the Union Address have all been developed to address this issue.

It is important to note that the rise of external accountability is partly due to the lack of internal accountability. Particularly in student affairs, administrators and educators were not doing an adequate job telling the story of their impact on student learning and the student experience. The assumption was that constituents on campus understood the work that student affairs educators performed. In the absence of internal accountability, external accountability filled the void. With the increased focus on external accountability in the national higher education conversation, the second grand purpose of assessment has been somewhat drowned out. In addition to demonstrating achievement of goals and outcomes, assessment should be used to identify opportunities for improvement. The assessment loop is closed when those improvements are made and assessed.

The challenge is that the data needed to demonstrate accountability are often not the same data needed to identify opportunities for improvement. If an aim is to demonstrate goal or outcome achievements, the focus will be on gathering summative data for accountability, whereas formative data are needed for improvement. Summative assessment questions, for example, could include the following: "What percentage of students graduated in five years?"; "What was the alcohol binge rate in the past academic year?"; "What did students learn by participating in the orientation program?" The data needed to answer these "what" questions is summative in nature and is different from the data needed to determine the "how" questions for improvement. If outcomes such as these are achieved, data must be gathered to help explain how they can be achieved. For instance, "How do we increase the five-year graduation rate?"; "How do we decrease the percentage of students who binge drink?"; "How can students learn what we want them to learn during orientation?" These are different questions with different answers. Although the data are different for accountability and improvement, there is additional tension between these concepts.

In 2009, Peter Ewell revisited the tension between accountability and improvement that he had discussed in 1987. In his more recent paper, entitled "Assessment, Accountability, and Improvement: Revisiting the Tension," Ewell discusses the challenges between these two grand purposes. He states that the incentives for each purpose are different.

> Accountability requires the entity held accountable to demonstrate, with evidence, conformity with an established standard of process or outcome. The associated incentive for that entity is to look as good as possible, regardless of the underlying performance. Improvement, in turn, entails an opposite set of incentives. Deficiencies in performance must be faithfully detected and reported so that they can be acted upon. (Ewell, 2009, p. 7)

The task is reconciling these two purposes. Sometimes both can be addressed in the same assessment project; sometimes they cannot. It is up to the student affairs staff to navigate and balance these competing purposes.

Embedded

For many staff members assessment is a burden—an additional task added to an already heaping plate of responsibilities that keeps getting higher and higher. Assessment should not be seen as an additional task. It should not be seen as a singular activity that is performed at the end of a program or a service. Staff should no longer be sending out surveys a week after a program. Rather, they should be identifying ways to integrate assessment into the activity, program, or service, making it a seamless component.

This type of assessment, embedded in practice, is also called *authentic assessment*, as it is aligned with teaching and learning and is not an add-on, stand-alone assessment. Both Angelo (1999) and Maki (2010) have remarked that authentic assessment provides direct evidence of application of learning. Goff et al. (n.d.) identify a number of benefits of this embedded approach to assessing student learning. First, this approach directly engages educators in the process of assessment, providing them control in the process to develop assessment in a way that is useful to them. Second, students are more motivated to participate since the assessment is not isolated from the learning itself. Third, resource expenditures are minimized no additional staff, time, or expensive tools are needed for the assessment. Fourth, since this type of assessment is educator-driven, there are direct implications for teaching and learning. Authentic assessment can also support program-level assessment. Finally, this type of assessment is flexible and can be adapted to different educational styles and content.

There are additional benefits to the use of authentic assessment. In the book *Switch: How to Change Things When Change Is Hard*, brothers Chip and Dan Heath (2010) discuss one way to make change is to shape the path making it easy for people to change behaviors. Within that category, one specific strategy is to "build habits" (p. 112). By this, the Heath brothers mean that habits need to be encouraged to make behavior automatic. In other words, staff should develop ways to do assessment so assessment is no longer an activity but a state of mind. Embedding assessment into the activity itself is a way to build habits. Assessment methods such as one-minute papers, "muddiest point," focused listing, and others not only provide evidence regarding what students know or have learned but also foster learning. These methods create "reflection traps," permitting students to take a few minutes to process or reflect on what they have learned. With some creativity, these methods can even be scaled up for large groups of students. Assessment methods that provide assessment evidence as well as foster learning are the ideal methods as they serve two purposes at once.

Although it may be easier to embed assessment methods into learning activities, they can also be embedded into service activities. Point-of-service assessments are brief assessments done right before, during, or after a service is provided; they are useful tools toward achieving this goal. To better understand sleeping behavior on campus, rather than doing a survey students receive in their campus email, students could complete a one- to two-question minisurvey when they visit a health care provider at the health center. Upon check-in, students could either complete the questions on a tablet in the waiting area or on a small piece of paper, placing the paper in a locked box similar to a comment box. Although such a sample may not be representative, this is an easy way to embed assessment into another activity. This approach is likely to be just as valid as a campus survey that has a 25% response rate.

Embedded assessments are usually easier, more interesting, and more useful than traditional after-event assessments.

Collaborative

As John Schuh (2013) has stated, "While someone needs to be in charge, all student affairs staff members should pitch in when it comes to assessment" (p. 94). It is easy for staff and even division leaders to rely too much on the assessment coordinator to do all of the assessment in the division. The coordinator has the formal responsibility and expertise and enjoys the work. However, depending on one person to do all or most of the assessment in the division is not sustainable over the long term. In addition, a culture of assessment cannot evolve if everyone is not investing in performing assessment.

It is essential that expectations be established for all staff to engage in assessment even if there is a division coordinator and/or departmental point person. These expectations need to come from the leadership. There also should be opportunities created that bring people together to discuss the assessments that they are doing. These activities reinforce the expectations. Another strategy is to identify goals and outcomes that transcend multiple offices and have staff from those offices discuss how those goals and outcomes can be assessed collaboratively. A final strategy that institutionalizes these expectations is to integrate assessment responsibilities into every job description and make assessment a component of annual performance evaluations. It is important to note that the focus on the evaluations is simply engaging in assessment, not the results themselves. If staff feel that their personal performance is based on the results of the assessments, they will be less likely to perform assessment for fear of the impact on their evaluation.

Transparent

It is easy to be transparent with assessment data when the information demonstrates that programs are successful and students are learning what they are expected to learn. Transparency is not so easy when the results show the opposite. It is difficult to show warts. However, good, bad, or ugly, it is critical to be transparent with both assessment results and assessment processes. There are a number of reasons for this. Schuh and Associates (2009) describe two related reasons. First, students and parents are becoming consumers of higher education assessment data. They are beginning to question the return on investment of college tuition and fees. Second, the federal government is nudging institutions to share more data and soon the nudge will turn into policy.

Aside from the external factors influencing transparency, there are internal reasons as well. The more student affairs professionals are open about assessment processes and data, the more credibility they garner. With greater transparency, assessment is no longer seen as some political process that takes place in a darkly lit room to produce data that spin the right story. By sharing both positive and negative assessment data, professionals can tell the "whole" story. More importantly, when stakeholders see how the data are being used to create change, they are more supportive of assessment and more willing to participate in assessment processes, as they know there will be some larger benefit to their participation.

Ongoing and Never Ending

Many readers will recognize the Energizer bunny commercials. In those commercials, Energizer batteries were put into a pink toy bunny with blue- and white-striped sandals that walks and plays a bass drum simultaneously. The tagline was that Energizer batteries "keep going and going and going." That is the same way to think about assessment. Assessment cannot be "one and done." It cannot be episodic when a program needs to be defended. And it cannot also happen for 18 months every 10 years in preparation of a reaccreditation visit. Assessment has to be ongoing. This doesn't mean that everything has to be assessed all of the time. That is just not possible. But it is important to develop an assessment plan for the department or division so that there is a clear blueprint for how assessment will be done and integrated into the work of the unit. Again, assessment cannot just be an activity. It has to be a state of mind.

Support for Assessment

The final domain in cultivating a culture of assessment is providing support for assessment efforts. Even with a strong foundation and solid principles for implementation, a culture of assessment isn't sustainable without support.

Vocal and Unyielding Leadership

Vocal and unyielding leadership is a critical component of building and maintaining a culture of assessment. Often the prime mover for a culture of assessment is a divisional leader who values assessment inherently and is not motivated by external accountability. This leadership is a strong cornerstone in creating a culture of assessment. Leaders of cultures of assessment understand the importance of data to inform decision making and thus set expectations regarding the use of data (Yousey-Elsener, 2014).

The leader needs to continually vocalize the importance of assessment and its benefits while supporting those comments with examples and evidence regarding how assessment has been used to tell the division's story and make improvements. Simply saying that assessment is important is not enough no matter how often it is repeated. The benefits need to be substantiated to convince others that assessment is a valuable process in which to engage.

The leader also has to be unyielding, as there will undoubtedly be push-back. Staff will make comments such as "I don't have time to do assessment"; "How am I supposed to fit this in among my million other responsibilities?" "I don't know how to do assessment"; "This will take away from my direct work with students"; or "Can't we just hire a work-study student to do this?" Rather than shunning these responses, an effective leader must understand that these comments often come from staff who care about their work and students but are frightened, insecure in their ability, and overworked. Thus, there is some validity to their responses even if they seem petty. The leader cannot give in to these reactions, but must seek to understand them in order to provide the support and resources needed to convert these detractors into advocates of assessment. This action takes perseverance and compassion on the part of the divisional leader.

Championed Across the Division

A vocal, unyielding leader is a necessary component of support when building and maintaining a culture of assessment, but that is not sufficient. A culture of assessment needs a champion. This is a person who motivates people when assessment gets difficult. The champion has her eye on the "big picture" of assessment in the division seeing how all of the parts fit together and campaigns for resources to continue to develop the culture of assessment. Often the champion is not the divisional leader, as the chief student affairs officer doesn't have the time to attend to all of these assessment-related responsibilities. For institutions with a student affairs assessment coordinator, this person will serve as the champion. For institutions that do not have a coordinator, usually the associate or assistant vice president whose portfolio includes assessment will play this role.

Strong Infrastructure

Building an infrastructure to support assessment efforts is one of the most critical components to sustaining a culture of assessment. Established policies and practices provide the scaffolding that supports assessment efforts by the staff. The Heath brothers (2010) defined this as "tweaking the environment" as a way to shape the path to make it easy to change behavior. In their book *Switch: How to Change Things When Change Is Hard* (2010), Chip and Dan Heath discussed that changing the environment helps to change behavior. To support this notion, they discuss the research that suggests that by simply using a smaller plate, people will consume less food.

Thus, in order to encourage assessment, processes and policies should be developed that make it easier to perform assessment. The development of an assessment coordinator position is a key element of the infrastructure to develop and maintain a culture of assessment. Another common tool is the development of templates for curricular mapping, assessment reports, and the like. These templates make it easier for staff to engage in assessment activities. Some institutions revise their annual reporting process by creating quarterly reports that focus primarily on assessment data. Still other divisions invest in software systems that track and report assessment information. The assessment champion has to scan the environment and understand the divisional and institutional culture to determine what infrastructure needs to be built and the divisional leader needs to finance that infrastructure.

Continuous Development of Skill and Knowledge

As stated earlier in the discussion of collaboration, one person cannot and should not perform all assessment in a division. In order to involve all staff members in assessment efforts they need the skills, knowledge, and confidence to do assessment themselves.

Good starting points in building capacity are the ACPA/NASPA professional competencies (ACPA, 2015) as one of the competencies is focused on assessment, evaluation, and research (AER). The AER competency can provide a framework for the development of a professional development curriculum that can be used to help staff develop the valuable skills and knowledge to perform assessment.

A rubric has also been developed for the 2010 version of AER competency (www.myacpa.org/files/professional-comp-rubricspdf) (Yousey-Elsener & Elkins, 2012). This rubric, which also applies to the 2015 edition of the AER competency, can be used as a needs assessment or as an evaluation of a professional development activity. Perhaps more usefully, the dimensions of the ACPA/NASPA AER competency identified in the rubric could serve as domains for skill and knowledge development. The dimensions include the following: define terms and concepts, value of assessment, define purpose, design, data collection, analysis, interpreting results, reporting, use of results, politics, creating systems, and ethics.

Once the content areas for capacity building have been defined, delivery methods need to be identified. These methods could include on-campus workshops, readings, and discussions; attendance at assessment programs at the NASPA and/or ACPA annual conventions; as well as participation in national assessment events such as the ACPA Student Affairs Assessment Institute or the NASPA Assessment and Persistence Conference. Divisions may hire a consultant to provide the training or staff may also choose to use the AER competency to develop their own professional development plan. Many campuses have useful resources such as centers for teaching and learning as well as institutional research offices. There can be many components to an intentional plan to build the assessment capacity of staff.

Robust Resources

Resources to support assessment can take many forms. They can include financial support for staff to attend conferences or hire an external consultant to provide training. Release time to work on assessment projects or reallocation of responsibilities freeing up workload for assessment practices can also be a form of resources. And access to books, literature, and other readings can help to sustain assessment practice.

Divisional leaders and champions need to decide what types of resources are required and which are financially feasible. The choice of resources will depend on the needs of the organization and the funding available. Leaders and champions should visit the NASPA and ACPA web pages to view professional development events offered by each association. They may also want to visit www.assessmentconferences.com to view upcoming conferences. Champions may also wish to build an assessment library for staff.

Tips for Cultivating a Culture of Assessment

Armed with a framework for cultivating a culture of assessment, where does one begin to actually develop this culture? The following are tips for next steps.

Identify a Mentor

Professionals new to the field of student affairs or assessment benefit from having a mentor who can help them continue to develop and hone assessment skill and knowledge. The mentor can provide feedback on assessment plans, answer questions, and provide advice for how to integrate assessment across a department.

Build Relationships

One of the most important steps is to develop relationships. Volunteering for assessment projects or becoming a member of a divisional or institutional assessment team is a way to form relationships with others doing assessment. Join groups such as Student Affairs Assessment Leaders; the NASPA Assessment, Evaluation, and Research Knowledge Community; or the ACPA Commission for Assessment and Evaluation. In these groups staff interested in assessment will find people in similar positions who can provide support and guidance.

Participate in Professional Development

To continue to develop capacity to perform assessment, one should participate in professional development, including webinars and conferences. The organizations discussed previously offer opportunities for skill building. There are numerous assessment books now available, which provide information for beginning to advanced assessment work.

Develop a Resource Library

A personal assessment library will be a useful resource. This library may contain assessment articles, a list of assessment books (and maybe the books themselves), conference presentation materials, and a list of helpful online resources. Student Affairs Assessment Leaders has a growing repository of assessment resources that members have shared. The personal library could be converted into an assessment resource clearinghouse for an entire department or division of student affairs.

Conclusion

All staff contribute to a culture of assessment. Cultivating one is not an easy task. Change is difficult. The status quo is comfortable. However, the benefits foster change, and building a culture of assessment is well worth the effort. A culture of assessment helps all staff members to be more effective in delivering services and fostering learning. Resources in all forms—money, space, and staff time—will be used more efficiently. Priorities will be easier to implement and the division will be able to successfully tell the story of how it adds value to the institution by helping students learn and develop. This chapter has provided the blueprint for developing a culture of assessment.

Key Points

- A culture of assessment is one in which there are shared beliefs, values, and behaviors regarding the use of data for accountability and improvement.
- The 3 x 5 model for cultivating and sustaining a culture of assessment focuses on three domains—foundation, implementation, and support—each of which includes five components.

Discussion Questions and Activities

- Describe what a culture of assessment would look like in an admissions office. How would a culture of assessment look different in an office of multicultural affairs, if at all?
- You are an assistant director in a financial aid, residence life, or student activities office. How would you go about developing a culture of assessment? What is the impact of not being the director of the office?
- What are the biggest challenges to developing a culture of assessment? How might these challenges differ by functional area, institutional type, or some other characteristic?
- What are the implications of politics and power for cultivating and sustaining a culture of assessment? What types of power would be useful in this task?

18

TECHNOLOGY

By the time this book is published, this chapter will already be out of date. Technology changes on a daily basis. In many ways, technology makes student affairs assessment much easier than it was even a few years ago. Technology has increased the options for data collection, data analysis, and information sharing. Information from around the world is more readily available, and it is easier to collaborate with other institutions across the country and the world. The examples given in this chapter are not endorsements of any products, but they illustrate types of options we investigated.

Although technology has made assessment easy in some ways, it also complicates assessment if not used well. As technology becomes pervasive and less expensive, more people will invest in it. One challenge is that people are relying on technology without understanding assessment principles or ethical principles. As with anything, the saying "garbage in, garbage out" applies here. No matter how convenient an electronic survey is, if the right questions are not asked of the right people and using the correct methodology, the information will be useless. Anyone can send out a survey without considering the ethical principles: They may ask invasive questions without providing appropriate support, they may not have a way to secure the data collected, and they may not be able to protect the confidentiality of respondents. Others will just implement bad assessment practices by surveying their whole population, not knowing their audience's characteristics and not considering the time frame of data collection, analysis, and sharing.

Staff should be using technology in the assessment process to improve effectiveness, efficiency, and knowledge. Technology can help in data collection, data analysis and integration, and data presentation. Student affairs staff should collaborate with information technology (IT) professionals to ensure the products used meet the standards for individual work as well as the standards for the department, division, institution, and profession.

Data Collection

Survey Software

Technology has greatly expanded the ability to access data and collect information from a variety of places. Before the advent of the Internet, people had to collect data by writing on a piece of paper and then manually entering data points into a computer program (e.g., using Excel or SPSS), or even calculate statistics by hand. Data collection, storage, and analysis took a long time and required people with expertise and attention to detail.

Most people remember taking tests using a Scantron or bubble sheet to record answers. Those technologies still exist and have been built upon. New technology has allowed staff to collect data on plain paper forms that can be scanned to collect data points and read handwriting. Teleform is one example of this technology. This survey technology allows for multiple types of questions (select one, check all that apply, open-ended, etc.), which makes it a flexible option for data collection. The answers are noted by marking locations on the page and coded in the design phase. When the responses are scanned in, the data can be saved in Excel or SPSS, for example, for easy analysis. Other scannable technology will provide a picture of the comments, without the ability to edit.

The Internet has increased the ability to collect data from respondents anywhere at any time. Numerous companies have filled the niche, making survey creation and distribution incredibly easy. Some companies offer free versions for basic data collection, but they also typically offer an expanded version for a price. Survey software products, such as SurveyMonkey (www .surveymonkey.com) and Qualtrics (www.qualtrics.com), have become very user-friendly, so novice assessors can create professional-looking surveys that gather useful information in an efficient manner. These survey software packages offer sample questions, mobile applications, skip logic, data analysis within the software, and customer support.

Card Scanners

Many campuses are using ID card scanners to track students who attend campus programs, enter their recreation centers, and check in for their advising appointments. Card scanning can be used not only by program staff but also by students themselves to track attendance at organization meetings. At the least, card scanning allows staff to know who is using their services. In a more complex environment, these data can be combined with campus data to clarify the relationship of student attendance to use of other resources, GPA, retention, graduation, and student learning. In terms of follow-up assessment, this method allows staff to survey only those students who have attended a particular event, rather than a random sample of students, many of whom may not fit the population of interest.

Electronic Response Capture Technology

In working with a group of students, clickers may be appropriate for immediate data collection and visual display of results (Oaks & Kennedy-Phillips, 2015). Students are given a keypad with which to answer questions, and the results are displayed in a PowerPoint presentation or similar program. Some technologies use smartphones to accomplish the same thing through text messaging. This type of technology engages participants in active data collection and can demonstrate immediate learning or differences in individual behavior versus perceptions (e.g., "How many alcoholic beverages do you consume in an average week?" "How many alcoholic beverages do you think your peers at this institution consume in an average week?").

Products such as PollEverywhere (www.polleverywhere.com) can engage participants by asking questions through smartphones, Twitter, or websites. A variety of question types can be used, including scaled and free-response questions. The live responses are then illustrated immediately on a website or in a PowerPoint presentation. Students may appreciate the immediate feedback, but it is also important to make sure that all participants have access to the needed hardware or software.

Social Media

As social media change, so do the data-collection opportunities. For example, student affairs staff can use Twitter in a program to have participants comment using a specific hashtag (#). Staff can then analyze the comments (at most 140 characters) per tweet. Facebook posts, "likes," and followers can also be analyzed. Students may be posting pictures, blogging, and creating videos. Although those data-collection methods do not provide expansive in-depth answers, they do provide a snapshot of participants' thoughts and opinions. As more networking applications are invented and adopted by college students, there will be more information for student affairs staff to assess.

Learning Management Systems

Learning management systems (LMSs), also called course management systems (CMSs), can be used to collect data using discussion boards and document collection. This can be especially appropriate for intact groups that have structured systems for assessment (Oaks & Kennedy-Phillips, 2015).

Many institutions have adopted a CMS system that can be used by student affairs staff for cocurricular experiences. If students are already using a platform for their academic work, they can easily adapt this technology for their involvement in work.

In higher education, Blackboard (www.blackboard.com) and Moodle (https://moodle.org) are fairly common products to supplement in-person courses or provide online learning. They can provide content, track engagement, and document individual learning. For student affairs, these systems could be used to provide resources for student leaders, engage students in online discussions, and provide certification for completion of leadership programs or other workshops. Student affairs staff could have their own "course" as well, providing a learning community for student organization advisors or supervisors who want to engage with their peers across campus.

Voice Recording

In terms of qualitative research, technology is helping to record the human voice and potentially converting that into text. Digital recorders and smartphones have increased the quality of recordings. Current technology is fairly accurate for speech recognition. At the time of this printing, many speech-to-text applications provide workable accuracy without training. In the future, they may change how interviews and focus group data are collected. Nuance's Dragon software (www.nuance.com/dragon/index.htm) is a type of speech recognition software that claims 99% accuracy, with a brief setup time and training. Siri (Apple's voice recognition agent) claims 76% accuracy without training.

As technology changes, the data-collection options will clearly expand for the everyday consumer. In student affairs, this means that staff should follow the trends but also be proficient in new technologies as well as maintaining a high level of ethical conduct in data use.

Data-Analysis Tools

Qualitative Analysis Software

For *qualitative* data, computer-assisted qualitative data-analysis software (CAQDAS) can assist with the analysis and coding themes. Products such as ATLAS.ti, NVivo, Dedoose, and Leximancer help the analyst organize large amounts of data. These programs do not automatically analyze the data; the analyst still needs to use professional judgment in the process.

For example, ATLAS.ti (http://atlasti.com) can import responses from an online survey to a useful data file for coding. It also provides coding options for text (including PDFs), audio, and video material and allows the user to work on multiple documents simultaneously and search for quotations using the code assigned. In the analysis phase, the software allows for not only frequency calculations but also the cross-tabulation of codes. The program works on multiple operating systems, which allows for the flexibility of data collection, storage, analysis, and sharing. Trial versions and student licenses are available, as are educational and campus licenses.

Similarly, NVivo (www.qsrinternational.com) also collects data on multiple types of devices and even provides transcript processing. Survey responses can be imported from SurveyMonkey, and NVivo can import data from Twitter, Facebook, YouTube, LinkedIn, websites, and PDFs. Notes, articles, and images can be transferred from OneNote to NVivo. NVivo also has query, tracking, and visualization tools. The software works in both the Windows and Mac environments. Blaney, Filer, and Lyon (2014) used NVivo to analyze 171 student high-impact practice reflection essays using the text search query to automate their theming process. They used a sample of essays to code manually. Once themed, the themes were analyzed for the specific wording/syntax students used to describe that theme. The search query function was tested and used in NVivo to find specific examples in the text.

Dedoose (www.dedoose.com) is a web-based program for qualitative and mixed-methods assessment. It uses text, photos, audio, video, and even spreadsheet data for coding, analysis, and visualization. Because it is strictly an online product, it can be accessed through any Internet connection. Dedoose has one fee for all of its services, which is slightly different from other products.

Leximancer (info.leximancer.com) is another qualitative analysis software option based on the philosophy that words form clusters of terms that create concepts. The meaning, then, is implied by the context. Leximancer does not require predefined dictionaries but uses a thesaurus and concepts to build a visual representation. Because of this emergent process, the meaning is not biased based on preconceptions. The process also uses a thesaurus for greater flexibility in finding similar concepts and words. The very visual output is a concept map or network and can be divided by categorical data for further analysis. The product can be used with traditional data sources, such as Word or Excel, but also has the flexibility to use social media.

Quantitative Analysis Software

Student affairs professionals should also be at least somewhat familiar with quantitative data-analysis software even if they are not the ones who will be performing the actual data analysis. Staff can perform basic and intermediate statistical functions in Excel. Some staff prefer to work in SPSS (www-01.ibm.com/software/analytics/spss), SAS (www.sas.com/en_us/home.html), or STATA (www.stata.com), which are statistical packages with advanced capability in addition to the basic statistical functions used by most student affairs staff. R (www.r-project.org) is a web-based open-source quantitative data-analysis tool. The online and paper-based survey software is typically compatible with Excel, SPSS, or SAS. Data in an Excel file can be imported easily to SPSS, for example, if that is how the data were originally collected. Some survey software products also have data-analysis tools built into the product, which eliminates the step of transferring data to another program.

Data Presentation and Visualization

Being able to present information in a coherent and meaningful way to multiple audiences is a useful skill. Technology can assist in that endeavor, from the very simple to the very complex. For example, Wordle (www.wordle.net) is an easy-to-use website to create word clouds. The user copies text into the system, which then creates a visual effect in a variety of colors and fonts, where the largest words represent the most commonly mentioned. Wordle can also analyze text on a website when the user provides the link that has an RSS (rich site summary) feed.

Social media can be used not only to collect data but also to share information. This is particularly useful for sharing small bits of information—for example, in a Facebook post or a 140-character tweet. Some institutions use Instagram or Pinterest to share information visually.

For quantitative data, infographics are currently popular. They use data, typically quantitative, to create graphics, charts, and tables that can be used in print or web material. Some companies, like Piktochart (http://piktochart.com), provide a few free templates and resources but rely on organizations to purchase a license. The caveat is that the person creating the infographic has to have an eye for how data can be clearly and simply illustrated while also being sensitive to color, font, and space. Information presented poorly will not help to tell a story. Alternatively, a creative, eye-catching document can invite the audience to learn more.

Dashboards are becoming more common in student affairs and higher education. A dashboard is a visual representation of current information that "allows users to track and respond to organizational or institutional activities based on key goals-based and objectives-based metrics or indicators" (Mitchell & Ryder, 2013, p. 73). Dashboards display information visually so that the user typically can choose variables to include in analysis. Mitchell and Ryder have highlighted three functions of dashboards: monitoring, analysis, and management. These features can provide information on progress toward a goal, historical comparisons and trends, and performance. Mitchell and Ryder also described three types of dashboards: operational, analytical, and strategic. The dashboards can range from simple to complex and static to dynamic. In student affairs, they can be used to describe student engagement, residence hall occupancy, recreation center usage, and student retention (Mitchell & Ryder, 2013). Before a dashboard is created, its purpose, cost, technology, and features need to be determined. Done well, a dashboard can provide clear and comprehensive information about the effectiveness of a unit.

On a very complex level, software such as Tableau (www.tableausoft ware.com) can create interactive dashboards that combine multiple live data sets and allow the user to interact with the data. Databases, spreadsheets, and large data sets can be combined and analyzed in a variety of ways. As Oaks and Kennedy-Phillips (2015) observe, users drill down to view the most relevant information.

Integrated Products and Data

Some companies are providing integrated assessment, data management, and planning products and services. As an example, Campus Labs (formerly Student Voice) provides products and support for survey design, data collection, data analysis, reporting, and dashboards; strategic planning, accreditation and program review, action plans, and institutional effectiveness; student organization and event management, aligning learning and involvement, and marketing services; early alert and intervention services; and course evaluations. Campuses can choose one or more of the products that ideally will bring student affairs, academic affairs, and institutional research together. The multiple platforms can integrate data to provide a more complete picture of student success and involvement.

Regardless of how data are collected and analyzed, it is important to think about how data are integrated with other files and data sets following campus policies and practices. Most new professionals and graduate students are not at the level to create a data integration system, but they should be thinking about the value of their data to others and what information they need to better support the students they work with. For example, how can the housing department and the academic support office work together to identify and engage early with first-year students who are having academic and transition difficulties? How can the recreation center, which uses a card access system, collaborate with the institutional research office to clarify the connections between students exercising on a regular basis and making good grades and persisting at the institution (being careful not to make a causal relationship)?

As more data files are created and shared across campus and as higher education professionals are becoming more data analysis savvy, more attention is being paid to predictive analytics, business intelligence, and big data. For example, data integration and analysis can predict which students will be academically successful or will graduate in four years. It is important to not only collect meaningful data but also use multiple sources to draw conclusions about the big picture. At the same time, student affairs staff should continue to serve individual students who may not fit the trend data.

Technology Requirements

There are software and hardware requirements to consider before investing in any product. Some software programs require a license and maintenance agreement, which can be expensive, whereas some resources cost little or nothing. There may be significant differences in pricing depending on quantity, license type (per seat versus concurrent), or user type (student versus staff). Software programs have process, memory, disk space, operating system, or server/desktop requirements that need to be verified before purchasing a product. Web-based products may work better with certain devices or browsers (e.g., Internet Explorer, Google Chrome). As products are upgraded, the user must make sure that the technical requirements are continually met. Some products are available for purchase on a semester or annual basis for full-time students, as these companies recognize that the product may be used for a class, a specific project, or thesis/dissertation research. Some products provide online training through videos and step-by-step instructions on how to use the application.

In terms of hardware, if you choose the scannable paper technology you will need a scanner to read the forms. A different type of mobile scanner is needed to read ID cards and import the information to another computer for analysis or integration with other information. Some institutions purchase products campuswide that student affairs can use, although there may be specialized software that needs to be purchased separately. Before purchasing a product, accessibility and security should also be investigated so as to meet institutional standards. Assessment professionals should work closely with their IT office for specifications and advice.

Information Technology Staff

IT professionals will be able to give well-informed advice about which off-the-shelf products, hosted solutions, or homegrown products are the best options. The advantages of off-the-shelf products include implementation time, the update process, and sometimes the price. The main disadvantage is that the product may not meet the exact needs of the organization. In addition, there are some off-the-shelf products that can be enhanced by campus IT professionals. Similarly, hosted solutions are web-based products run by another company. They are also fairly quick to implement, and the companies spend time continually improving their products. On the other hand, they may not always meet organizational needs. Homegrown products are designed, tested, upgraded, and maintained by campus IT professionals. The main advantage is that the product will meet the specific needs of the organization. The potential disadvantages are the time for development and the potential difficulty in maintaining and updating the product. IT professionals are also skilled in data and system security, which is highly important in working with data, especially if there are data classification requirements such as those of the Family Educational Rights and Privacy Act (FERPA) and the Health Insurance Portability and Accountability Act (HIPAA).

Technology changes frequently and should support the educational and business practices of the unit, department, or division rather than the other way around. Further, technology can be expensive, so not every assessment project needs the latest, state-of-the art software or piece of hardware. New professionals need to understand the balance of priorities on a larger scale and to be able to seek out less expensive resources as needed. At the same time, campuses may invest in technology at the institutional level, and departments and divisions may be able to access products at a reduced cost. By investigating the benefits of large-scale purchases through collaboration, much time and money can be saved.

For all technology, it is important to ensure that websites, applications, and other products are accessible to people with disabilities. IT professionals can also review the accessibility of the products to ensure that all users are able to interact with a specific software, most commonly those with visual impairments.

Can a person with a visual impairment use a screen reader to respond to a survey? Can a person without fine motor skills use a clicker or other devices? Companies providing technology should be able to demonstrate their accommodations, but the campus staff need to be diligent about testing products and services to make sure they are accessible to all. Section 508 of the Rehabilitation Act of 1973 (U.S. Department of Education, n.d.) provides guidance and expectations for higher education electronic information technology. Campuses have Americans with Disabilities coordinators who can be excellent resources. The best advice is to consult the department, division, or campus IT professionals early and often about all needs and options.

Conclusion

Technology has clearly enhanced the assessment process, especially through the data-collection, analysis, and sharing stages. Although there are many options for products, student affairs staff should consult IT staff to make sure that the products are compatible and secure in the campus infrastructure. In addition, because technology changes rapidly, staff should keep up to date with new innovations that may make the assessment process easier. At the same time, the assessment goals should be driving technology decisions, which may mean that staff do not always adapt the newest technology as soon as it becomes available.

Key Points

- Technology has improved the ability to collect, store, analyze, and share data and information.
- Although technology products are on the market, student affairs professions need to determine their specific needs before investing in them.
- The availability of technology does not relieve staff of the responsibility to perform quality assessments.

Discussion Questions and Activities

- What technology are you most comfortable with? Least comfortable?
- Describe how you might use social media as an assessment strategy.
- What resources are available on your campus?
- How can you incorporate technology into your assessment planning and implementation?

19

THE FUTURE

Where Are We Headed?

Although no one has a crystal ball that can predict the future, there are some certainties. Overall, assessment will continue to be an integral part of student affairs and higher education. This is not a fad that will come and go. It may take different forms at different times, but student affairs must continue to assess programs, services, and cocurricular learning to demonstrate efficiency and effectiveness as a part of the higher education mission. Higher education will continue to change and evolve; student affairs will follow. In a recent survey of college presidents, Selingo (2014) found that they acknowledged the economic, demographic, and technological forces that will continue to shape campuses, but they also have a positive outlook as they recognized the innovations in higher education.

Several authors have postulated what the future holds in terms of assessment in higher education and student affairs. Wehlburg (2008) has identified several areas of interest in the future of assessment in higher education: increasing accountability and comparability needs, changing student matriculation patterns, technology, increased authentic measures of learning, recognition of the complexity of higher education outcomes, intentional alignment of the educational process, assessing collaboration and teamwork, and team-based transformative assessment. She also recognized that institutions will be expected to have greater documentation about job placement and mission-related activities. Each of these areas will have a slightly different impact based on the uniqueness of institutions: public/private, urban/rural, large/small, traditional/nontraditional student population.

Similarly, in *Assessment Methods for Student Affairs*, Schuh and Associates (2009) also anticipated several other areas of how student affairs assessment will continue to evolve. They identified areas such as increased accountability for degree-granting and non-degree-granting units, increased use of institutional databases, increased use of databases such as the Integrated

Post-Secondary Education Data System (IPEDS) and revamped Carnegie System, increased use of comparative data, more time for collecting and managing databases, greater use of data in decision making, greater demand for transparency, more sophisticated studies, more mixed-methods studies, increased need for assessment skills, more use of technology in collecting data, increased scrutiny in human subjects protection, and survey fatigue. Since the publication of that book, several of those premonitions have been accurate. As it continues to impact all aspects of society, technology has an important impact on how people conduct assessment, how data are analyzed and integrated, and how people can access and interpret data.

Other authors see an opportunity in the future for higher education and student affairs to improve skills, resources, and collaborative efforts to respond to the issue of accountability. Banta, Suskie, and Walvoord (2015) identified a move from denial to acceptance, ongoing calls for accountability, increasing experience with assessment, growing and maturing assessment resources, balancing standardization with individualization, moving from silos to integration, and closing the loop as a challenge. Clearly, accountability impacts higher education initiatives, but individual institutions can begin to build internal processes that ingrain assessment in what they do for the benefit of the students. In addition, institutions can promote professional development to ensure that staff have the knowledge, skills, and abilities to do and use assessment wisely.

Ikenberry and Kuh (2015) postulate five broad trends affecting higher education institutions:

> changing student characteristics and needs; unrelenting technological advances that stretch institutional resources and revolutionize when, where, and how students learn; more intense competition for students; less forgiving economic circumstances that make efficient, effective management of the academic enterprise more challenging; and widespread skepticism about the quality of higher education. (pp. 9–10)

They recognized the business of higher education and how it impacts the teaching and learning mission of institutions more so than in the past. Assessment plays a key role in responding to and shaping the societal trends in place today.

More recently, Kevin Kruger (2015), NASPA president, made several predictions about higher education and student affairs that have implications for assessment. Among others, he emphasized documenting learning outside the classroom, stressing degree progress and graduation for populations such as low-income and first-generation students, and addressing career development and employability. Each of these areas alone is significant to student affairs assessment; all of them together challenge the direction, priorities, and resources in student affairs divisions and the profession. The following areas will be highlighted as impacts on student affairs assessment: technology, accountability and compliance, student success, employment and postgraduation life, politics, and student affairs professional skills.

Technology

Technology will continue to impact assessment work in multiple ways. Data-collection techniques will continue to be more sophisticated—right now the Internet, text messages, card swipes, and the like allow data to be collected much faster and with more accuracy than ever before. Technology can continue to provide creative ways to engage students in the assessment process. The challenge is to keep up with the next technology that can be leveraged in responsibly collecting information without violating confidentiality. The ability to integrate data from multiple sources provides a larger picture. Big data has the potential to impact higher education and student affairs as it can be used not only to describe students but also to predict success for specific groups.

Technology can continue to assist in data analysis. The quantitative statistical packages on the market today are excellent at calculating any number of analyses in a very short period of time and even create predictive models. New technologies have been created to manipulate data in real time for specific analysis. Qualitative software applications are also improving to analyze large quantities of written comments in a relatively short period of time. Those advancements in technology do not relieve student affairs staff of their professional judgment about using data in decision making.

Technology has allowed the integration of data from multiple sources, such as student information, survey data, and program/service attendance/usage. This provides the development of models to predict performance, a more accurate picture of programs and services, and an indication of improvements. It also creates more efficiency by not collecting information that is already available.

Technology has helped the profession, institutions, divisions, and departments tell their story. Information can be shared on websites, electronic social media, and print media quickly and for little cost. Information can be distributed around the world in a matter of seconds, but someone stills needs to decide what needs to be disseminated when to have the most impact. Having too much information pushed can dilute an important message or send the wrong message entirely. Leadership needs to be on the same page about a consistent message and address who has the authority to tell the story.

Accountability and Compliance

Higher education institutions, academic colleges, and divisions of student affairs are undergoing increased levels of scrutiny. Federal and state governments are demanding institutional accountability regarding cost, retention and persistence, graduation rates, postgraduation employment, loan default rates, and so on. They are also making decisions about resource allocation and policies that have a far-reaching impact on campus resource allocation, policies, and practices. More voices are calling for transparency on a variety of levels.

Accreditors are taking an increased interest in the effectiveness of educational institutions. They have not been without controversy in recent years. Even Congress has been engaged in the debate about the effectiveness of the accreditation process. Some say it holds institutions accountable, whereas others say it is too expensive and time-consuming, without an increase in quality (Kelderman, 2015). The debate will continue to find the most effective way to measure quality without increasing the federal government's intrusion and regulation of the educational system.

Institutions are being asked to assess more about student experiences. For example, in 2014 the White House Task Force to Protect Students From Sexual Assault (2014) requested that every higher education institution implement a sexual assault climate survey on an annual basis. Because student affairs traditionally addresses sexual assault on campus through education and the counseling, health, and conduct processes, student affairs staff are integral to the assessment. The long-term plan is to mandate institutions to submit data to the federal government to be posted on a website for comparison. Similar mandates will continue to increase the complexity of the assessment agenda.

Finley (2012) has identified several national initiatives, though not government compliance driven, that are shaping accountability and the future of higher education. She highlights the Degree Qualifications Profile (DQP) through the Lumina Foundation (Adelman, Ewell, Gaston, & Schneider, 2014). The DQP provides overarching learning outcomes across the associate's, bachelor's, and master's degrees. The framework addresses learning within and across institutions, as well as within and across systems. Obviously, the assessment of student learning will play a key role in the DQP as it organizes learning into five categories: specialized knowledge, broad and integrative knowledge, intellectual skills, applied and collaborative learning, and civic and global learning.

Finley (2012) also highlights the Association of American Colleges and Universities' (AAC&U) Liberal Education and America's Promise (LEAP) States Initiative and the Compass, Roadmap, and Quality Collaboratives projects encouraging partnerships at the campus, system, and state levels. The initiatives include "intentional assessment of learning, high impact practices, and educational gains for underserved students" (Finley, 2012, p. 27). The LEAP campaign addresses essential learning outcomes through the VALUE rubrics (Valid Assessment of Learning in Undergraduate Education) addressed in Chapter 12. AAC&U also recognized the important role of community colleges through its Developing a Community College Student Roadmap (Finley, 2012). In 2015, AAC&U, building on the Lumina Foundation's DQP, produced the General Education Maps and Markers (GEMs) initiative. It provides guidelines and principles for engaging students in integrative and problem-based learning both in and out of the classroom that will lead to student proficiency (Association of American Colleges & Universities, 2015a).

On the surface these initiatives do not specifically refer to the impact of student affairs, but that does not mean that student affairs can stand on the sidelines; student affairs needs to be part of the student learning initiatives and assessment movement. Student affairs contributes to learning and student success, provides opportunities for students to practice important learning domains, and adds to the knowledge base about the student experience.

Stakeholders will continue to demand accountability and transparency. Student affairs needs to be proactive in assessment to share information and document efficiency, effectiveness, contribution to academic success and employability, while still meeting the compliance requirements imposed by external stakeholders.

Student Success

While external stakeholders have an influence in higher education assessment, individual campuses are also committing to using data for student success. Many institutions focus on retention, persistence, graduation, and employment, but there are even more opportunities to collaborate on deeper topics of student success. Faculty and student affairs staff can collaborate on areas such as service-learning, leadership development, inclusion, and reflection.

The demographics of students in college today are changing, and individual institutions need to predict those trends to change with the environment. For example, institutions that used to serve traditionally aged (18- to 22-year-old) students may be seeing an influx of older students who may be wanting a career change as the economy fluctuates, who may attend during or after military service, who have dependent children, or who need to balance a full-time job with their educational pursuits. Traditional undergraduate curricula are typically four years, but many students today may not fit the full-time student role. Each of those groups has specific needs that do not fit into the traditional service model. At the same time, the longer it takes students to graduate, the more debt they accumulate. Student affairs professionals must be attuned to the challenges and provide support, resources, and knowledge about student success.

In addition, more research is being done in terms of brain development and how people learn. While neuroscience is beyond the scope of this book, Bresciani (2013a) has challenged higher education professionals to grapple with "what we *do* know about learning and development . . . [and] what we do *not* know" (p. 103), and what that means in terms of decision making, resource allocation, and policy. She asks readers to reflect on what they communicate about what they know and do not know about student learning. How often do higher education staff admit to what they do not know? She proposes that this area of research can provide opportunities for all in higher education to talk about student learning and accountability, rather than focusing on either/or. This may mean changing part of the curriculum in student affairs preparation programs. While many programs currently teach student development theories based in psychology, neuroscience enhances the discussions about student development in a different way. In *The Neuroscience of Learning and Development: Enhancing Creativity, Compassion, Critical Thinking, and Peace in Higher Education* (2016), Bresciani Ludvik and colleagues articulate how the use of integrative inquiry is effective in fostering learning and development as a pedagogical method consistent with how the brain operates.

Emerging trends also include how content is delivered and credit given. Massive online open courses, hybrid courses (i.e., both online and in person), and competency-based credit have raised questions about the value of a traditional education on a physical campus. Selingo (2014) found that college presidents were "concerned that in the future only the wealthy students will get immersive, in-person experiences at elite colleges" (p. 20). This brings up questions of quality and access for all students seeking higher education. In 2015, NASPA–Student Affairs Administrators in Higher Education and AACRAO (the American Association of Collegiate Registrars and Admissions Officers) launched a partnership to determine how to document the competencies that students are learning outside of the classroom in some form of transcript-like document to fill the current void (Fain, 2015).

As these areas continue to develop, assessment can provide an indication of student success before, during, and after graduation. Student affairs staff need to understand their contributions to new models of higher education delivery.

As a part of the student success discussion, student affairs has the opportunity to assess its specific contribution to student achievement, through tracking students in specific experiences (living on campus the first year, participating in a transition program, etc.), or even by asking graduates about the impact of specific programs. As Bresciani, Moore Gardner, and Hickmott (2009) predicted regarding transparency of outcomes and assessment, "If we do not choose to find a meaningful way to do this on our own as professionals in the various disciplines of student affairs, others will do it for us" (p. 183). Clearly, student success cannot be attributed to one out-of-class experience, but with no assessment, student affairs will be ignored as an important component in the student success formula. As Schuh and Gansemer-Topf (2010) conclude, "We are confident that student affairs practitioners are ready, willing, and prepared to embrace these challenges . . . and will continue to make progress in assessing how student affairs activities and the out-of-class experience contribute to student learning" (p. 12).

Employment and Postgraduation Life

The industries and companies that employ graduates will continue to influence the formal and informal curriculum. Student affairs professionals have a role in preparing students for the work world. Additionally, they have a responsibility to assess the learning that takes place in the cocurricular area and assist students in articulating their knowledge and skills.

In a blog post, Morse (2014) states that student affairs should be involved in the postgraduation assessment that most institutions implement. Student affairs leaders should collaborate with other institutional entities and bring resources and expertise to generate knowledge, not only about employment but also about other areas of life after graduation. Specifically, Morse (2014) asks:

- Are graduates civically engaged, and are they involved in activities that continue to develop their competencies as leaders and professionals?
- Have they built relationships with peers and colleagues?
- In what kind of activities are graduates engaging that build upon personal identity?
- Are graduates engaging in behaviors that promote mental health and physical well-being? (para. 15)

These questions address the holistic development of students who are expected to be productive members of society when they leave campus. The answers to the questions illustrate the impact of student affairs on student learning and development.

Student affairs professionals are in a unique position to help students articulate their learning, synthesize learning across all experiences, and transfer the learning to a variety of situations after graduation. Student organization advisors and student supervisors interact with students in ways not always possible in the classroom. They can promote reflection, challenge conventional thought, and encourage students to take risks. In addition, staff can implement meaningful assessment to capture learning and development. As highlighted in the section on accountability and compliance, national associations are calling for a focus on student learning and preparation for postgraduation success. This philosophy is a shift in traditional student affairs thinking, but it is a necessary change in the profession.

Politics

As noted in previous chapters, no one can deny that politics intrudes on higher education, potentially now more than ever. A recent survey of college presidents (Selingo, 2014) concludes that "two-thirds of public-institution presidents think that politicians are the most influential drivers of change in higher education and half of private-campus presidents agree with that assessment" (p. 5). They would prefer that faculty, college presidents, and students be the drivers. Politicians do not always understand the higher education context. They may only have a reference of their time in college or sending their children to college. If they do not have good information about the intricacies of student learning, the sources of educational revenue and expenses, and the value-added nature of out-of-class experiences, they will make decisions without the full picture. In student affairs, staff need to be sure that change agents and decision makers have accurate assessment results about the impact of the cocurricular experiences and services.

Public institutions are in a unique relationship with politicians who make decisions about funding. Politicians answer to their constituents, who question the cost and benefits of higher education. It is challenging in these uncertain economic times for a politician to promote increased spending in any one area, which inevitably decreases spending in another area. As state funding fluctuates, there is increased competition to receive a large portion of a pie of unknown size. National politicians have similar challenges. Although they agree that education is an important public good, they do not agree on who should fund it and who should get it. They also do not agree about how it should be judged and how much the government should be involved. If institutions do not provide an indication of their efficiency and effectiveness, it seems that the government is more likely to intervene. That is all the more reason for institutions, and areas within institutions, to be leaders in providing high-quality, meaningful assessment results about the value of higher education and particular programs.

Student Affairs Professional Skills

Student affairs professionals will need to be prepared to follow the assessment cycle and, most importantly, to use assessment results for effectiveness, efficiency, and evidence of student learning. Staff cannot rely on others to do it—assessment is everyone's job. As the student affairs profession and higher education environment change and develop, assessment will continue to be an important piece of the conversation, as will research on student learning, student development, and student success. Professionals need to be proficient in multiple assessment methods to illustrate success in containing costs, providing value in programs and services, and ensuring satisfaction.

Student affairs preparation programs have a responsibility to prepare graduates to enter the profession with at least a basic understanding of assessment techniques. The CAS standards (CAS, 2015) provide guidance to master's degree programs about courses and experiences that should be included in preparation programs. Currently some programs have at least one required course in assessment whereas others have electives, and some do not have any formal assessment experiences as part of the curriculum. One of the other challenges related to staff entering the profession is that many staff enter without a student affairs background or education. Those individuals may be at a disadvantage and need to have a plan to develop competence.

As described at the beginning of this book, the ACPA/NASPA competencies (ACPA and NASPA, 2015) and the ACPA *ASK Standards* (2006) provide guidance about what student affairs professionals should know and be able to do. The *ASK Standards* describe 13 focus areas: assessment design, articulating learning and development outcomes, selection of data collection and management methods, assessment instruments, surveys used for assessment purposes, interviews and focus groups used for assessment purposes, analysis, benchmarking, program review and evaluation, assessment ethics, effective reporting and use of results, politics of assessment, and assessment education. This document provides specific outcomes in each area that all student affairs professionals should develop competence, regardless of their functional area.

ACPA and NASPA (2015) also provide guidance for all student affairs professionals related to assessment competencies. They identify competency levels needed in assessment, based on foundational, intermediate, and advanced levels. The assessment, evaluation, and research category includes using qualitative and quantitative methods, critiquing assessment, managing processes, and shaping the political environment. Currently, the student affairs profession does not have a formal certification process, so this set of competencies serves as a set of guidelines for staff to follow throughout their careers. In the future, student affairs professionals will continue to have qualifications scrutinized related to assessment, and the competencies will be reviewed to meet current environments.

Because technology has such an impact on the assessment process, student affairs professionals must also be competent in technological skills. This may be a challenge for seasoned professionals without the day-to-day or early exposure that younger staff have experienced. Technology has also changed the student experience in ways that student affairs as a profession is still grappling with (cyberbullying, anonymous communication, information security, etc.). Endersby (2015) describes the ACPA and NASPA technology competency, a newly created competency in the 2015 revision of the ACPA and NASPA professional competencies, which recognizes its importance in professional development and the ability to best serve students and higher education. Rather than have the competency woven through the other competency areas, its stands on its own with levels of competence expected for all professionals.

As a profession, there is a call to continue assessing and documenting the learning that takes place outside the classroom, especially using direct measures. Learning assessment is no longer confined to academic courses, but student affairs professionals should also be clear that a significant amount of learning does occur within the classroom. Staff need to be able to write student learning outcomes, as well as be able to competently use a variety of assessment methods to provide meaningful evidence of learning. As a part of that process, staff also need to be able to share that information with a variety of audiences and implement programmatic changes to improve learning. While not every program, event, activity, or service has a learning component, those that do should be expected to participate in learning assessment. As Collins (2012) has stated, "Student affairs staff need to initiate action related to assessment of student learning outcomes. Failure to do so could eventually result in elimination of staff, departments, or divisions of student affairs" (p. 191).

To meet the skill needs, professional associations and higher education institutions have contributed to staff development. The ACPA Student Affairs Assessment Institute; the NASPA Assessment and Persistence Conference; institutional certificate programs; and state, regional, and national conferences continue to provide cutting-edge information. In the future, the professional development can become more focused and sophisticated, following adopted competencies and being integrated into functional areas.

Student affairs assessment does not happen in a vacuum. Kuh, Gonyea, and Rodriguez (2002) conclude that

> as with other areas of policy and practice focused on improving undergraduate education, the scholarship of assessment will be furthered through collaboration between student affairs professionals who often are knowledgeable about student development theory, survey research methods, and the out-of-class experiences of students, faculty members who are experts in pedagogy and curricular matters, and institutional research and assessment specialists who are familiar with assessment theory, research methods, and technology. (p. 127)

Although that statement was made over a decade ago, it still rings true today; student affairs professionals bring expertise to the table. As the higher education environment continues to evolve, student affairs staff need to proactively engage other campus constituents for assessment and research collaborative opportunities.

Not every student affairs division will have a dedicated person whose job is assessment. Even if they did, assessment is everyone's responsibility. Because the profession, institutions, divisions, and a myriad of stakeholders expect more transparency and value-added evidence, staff must be developing themselves professionally in the area. It's no longer acceptable to say, "I don't do assessment." The expectation is for staff to say, "I used quality assessment to improve how I serve students and the institution. Let me tell you about it."

Conclusion

Student affairs assessment will continually change and develop as the higher education environment becomes even more complex, with increasing demands from multiple stakeholders for accountability, added value, and a demonstration of learning. Professionals must keep up with current issues to predict and guide the impact of changes. The issues can come from national conversations, state demands, employer desires, campus events, and more. Student affairs professionals should be using assessment to lead change efforts and decisions, provide evidence of improvement, and contribute to the body of knowledge.

Key Points

- Higher education exists in a dynamic environment with multiple and sometimes conflicting forces shaping policy and practice.
- Student affairs professionals must stay abreast of issues that may not, on the surface, seem to impact their work but can result in significant changes.
- Student learning, development, and success still remain at the forefront of student affairs work; now, more than ever, professionals must be actively engaged in assessment practices.

Discussion Questions and Activities

- Describe the trends and impact you foresee in the next 10 years and how they will affect assessment in student affairs.
- What trends have you seen on your campus that could change the nature of student affairs work?
- What assessment has influenced the changes mentioned in the first question?
- What changes do you predict in the next decade that will demand increased assessment?

REFERENCES

Accreditation Association for Ambulatory Health Care. (2015). *Accreditation programs*. Retrieved from http://www.aaahc.org/en/accreditation/

ACPA—College Student Educators International. (n.d.). *Statement of ethical principles and standards*. Retrieved from http://www.acpa.nche.edu/sites/default/files/Ethical_Principles_Standards.pdf

ACPA—College Student Educators International. (1994). *The student learning imperative: Implications for student affairs*. Washington, DC: Author.

ACPA—College Student Educators International. (2006). *ASK standards: Assessment skills and knowledge content standards for student affairs practitioners and scholars*. Washington, DC: Author.

ACPA—College Student Educators International & NASPA–Student Affairs Administrators in Higher Education. (2010). *Professional competency areas for student affairs practitioners*. Washington, DC: Author.

ACPA—College Student Educators International & NASPA–Student Affairs Administrators in Higher Education. (2015). *Professional competency areas for student affairs practitioners*. Washington, DC: Author.

Adelman, C., Ewell, P., Gaston, P., & Schneider, C. G. (2014). *The degree qualifications profile*. Indianapolis, IN: Lumina Foundation.

American Association for Higher Education. (1992). *Principles of good practice for assessing student learning*. Washington, DC: Author. Retrieved from http://www.learningoutcomesassessment.org/PrinciplesofAssessment.html

American College Health Association. (2014). *National college health assessment*. Retrieved from www.acha-ncha.org

American Council on Education. (1937). *The student personnel point of view*. Washington, DC: Author.

American Council on Education. (1949). *The student personnel point of view* (Rev. ed.). Washington, DC: Author.

American Psychological Association. (2010). *Publication manual of the American Psychological Association* (6th ed.). Washington, DC: Author.

American Psychological Association Commission on Accreditation. (2015). *Commission on accreditation*. Retrieved from http://www.apa.org/ed/accreditation/about/coa/

Anderson, L., Krathwohl, D., Airasian, P., Cruikshank, K., Mayer, R., Pintrich, P., . . . Wittrock, M. (2000). *A taxonomy for learning, teaching, and assessing: A revision of Bloom's taxonomy of educational objectives* (abridged ed.). New York, NY: Pearson.

Angelo, T. (1999, May). Doing assessment as if learning matters most. *American Association for Higher Education Bulletin*. Retrieved from http://www.aahea.org/aahea/articles/angelomay99.htm

Angelo, T., & Cross, K. (1993). *Classroom assessment techniques: A handbook for college teachers* (2nd ed.). San Francisco, CA: Jossey-Bass.

Association of American Colleges and Universities. (n.d.). *Essential learning outcomes*. Retrieved from https://www.aacu.org/leap/essential-learning-outcomes

Association of American Colleges and Universities (2015a). *General education maps and markers: Designing meaningful pathways to student achievement*. Washington, DC: Author.

Association of American Colleges and Universities (2015b). *VALUE*. Retrieved from http://www.aacu.org/value

Astin, A., Banta, T., Cross, K., El-Khawas, E., Ewell, P., Hutchings, P., . . . Wright, B. (1992). *Nine principles of good practice for assessing student learning*. Washington, DC: American Association for Higher Education.

Astin, A. W. (1993). *Assessment for excellence: The philosophy and practice of assessment and evaluation in higher education*. Phoenix, AZ: Oryx Press.

Baker, G., Jankowski, N., Provezis, S., & Kinzie, J. (2012). *Using assessment results: Promising practices of institutions that do it well*. Champaign, IL: National Institute for Learning Outcomes Assessment.

Banta, T., Jones, E., & Black, K. (2009). *Designing effective assessment: Principles and profiles of good practice*. San Francisco, CA: Jossey-Bass.

Banta, T., & Kuh, G. (1998). A missing link in assessment. *Change, 30*(2), 40–46.

Banta, T., & Palomba, C. (2015). *Assessment essentials: Planning, implementing, and improving assessment in higher education* (2nd ed.). San Francisco, CA: Jossey-Bass.

Banta, T., Suskie, L., & Walvoord, B. (2015). Three assessment tenors look back and to the future. *Assessment Update, 27*(1), 14–15.

Bass, R. (2014). The next whole thing in higher education. *Peer Review, 16*(1), 35.

Blaney, J., Filer, K., & Lyon, J. (2014, Summer). Assessing high impact practices using NVivo: An automated approach to analyzing student reflections for program improvement. *Research and Practice in Assessment, 9*, 97–100.

Blumenstyk, G. (2015, April 13). State spending on higher education shows "sizable" increase. *The Chronicle of Higher Education*. Retrieved from http://chronicle.com/article/State-Spending-on-Higher/229265/

Bolman, L., & Deal, T. (2013). *Reframing organizations: Artistry, choice, and leadership* (5th ed.). San Francisco, CA: Jossey-Bass.

Bresciani, M. (2010). Data-driven planning: Using assessment in strategic planning. In S. Ellis (Ed.), *Strategic Planning in Student Affairs*. Spec. issue of *New Directions for Student Services*, 2010(132), 39–50.

Bresciani, M. (2012). Changing roles and responsibilities in student affairs research and assessment. In A. Tull & L. Kuk, *New realities in the management of student affairs* (pp. 114–125). Sterling, VA: Stylus.

Bresciani, M. (2013a). Afterword: Considerations for future practice of assessment and accountability. In J. H. Schuh (Ed.), *Selected contemporary assessment issues*. Spec. issue of *New Directions for Student Services*, 2013(142), 99–105.

Bresciani, M. (2013b). Developing outcomes. In D. Timm, J. Davis Barham, & K. McKinney (Eds.), *Assessment in practice: A companion guide to the ASK Standards.* (pp. 19–29) Washington, DC: ACPA—College Student Educators International.

Bresciani, M. J. (2006). *Outcomes-based academic and co-curricular program review: A compilation of institutional good practices.* Sterling, VA: Stylus.

Bresciani, M., Moore Gardner, M., & Hickmott, J. (2009). *Demonstrating student success: A practical guide to outcomes-based assessment of learning and development in student affairs.* Sterling, VA: Stylus.

Bresciani, M., Zelna, C., & Anderson, J. (2004). *Assessing student development and learning: A handbook for practitioners.* Washington, DC: NASPA–Student Affairs Administrators in Higher Education.

Bresciani Ludvik, J. (Ed.). (2016). *The neuroscience of learning and development: Enhancing creativity, compassion, critical thinking, and peace in higher education.* Sterling, VA: Stylus.

Bresciani Ludvik, M., Kline, K., & Moore Gardner, M. (2014). Showing promise: Assessment in community and two-year colleges. *Leadership Exchange, 12*(2), 25.

Bryson, J. (2011). *Strategic planning for public and nonprofit organizations: A guide to strengthening and sustaining organizational achievement* (4th ed.). San Francisco, CA: Jossey-Bass.

Capela, S., & Brooks-Saunders, A. (2012). *A different approach to strategic planning: SOAR-building strengths-based strategy.* Retrieved from http://www.coanet.org/conference/ppt/A7Presentation.pdf

Carreon, J. (2011). A commitment to serving our changing communities. In G. J. Dungy & S. E. Ellis (Eds.), *Exceptional senior student affairs administrators' leadership: Strategies and competencies for success* (pp. 145–152). Washington, DC: NASPA.

Center for Community College Student Engagement. (2015). *About the center.* Retrieved from http://www.ccsse.org/center/

Center for Postsecondary Research. (2015). *National survey of student engagement.* Retrieved from http://nsse.iub.edu/

Chickering, A., & Reisser, L. (1993). *Education and identity* (2nd ed.). San Francisco, CA: Jossey-Bass.

Christians, C. (2011). Ethics and politics in qualitative research. In N. Denzin & Y. Lincoln (Eds.), *Handbook of qualitative research* (pp. 139–164). Los Angeles: SAGE.

College of American Pathologists. (2015). *Experience the CAP.* Retrieved from http://www.cap.org/web/home

Collins, J. (2011). *Good to great: Why some companies make the leap . . . and others don't.* New York, NY: HarperBusiness.

Collins, K. (2012). The future of student learning in student affairs. In K. Collins & D. Roberts (Eds.), *Learning is not a sprint: Assessing and documenting student leader learning in cocurricular involvement* (pp. 185–196). Washington, DC: NASPA.

Colton, D., & Covert, R. (2007). *Designing and constructing instruments for social research and evaluation.* San Francisco, CA: Jossey-Bass.

Cook, K., & Buck, G. (2010). Photovoice: A community-based socioscientific pedagogical tool. *Science Scope, 33*(7), 35–39.

Cooper, R. (2009). Planning for and implementing data collection. In J. H. Schuh & Associates, *Assessment methods for student affairs* (pp. 51–75). San Francisco, CA: Jossey-Bass.

Corbin, J., & Strauss, A. (2015). *Basics of qualitative research: Techniques and procedures for developing grounded theory* (4th ed.). Thousand Oaks, CA: SAGE.

Council for Higher Education Accreditation. (2015). *About CHEA*. Retrieved from http://www.chea.org/pdf/chea-at-a-glance_2012.pdf

Council for the Advancement of Standards in Higher Education. (n.d.). *CAS program review process*. Retrieved from http://www.cas.edu/Files/CLabs_resources/Resources.HowTo.pdf

Council for the Advancement of Standards in Higher Education. (2012a). Assessment services standards. In D. Mitstifer (Ed.), *CAS professional standards for higher education* (8th ed). Washington, DC: Author. Retrieved from http://www.cas.edu/files/CASethicsstatement.pdf

Council for the Advancement of Standards in Higher Education. (2012b). CAS learning domains and dimensions. In D. Mitstiter (Ed.) *CAS professional standards for higher education* (8th ed.). Washington, DC: Author.

Council for the Advancement of Standards in Higher Education. (2012c). CAS statement of shared ethical principles. In D. Mitstifer (Ed.), *CAS professional standards for higher education* (8th ed.). Washington, DC: Author.

Council for the Advancement of Standards in Higher Education. (2012d). *Standards*. Retrieved from http://www.cas.edu/

Council for the Advancement of Standards in Higher Education. (2015). *CAS professional standards for higher education* (9th ed.). Washington, DC: Author.

Creswell, J. (2012). *Qualitative inquiry and research design: Choosing among five approaches* (3rd ed.). Los Angeles, CA: SAGE.

Creswell, J., & Plano Clark, V. (2010). *Designing and conducting mixed methods research* (2nd ed.). Los Angeles, CA: SAGE.

Culp, M. (2012). Starting the culture of evidence journey. In M. Culp & G. Dungy (Eds.), *Building a culture of evidence in student affairs: A guide for leaders and practitioners*. Washington, DC: National Association of Student Personnel Administrators.

Dave, J. (1967). *Psychomotor domain*. Presented at the International Conference of Educational Testing, Berlin, Germany.

Denzin, N. (1978). *The research act: A theoretical introduction to sociological methods* (2nd ed.). New York, NY: McGraw-Hill.

Denzin, N., & Lincoln, Y. (Eds.). (2011). *The SAGE handbook of qualitative research* (4th ed.). Thousand Oaks, CA: SAGE.

Denzin, N., & Lincoln, Y. (Eds.). (2013). Introduction: The discipline and practice of qualitative research. In *Strategies of qualitative inquiry* (4th ed., pp. 1–41). Thousand Oaks, CA: SAGE.

Dillman, D. (2007). *Mail and Internet surveys: A tailored design method*. Hoboken, NJ: John Wiley & Sons.

Dillman, D., Smyth, J., & Christian, L. (2009). *Internet, mail, and mixed-mode surveys: The tailored design method* (3rd ed.). Hoboken, NJ: John Wiley & Sons.

Doyle, J., & Meents-DeCaigny, E. (2015). Tenet Seven: Connecting assessment to planning, decision-making, and resource allocation. In K. Yousey-Elsener, E. Bentrim, & G. Henning (Eds.), *Coordinating student affairs divisional assessment: A practical guide* (pp. 105–118). Sterling, VA: Stylus.

Driscoll, A., & Wood, S. (2007). *Developing outcomes-based assessment for learner-centered education: A faculty introduction.* Sterling, VA: Stylus.

Easton, D. (1965). *A framework for political analysis* (5th ed.). Englewood Cliffs, NJ: Prentice Hall.

Education Advisory Board. (2011). Aligning co-curricular initiatives with learning outcomes: Key challenges facing student affairs leaders. Washington, DC: The Advisory Board Company.

Egbert, J., & Sandeen, A. (2014). *Foundations of education research: Understanding theoretical components.* New York, NY: Routledge.

Elkins, B. (2009). *Diving deeper: Qualitative analysis and interpretation.* Presented at the ACPA Student Affairs Assessment Institute, Austin, TX.

Endersby, L. (2015, June 16). A new addition to our competencies. [Web log post]. Retrieved from http://www.naspa.org/about/blog/a-new-addition-to-our-com petencies

Evans, N., Forney, D., & Guido-DiBrito, F. (1998). *Student development in college: Theory, research, and practice.* San Francisco, CA: Jossey-Bass.

Ewell, P. (2009). *Assessment, accountability, and improvement: Revisiting the tension.* (Occasional Paper No. 1). Urbana, IL: University of Illinois and Indiana University, National Institute for Learning Outcomes Assessment.

Fain, P. (2015, July 13). *Beyond the transcript.* Retrieved from https://www.inside highered.com/news/2015/07/13/project-create-models-broader-form-student -transcript

Fink, L. (2013). *Creating significant learning experiences: An integrated approach to designing college courses* (2nd ed.). San Francisco, CA: Jossey-Bass.

Finley, A. (2012). *Making progress? What we know about the achievement of liberal education outcomes.* Washington, DC: Association of American Colleges and Universities.

Forehand, M. (2005). Bloom's taxonomy: Original and revised. In M. Orey (Ed.), *Emerging perspectives on learning, teaching, and technology.* Athens, GA: University of Georgia.

Fraenkel, J., Wallen, N., & Hyun, H. (2014). *How to design and evaluate research in education* (9th ed.). New York, NY: McGraw-Hill.

French, J., & Raven, B. (1959). The bases of social power. In D. Cartwright & A. Zander (Eds.), *Group dynamics* (pp. 259–269). New York, NY: Harper & Row.

Fulcher, K., Good, M., Coleman, C., & Smith, K. (2014, December). *A simple model for learning improvement: Weigh pig, feed pig, weigh pig* (Occasional Paper No. 23). Urbana, IL: University of Illinois and Indiana University, National Institute for Learning Outcomes Assessment.

Gall, M., Gall, J., & Borg, W. (2007). *Educational research: An introduction* (8th ed.). Boston, MA: Pearson.

Giedd, J., Lalonde, F., Celano, M., White, S., Wallace, G., Lee, N., & Lenroot, R. (2009). Anatomical brain magnetic resonance imaging of typically developing children and adolescents. *Journal of the American Academy of Child Adolescent Psychiatry ,48*(5), 465–470.

Goff, L., Potter, M., Pierre, E., Carey, T., Gullage, A., Kustra, E., . . . Van Gastel, G. (n.d.). *Learning outcomes assessment: A practitioner's handbook.* Toronto, Ontario, Canada: Higher Education Quality Council of Ontario.

Goffee, R., & Jones, G. (1998). *The character of a corporation.* New York, NY: Harper Business.

Guest, G., Bunce, A., & Johnson, L. (2006). How many interviews are enough? An experiment with data saturation and variability. *Field Methods, 18*(1), 59–82. Retrieved from http://doi.org/10.1177/1525822X05279903

Harper, D. (1988). Visual sociology: Expanding sociological vision. *The American Sociologist, 1988*(1), 54–70.

Harper, S., & Kuh, G. (2007). Myths and misconceptions about using qualitative methods in assessment. In S. Harper & S. Museus (Eds.), *Using qualitative methods in institutional research* (pp. 5–14). *New Directions for Institutional Research,* no. 136. San Francisco, CA: Jossey-Bass.

Harrington, C., & Schibik, T. (2003). Reflexive photography as an alternative method for the study of the freshman year experience. *NASPA Journal, 41*(1), 23–40.

Harrow, A. (1972). *A taxonomy of the psychomotor domain: A guide for developing behavioural objectives.* New York, NY: David McKay.

Hart, J., & Fellabaum, J. (2008). Analyzing campus climate studies: Seeking to define and understand. *Journal of Diversity in Higher Education, 1*(4), 222–234.

Hart Research Associates. (2015). *Falling short? College learning and career success.* Washington: DC: Association of American Colleges and Universities.

Heath, C., & Heath, D. (2010). *Switch: How to change things when change is hard.* New York, NY: Crown Business.

Henning, G. (2007). *An overview of the whats, whys, and hows of student affairs assessment.* Presented at the Association of College Unions International (ACUI) Region I Conference, Boston, MA.

Henning, G. (2009, April). *Using what you have ASKed for: Turning assessment into action.* Presented at the ACPA Annual Convention, Washington, DC.

Henning, G. (2013a). *Assessment isn't an activity. It's a state of mind.* Presented at the 2nd Annual International Forum on Student Affairs, Monterrey, Mexico.

Henning, G. (2013b). *Get SMART: Developing outcomes.* Presented at the Systematizing Assessment Across Student Affairs, Portland, OR: Academic Impressions.

Henning, G. W. (2015). Tenet two: Cultivating a culture of assessment. In K. Yousey-Elsener, E. M. Bentrim, & G. W. Henning (Eds.), *Coordinating student affairs divisional assessment: A practical guide* (pp. 11–34). Stylus Publishing, Sterling, VA.

Higher Education Research Institute. (1996). *A social change model of leadership development: Guidebook version III.* College Park, MD: National Clearinghouse for Leadership Programs.

Holstein, J., & Gubrium, J. (2011). The constructionist analytics of interpretive practice. In N. Denzin & Y. Lincoln (Eds.), *Handbook of qualitative research* (4th ed., pp. 341–358). London: SAGE.

Huba, M., & Freed, J. (2000). *Learner-centered assessment on college campuses: Shifting the focus from teaching to learning.* Boston, MA: Allyn & Bacon.

Ikenberry, S., & Kuh, G. (2015). From compliance to ownership: Why and how colleges and universities assess student learning. In G. D. Kuh, S. O. Ikenberry, N. A. Jankowski, T. R. Cain, P. T. Ewell, & P. Hutchings (Eds.), *Using evidence of student learning to improve higher education* (pp. 1–26). San Francisco, CA: Jossey-Bass.

Janesick, V. (1998). The dance of qualitative research design: Metaphor, methodolatry, and meaning. In N. K. Denzin & Y. S. Lincoln (Eds.), *Strategies of qualitative inquiry* (pp. 35–55). London: SAGE Publications.

Jones, S., Torres, V., & Arminio, J. (2006). *Negotiating the complexities of qualitative research in higher education.* New York, NY: Routledge.

Junco, R., Heiberger, G., & Loken, E. (2011). The effect of Twitter on college student engagement and grades. *Journal of Computer Assisted Learning, 27*(2), 119–132.

Kaufman, R., & Guerra-López, I. (2013). *Needs assessment for organizational success.* Alexandria, VA: American Society for Training and Development.

Keeling, R. (Ed.). (2004). *Learning reconsidered: A campus-wide focus on the student experience.* Washington, DC: ACPA—College Student Educators International and NASPA–Student Affairs Administrators in Higher Education.

Keeling, R., Wall, A., Underhile, R., & Dungy, G. (2008). *Assessment reconsidered: Institutional effectiveness for student success.* Washington, DC: International Center for Student Success and Institutional Accountability.

Kelderman, E. (2015, April 10). Support for overhauling accreditation raises hard questions. *The Chronicle of Higher Education.* Retrieved from http://chronicle.com/article/Support-for-Overhauling/229237/

Keller, D. K. (2005). *The Tao of statistics: A path to understanding.* Thousand Oaks, CA: SAGE.

Kimbrough, W. (2011). Just the facts. In G. J. Dungy & S. E. Ellis (Eds.), *Exceptional senior student affairs administrators' leadership: Strategies and competencies for success* (pp. 183–187). Washington, DC: NASPA.

Kincheloe, J., & McLaren, P. (1994). Rethinking critical theory and qualitative research. In N. Denzin & Y. Lincoln (Eds.), *Handbook of qualitative research* (2nd ed., pp. 138–157). London: SAGE.

Kincheloe, J., McLaren, P., & Steinberg, S. (2011). Critical pedagogy and qualitative research: Moving into the bricolage. In N. Denzin & Y. Lincoln (Eds.), *Handbook of qualitative research* (4th ed., pp. 163–178). Los Angeles, CA: SAGE.

Kinzie, J., Hutchings, P., & Jankowski, N. (2015). Fostering greater use of assessment results: Principles for effective practice. In G. D. Kuh, S. O. Ikenberry, N. A. Jankowski, T. R. Cain, P. T. Ewell, & P. Hutchings (Eds.), *Using evidence of student learning to improve higher education* (pp. 51–72). San Francisco, CA: Jossey-Bass.

Kitchener, K. (1985). Ethical principles and ethical decisions in student affairs. In H. Canon & R. Brown (Eds.), *Applied Ethics in Student Services.* Spec. edition for *New Directions for Student Services, 30,* 17–29.

Kitchener, K. (2000). *Foundations of ethical practice, research, and teaching in psychology.* Mahwah, NJ: Erlbaum.

Klatt, J., & Taylor-Powell, E. (2005). *Program development and evaluation. Quick tips #28: Designing a retrospective post-then-pre question.* Retrieved from http://www.uwex.edu/ces/pdande/resources/pdf/Tipsheet28.pdf

Knoblauch, H., Baer, A., Laurier, E., Petschke, S., & Schnettler, B. (2008). Visual analysis. New developments in the interpretative analysis of video and photography. *Forum: Qualitative Social Research Sozialforschung, 9*(3). Retrieved from http://www.qualitative-research.net/index.php/fqs/article/view/1170

Kotter, J. (2007, January). Leading change: Why transformation efforts fail. *Harvard Business Review.*

Krathwohl, D., Bloom, B., & Masia, B. (1964). *Taxonomy of educational objectives, the classification of goals; handbook II: The affective domain.* New York, NY: David McKay.

Krueger, R. (1998). *Developing questions for focus groups: Focus group kit 3.* Thousand Oaks, CA: SAGE.

Krueger, R. (2006). *Focus group interviewing.* Minneapolis: University of Minnesota.

Kruger, K. (2015, January 5). NASPA right now—January: Thoughts and predictions for 2015 [Web log post]. Retrieved from http://www.naspa.org/about/blog/naspa-right-now-january-thoughts-and-predictions-for-2015

Kuh, G., & Banta, T. (2000, January/February). Faculty-student affairs collaboration on assessment: Lessons from the field. *About Campus,* 4–11.

Kuh, G., Gonyea, R., & Rodriguez, D. (2002). The scholarly assessment of student development. In T. W. Banta & Associates, *Building a scholarship of assessment* (pp. 100–127). San Francisco, CA: Jossey-Bass.

Kuh, G., Ikenberry, S., Jankowski, N., Cain, T., Ewell, P., Hutchings, P., & Kinzie, J. (2015). *Using evidence of student learning to improve higher education.* San Francisco, CA: Jossey-Bass.

Kuk, L. (2012). The changing nature of student affairs. In A. Tull & L. Kuk (Eds.), *New realities in the management of student affairs* (pp. 3–12). Sterling, VA: Stylus.

Lasswell, H. (1936). *Politics: Who gets what, when, how.* New York, NY: Whittlesey House.

Lichtman, M. (2012). *Qualitative research in education: A user's guide* (3rd ed.). Los Angeles: SAGE.

Lincoln, Y., & Guba, E. (1985). *Naturalistic inquiry.* Beverly Hills, CA: SAGE Publications.

Lincoln, Y., Lynham, S., & Guba, E. (2011). Paradigmatic controversies, contradictions, and emerging confluences, revisited. In N. Denzin & Y. Lincoln (Eds.), *Handbook of qualitative research* (4th ed., pp. 97–128). Los Angeles, CA: SAGE.

Lis Dean, J. (2013). Politics in assessment. In D. Timm, J. Davis Barham, & K. McKinney (Eds.), *Assessment in practice: A companion guide to the ASK Standards* (pp. 63–72). Washington, DC: ACPA—College Student Educators International.

Maki, P. (2010). *Assessing for learning: Building a sustainable commitment across the institution* (2nd ed.). Sterling, VA: Stylus.

Malaney, G. D. (1999). The structure and functions of student affairs research offices. In G. D. Malaney (Ed.), *Student affairs research, evaluation, and assessment: Structure and practice in a time of change.* Spec. edition for *New Directions for Student Services, 85,* 3–10. San Francisco, CA: Jossey-Bass.

Manning, K., Kinzie, J., & Schuh, J. (2006). *One size does not fit all: Traditional and innovative models of student affairs practice.* New York, NY: Routledge.

Martin, M. (2006). That's the way we do things around here: An overview of organizational culture. *Electronic Journal of Academic and Special Librarianship, 7*(1). Retrieved from http://southernlibrarianship.icaap.org/content/v07n01/martin_m01.htm

Merriam, S., & Tisdell, E. (2015). *Qualitative research: A guide to design and implementation* (4th ed.). San Francisco, CA: Jossey-Bass.

Middaugh, M. F. (2010). *Planning and assessment in higher education: Demonstrating institutional effectiveness.* San Francisco, CA: Jossey-Bass.

Mitchell, J., & Ryder, A. (2013). Developing and using dashboard indicators in student affairs assessment. In J. H. Schuh (Ed.), *Selected Contemporary Assessment Issues.* Spec. edition for *New Directions for Student Services, 2013*(142), 71–81. San Francisco, CA: Jossey-Bass.

Morse, A. (2014, December 12). Post-college outcomes assessment: Current initiatives and the vital role of student affairs leaders [Web log post]. Retrieved from http://www.naspa.org/rpi/posts/post-college-outcomes-assessment-current-initiatives-and-the-vital-role-of

Multi-Institutional Study of Leadership. (n.d.). *Home.* Retrieved from http://www.leadershipstudy.net

NASPA–Student Affairs Administrators in Higher Education. (n.d.). *Standards of professional practice.* Retrieved from https://www.naspa.org/about/student-affairs

National Institute of Standards and Technology. (2015). *2015–2016 Baldrige excellence framework (education).* Retrieved from http://www.nist.gov/baldrige/publications/education_criteria.cfm

Oaks, D. J., & Kennedy-Phillips, L. C. (2015). Making the grade: Using the technology to assess student affairs programs, activities. *Leadership Exchange, 12*(4), 14–17.

Pate, D. (2014). Wanted: Students who demonstrate work-world readiness. *Leadership Exchange, 11*(4), 36.

Patton, M. (2015). *Qualitative research and evaluation methods: Integrating theory and practice* (4th ed.). Los Angeles, CA: SAGE.

Perry, W. (1968). *Forms of intellectual and ethical development in the college years: A scheme.* New York, NY: Holt, Rinehart, and Winston.

Pfeffer, J. (1992). *Managing with power: Politics and influence in organizations.* Boston, MA: Harvard Business School Press.

Porter, S. R., & Whitcomb, M. E. (2004). Understanding the effect of prizes on response rates. In S. R. Porter (Ed.), *Overcoming Survey Research Problems.* Spec. edition for *New Directions for Institutional Research, 2004*(121), 51–62. San Francisco, CA: Jossey-Bass.

Porter, S., Whitcomb, M., & Weitzer, W. (2004). Multiple surveys of students and survey fatigue. In S. R. Porter (Ed.), *Overcoming survey research problems,* New Directions for Institutional Research, No. 121 (pp. 63–73). San Francisco, CA: Jossey-Bass.

Pulliam Phillips, P., Phillips, J., & Aaron, B. (2013). *Survey basics.* Alexandria, VA: ASTD Press.

Raven, B. (1965). Social influence and power. In I. Steiner & M. Fishbein (Eds.), *Current studies in social psychology* (pp. 371–382). New York, NY: Holt, Rinehart, and Winston.

Ravindra, G. (2011). The Nuremberg Code—A critique. *Perspectives in Clinical Research, 2*(2), 72–76. Retrieved from http://doi.org/http://dx.doi.org/10.4103%2F2229-3485.80371

Roberts, D. (2015). Tenet nine: Navigatiing politics. In E. Bentrim, G. Henning, & K. Yousey-Elsener (Eds.), *Coordinating student divisional affairs assessment* (pp. 133–147). Sterling, VA: Stylus.

Roberts, D., & Osters, S. (2006, June 14). The politics of assessment. *NASPA NetResults.*

Rutgers University Division of Student Affairs. (2015). *Assessment in action.* Retrieved from http://studentaffairs.rutgers.edu/mmc/magazine/

Saldaña, J. (2012). *The coding manual for qualitative researchers* (2nd ed.). Los Angeles, CA: SAGE.

Salkind, N. J. (2013). *Statistics for people who hate statistics* (5th ed.). Thousand Oaks, CA: SAGE.

Sandeen, A., & Barr, M. J. (2006). *Critical issues for student affairs: Challenges and opportunities.* San Francisco, CA: Jossey-Bass.

Sandeen, A., Winston, R., Jr., Creamer, D., & Miller, T. (2001). *The professional student affairs administrator.* New York, NY: Routledge.

Schuh, J. (2013). Developing a culture of student affairs. In J. Schuh (Ed), *Contemporary Issues in Student Affairs Assessment.* Spec. edition for *New Directions for Student Affairs, 2013*(142), 89–98. San Francisco, CA: Jossey-Bass.

Schuh, J. H., & Associates. (2009). *Assessment methods for student affairs.* San Francisco, CA: Jossey-Bass.

Schuh, J. H., & Gansemer-Topf, A. M. (2010, December). *The role of student affairs in student learning assessment* (NILOA Occasional Paper No. 7). Urbana, IL: University of Illinois and Indiana University, National Institute for Learning Outcomes Assessment.

Schuh, J. H., & Upcraft, M. L. (2001). *Assessment practice in student affairs: An applications manual.* San Francisco, CA: Jossey-Bass.

Schuh, J., & Upcraft, M. (2000, October). Assessment politics. *About Campus, 5*(4), 14–21.

Schwandt, T. A. (1997). *Qualitative inquiry: A dictionary of terms.* London: SAGE.

Schwartz, D. (1989). Visual ethnography: Using photography in qualitative research. *Qualitative Sociology, 12*(2), 119–154. Retrieved from http://sweb.cityu.edu.hk/sm6324/Schwartz_VisualEthno_using-photography.pdf

Selingo, J. (Ed.). (2014). *The innovative university: What college presidents think about change in American higher education.* Washington, DC: The Chronicle of Higher Education.

Shulze, S. (2007). The usefulness of reflexive photography for qualitative research: A case study in higher education. *South African Journal of Higher Education, 21*(5), 536–553.

Simon, J. (2015, January 8). Photo assessment [Electronic mailing list message]. Retrieved from https://listserv.tamu.edu/cgi-bin/wa?A2=SAA-Leaders;fcd02353.1501

Simpson, B. (1966). The classification of educational objectives: Psychomotor domain. *Illinois Journal of Home Economics, 10*(4), 110–144.

Smith, E., & Sponsler, B. (2014). Gainful employment and the federal crusade for higher education accountability. *Leadership Exchange, 11*(4), 29–30.

Southern Association of Colleges and Schools Commission on Colleges. (2012). *The principles of accreditation: Foundations for quality enhancement.* Decatur, GA: Author.

Spellings Commission. (2006). *A test of leadership: Charting the future of U.S. higher education.* Retrieved from https://www2.ed.gov/about/bdscomm/list/hiedfuture/reports/pre-pub-report.pdf

Stein, B., & Haynes, A. (2011). Engaging faculty in the assessment and improvement of students' critical thinking using the Critical Thinking Assessment Test. *Change, 43*(2), 44–49.

Sternberg, R., Penn, J., & Hawkins, C. (2011). *Assessing college student learning: Evaluating alternative models, using multiple methods.* Washington, DC: Association of American Colleges and Universities.

Stevens, D., & Levi, A. (2013). *Introduction to rubrics: An assessment tool to save grading time, convey effective feedback, and promote student learning* (2nd ed.). Sterling, VA: Stylus.

Stewart, D., Shamdasani, P., & Rook, D. (2006). *Focus groups: Theory and practice* (2nd ed.). Thousand Oaks, CA: SAGE.

Suskie, L. (2009). *Assessing student learning: A common sense guide* (2nd ed.). San Francisco, CA: Jossey-Bass.

Suskie, L. (2014). *Five dimensions of quality: A common sense guide to accreditation and accountability.* San Francisco, CA: Jossey-Bass.

Suskie, L. A. (1996). *Questionnaire survey research: What works* (2nd ed.). Tallahassee, FL: Association for Institutional Research.

Timm, D., & Lloyd, J. (2013). Ethical assessment. In D. Timm, J. Davis Barham, & K. McKinney (Eds.), *Assessment in practice: A companion guide to the ASK Standards.* Washington, DC: ACPA—College Student Educators International.

Umbach, P. D. (2004). Web surveys: Best practices. In S. R. Porter (Ed.), *Overcoming survey research problems* (pp. 23–38). *New Directions for Institutional Research,* no. 121. San Francisco, CA: Jossey-Bass.

Umble, K., Upshaw, V., Orton, S., & Matthews, K. (2000, June). *Using the post-then method to assess learner change.* American Association for Higher Education Assessment Conference, Charlotte, NC.

United Nations Economic Commission for Europe. (2009a). *Making data meaningful: Part 1. A guide to writing stories about numbers.* New York, NY: United Nations.

United Nations Economic Commission for Europe. (2009b). *Making data meaningful: Part 2. A guide to presenting statistics.* Geneva, Switzerland: United Nations.

University of Central Florida. (2004). *SMART guidelines.* http://www.fctl.ucf.edu/TeachingAndLearningResources/CourseDesign/Assessment/smart.php

University of Minnesota's Orientation & First-Year Programs (OFYP). (2014). *First year photo project.* Retrieved from https://www.ofyp.umn.edu/more/first-year-initiatives/first-year-photo-project

University of New Hampshire. (2013). *Institutional review board for the protection of human subjects in research: Guide for researchers.* Durham, NH: University of New Hampshire. Retrieved from http://www.unh.edu/research/sites/www.unh.edu.research/files/docs/RIS/irb_guide.pdf

University of North Carolina Wilmington. (n.d.). *Student affairs assessment, research & planning.* Retrieved from http://uncw.edu/studentaffairs/assessment/

Upcraft, M., & Schuh, J. (2002). Assessment vs. research: Why we should care about the difference. *About Campus, 7*(1), 16–20.

Urdan, T. C. (2010). *Statistics in plain English* (3rd ed., Kindle). New York, NY: Routledge.

U.S. Department of Education. (n.d.). *Protecting students with disabilities.* Retrieved from http://www2.ed.gov/about/offices/list/ocr/504faq.html

U.S. Department of Health and Human Services. (2009). Protection of human subjects, 45 C.F.R. 46.

U.S. Department of Health and Human Services. (2015, June 14). *Brief alcohol screening and intervention for college students (BASICS).* Retrieved from http://www.nrepp.samhsa.gov/ViewIntervention.aspx?id=124

U.S. Department of Health, Education, and Welfare. (1974). *The Belmont report.* Retrieved from http://www.hhs.gov/ohrp/humansubjects/guidance/belmont.html

Walvoord, B. E. (2010). *Assessment clear and simple: A practical guide for institutions, departments, and general education* (2nd ed.). San Francisco, CA: Jossey-Bass.

Wehlburg, C. M. (2008). *Promoting integrated and transformative assessment: A deeper focus on student learning.* San Francisco, CA: Jossey-Bass.

Wheelan, C. (2012). *Naked statistics: Stripping the dread from the data.* New York, NY: W. W. Norton & Company.

White House. (n.d.). *Education: Knowledge and skills for the jobs of the future.* Retrieved from https://www.whitehouse.gov/issues/education/higher-education

White House Task Force to Protect Students From Sexual Assault. (2014). *Not alone: The first report of the White House Task Force to Protect Students From Sexual Assault.* Washington, DC: Author.

World Health Organization. (2001). *Declaration of Helsinki* (pp. 373–374). Retrieved from http://www.who.int/bulletin/archives/79(4)373.pdf

Wyatt Knowlton, L., & Phillips, C. C. (2013). *The logic models guidebook: Better strategies for great results* (2nd ed.). Los Angeles, CA: SAGE.

Wyse, S. (2014, October 15). Advantages and disadvantages of face-to-face data collection [Web log post]. Retrieved from http://www.snapsurveys.com/blog/advantages-disadvantages-facetoface-data-collection/

Yousey-Elsener, K. (2013). Assessment fundamentals: The ABC's of assessment. In D. M. Timm, J. D. Barham, K. McKinney, & A. R. Knerr (Eds.), *Assessment in practice: A companion guide to the ASK standards* (pp. 9–18). Washington, DC: ACPA.

Yousey-Elsener, K. (2014). *Using data to inform decision making.* Presented at the University of Buffalo Supervisor's Learning Forum, Buffalo, NY.

Yousey-Elsener, K., & Elkins, B. (2012). *Professional competency areas for student affairs practitioners: Rubrics for professional development.* Washington, DC: American College Personnel Association.

Zeni, J. (2006). A guide to ethical issues and action research. *Educational Action Research, 6*(1), 9–19. doi.org/10.1080/09650799800200053

ABOUT THE AUTHORS

Gavin W. Henning is a college student educator with a reputation as an organizer, collaborator, and catalyst for educational change. His professional mission is to generate applied scholarship, bridge theory to practice, create systems and processes, and teach higher education professionals to foster college student learning, development, and success.

Having begun his career in residential life as a hall director, Gavin gained additional experience in judicial affairs and the prevention of excessive alcohol consumption and other drug abuse. The bulk of his career has been in student affairs assessment; he has 15 years of experience in this area, including coordinating assessment for the divisions of student affairs at two universities and working in institutional research at both.

Gavin has taught 15 student affairs assessment courses at two institutions and has also made numerous independent studies on the topic. His scholarship includes student affairs assessment standards, methods, and coordination; regional accreditation; student engagement; and roles of parents in college student success. An engaging speaker, Gavin has keynoted international, national, and regional conferences and has presented at numerous professional conferences. In addition, he has helped colleges and universities in the United States and other countries to develop and sustain cultures of assessment.

Through his involvement in professional associations, Gavin has helped to further a national agenda of accountability and continuous improvement in higher education. He is a founding member of Student Affairs Assessment Leaders (SAAL), an international organization supporting college student educators performing assessment. In ACPA, he served as president, director of professional development, and chair for the association's Commission for Assessment and Evaluation. Gavin is a member of the board of directors of the Council for the Advancement of Standards in Higher Education, where he also serves on the executive committee, which provides strategic direction for the organization.

In his current position as associate professor of higher education and director of the master of higher education administration and doctorate of education programs at New England College, Gavin is helping the next generation of professionals to improve educational organizations.

Gavin holds a doctor of philosophy degree in education leadership and policy studies and a master of arts degree in sociology, both from the University of New Hampshire, as well as a master of arts degree in college and university administration and a bachelor of science degree in psychology and sociology from Michigan State University.

Darby Roberts began her student affairs career in residence life, but she has always had an interest and ability in assessment and professional development. In 1998, she moved from residence life to student affairs assessment to help others in their efforts to improve programs and services for college students.

An educator at heart, Darby focuses on student learning outside of the classroom to move the profession, institutions, divisions, and departments forward in documenting the learning that occurs outside the classroom in students' holistic educational experience. She has offered numerous workshops, presentations, and webinars regionally, nationally, and internationally. She also consults with institutions that are developing cultures of assessment in student affairs.

In terms of professional association involvement, Darby has been the cochair for the NASPA Assessment, Evaluation, and Research Knowledge Community (AERKC). She has been recognized by NASPA through its excellence awards and the AERKC Innovation Award for efforts to improve student learning and assessment in the cocurricular area. In 2012, NASPA published *Learning Is Not a Sprint: Assessing and Documenting Student Leader Learning in Cocurricular Involvement*, which she coedited. She is also a founding member of SAAL.

As director of Student Life Studies in the Division of Student Affairs at Texas A&M University, Darby helps staff and student organizations collect data to inform decisions and action for program and student learning improvement. In addition, as a faculty member in the student affairs administration and higher education master's program, Darby guides and mentors graduate students in the process of becoming student affairs professionals with a strong assessment philosophy and ability.

Darby holds a doctor of philosophy in educational administration, a master of science in human resources management, and a bachelor of business administration from Texas A&M University.

INDEX

AAC&U. *See* Association of American Colleges and Universities

ABCD formula, 92–94, 102

access, in qualitative data collection, 156–57

accountability, 5–8, 12, 63, 77, 259
  in future of assessment, 293–94
  in implementation, 270–71
  in planning process, 38–39, 42, 52
  public, 42

accreditation, 6–7, 10–11, 39, 216–17
  assessment program, 68–69, 77–78

ACPA College Student Educators International, 4, 13, 245–46, 276–77

ACPA Student Affairs Assessment Institute, 276–77, 299–300

action plan, 38, 98, 221–23, 225, 229–30

action steps, in strategic planning, 89–91, 224

action verbs, 93–94, 96–97, 101

AER. *See* assessment, evaluation, research

affective taxonomy, 97–98, 102

agreement, with others, 19–20

American Association for Higher Education, 3, 230

American Council on Education, 1–2

American Psychological Association Commission on Accreditation (APA CoA), 78

analysis, 21–22, 26–27. *See also* data analysis
  qualitative data collection, 58, 158–61, 166–68, 170, 283–84
  quantitative data collection, 284–85

statistical, 58, 67–68, 81–82, 116, 137, 148–49

analysis of variance (ANOVA), 27, 108–9, 147–48

analyzing, in cognitive taxonomy, 97–98

Angelo, T., 33, 189, 194–95, 271–72

anonymity, 60–61, 73, 119, 213
  ethics and, 240–41, 245–46

ANOVA. *See* analysis of variance

APA CoA. *See* American Psychological Association Commission on Accreditation

application cards, 198

application domain, 100

applied learning, 10, 92, 186

applying, in cognitive taxonomy, 97–98

articulation, in psychomotor taxonomy, 99

ASK Standards. See Assessment Skills and Knowledge

assessment, evaluation, research (AER), 276–77

assessment cycle, 54–55, 82, 85–86
  Bresciani Ludvik on, 41–42
  goals in, 37–38, 40–42, 45–46, 49, 217
  mission in, 38, 41–42, 44–45
  PLAIR model, 45–46
  practical stage model in, 42–44
  priorities in, 7, 18, 46–49, 51, 83
  results sharing in, 14, 41, 44–45, 208, 242
  of Suskie, 45, 91

Assessment in Action, 209

Assessment in Student Affairs (Schuh and Associates), 290–91

"This book should be on the reading list of every senior student affairs officer, regardless of where his or her division is in implementation of its assessment program, as [it] not only offers a process for initiating assessment programs, but also provides a guide for evaluating the successful functioning of programs. Data will continue to be crucial to the success and survival of student affairs, as well as the successful stewardship of student affairs organizations and institutional resources. This book contributes greatly to our ability to have a positive and productive future."
—*Larry D. Roper*, *Oregon State University*

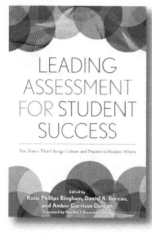

Leading Assessment for Student Success
Ten Tenets That Change Culture and Practice in Student Affairs
Edited by Rosie Phillips Bingham, Daniel A. Bureau, and Amber Garrison Duncan
Foreword by Marilee J. Bresciani Ludvik

"This book explains how to tell the story of assessment while engaging each student affairs team member on your campus, whether it is the senior student affairs officer or a frontline professional. Each chapter builds on the previous, making the case for why assessment matters and how to implement assessment practice so that inquiry becomes a priority, deeply embedded into the daily work of all who believe in and contribute to student success.

"It shares various ways to evaluate implementation of student success theory and practice in a manner that leads to improving relevant outcomes. Upon reading, you will likely gain ideas to cultivate a culture of inquiry along with important means to communicate results to stakeholders and garner their feedback for prioritizing recommendations. This book provides a 'how to' in making assessment an integral practice of the student affairs profession.

"It is my hope that the leaders (read: all of you) who are reading this book are the leaders who have that kind of courage—the courage to hold space for transformation to occur. If so, I invite you to read this book and fully engage in the lessons colleagues share. Explore how the ideas presented in these pages may be adapted and taken up within your organization. Then, collaboratively execute and enjoy the fruits of your investment in meaningful inquiry."—*Marilee J. Bresciani Ludvik*, *Professor, Postsecondary Education, San Diego State University*

22883 Quicksilver Drive
Sterling, VA 20166-2102   Subscribe to our e-mail alerts: www.Styluspub.com

Also available from Stylus

Assessing for Learning
Building a Sustainable Commitment Across the Institution
SECOND EDITION
Peggy L. Maki

"Peggy Maki's text . . . represents a comprehensive and realist approach to assessment and constructs a notion of assessment that is an uncommon blend of the pragmatic and sustainable, meaningful and valuable, theoretical and practical. Maki has artistically drawn together esoteric, philosophical foundations with pragmatic, real-world applications from which nearly any assessment practitioner will benefit. . . . The second edition of *Assessing for Learning* verges on being a seminal work in higher education assessment scholarship."—*The Review of Higher Education*

"This is a welcome second edition for Maki's well-known tome on assessment and learning. This volume stands out as a sentinel work in the area for three reasons. First, it is a comprehensive account of sustainable assessment across educational institutions. In this regard it looks at assessment not so much as something that occurs in universities and colleges but as something that defines them. Second, it provides a range of practical strategies that have been well tested at the 'coalface' of learning, that is, with students in classrooms and other educational settings. Finally, it provides a well-grounded practical focus without sacrificing conceptual depth. The book provides a wealth of theoretical material which creates and sustains a strong context for learning. This book is highly recommended."—*Teaching Theology and Religion*

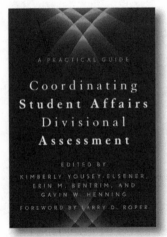

Coordinating Student Affairs Divisional Assessment
A Practical Guide
Edited by Kimberly Yousey-Elsener, Erin M. Bentrim, and Gavin W. Henning
Foreword by Larry D. Roper

AN ACPA / NASPA JOINT PUBLICATION

"*Coordinating Student Affairs Divisional Assessment* is a comprehensive A–Z guide to establishing, evolving, and sustaining a student affairs division assessment program. The authors offer a practical and professionally grounded model to inform and support successful leadership of student affairs assessment.

"The beauty and brilliance of [this book] is in the aggregate design it offers to demystify student affairs assessment and make successful leadership accessible.

(Continues on previous page)